RUNES

A HANDBOOK

MICHAEL P. BARNES

RUNES
A HANDBOOK

THE BOYDELL PRESS

First published 2012
The Boydell Press, Woodbridge
Paperback edition 2022

ISBN 978 1 84383 778 7 hardback
ISBN 978 1 78327 697 4 paperback

The Boydell Press is an imprint of Boydell & Brewer Ltd
PO Box 9, Woodbridge, Suffolk IP12 3DF, UK
and of Boydell & Brewer Inc.
668 Mount Hope Ave, Rochester, NY 14620-2731, USA
website: www.boydellandbrewer.com

A catalogue record for this book is available from the British Library

Designed and typeset in Monotype Albertus, Adobe Myriad Pro and
Adobe Warnock Pro by David Roberts, Pershore, Worcestershire

Contents

Illustrations

Plates

Figures

(All figures are the author's unless otherwise stated)

Maps

Preface

Runes: A Handbook aims to provide a rational and up-to-date introduction to runes and runic writing. It is based in part on courses in runology (the study of runes) I gave in the Department of Scandinavian Studies, University College London. Chapter 1 provides a general introduction to the subject, while chapters 2–11 are organised more or less chronologically, and take the reader from the origin of the script to its final demise in post-Reformation Scandinavia. Something is also said of modern uses of runes. Chapters 12–18 deal with topics that fall outside the main lines of development: runic cryptography; the appearance of runes in manuscripts; the names of the runes; how runic inscriptions were, or may have been, made; how runologists read and interpret runic texts; runes in literature and politics; the history of runology; where to look for inscriptions.

In a book of this size, it is necessary to be selective. Certain aspects of runes and runic writing are given greater prominence than others, and some are mentioned only in passing. Nevertheless, the aim has been to offer as comprehensive an introduction as possible, and one that will serve both the interested layman and the undergraduate student. With the interests of the layman in particular in mind, explanatory notes have been provided, including a glossary of grammatical and technical terms used. Most chapters conclude with a Select Reading List of works in English. The glaring omissions many will spot in these lists reflect the English-language bias. It seemed, however, unwise to assume a ready acquaintance with European tongues other than English. Those following up the suggested reading will of course find further references aplenty to books and articles in a range of languages, not least German and the various Scandinavian idioms.

The exploration of so many different aspects of runology has made it difficult to avoid repetition. One and the same phenomenon can be relevant in several contexts, and there is a limit to the number of cross-references that can be provided. It is also my view that retelling and re-explanation help fix important matters more firmly in the reader's mind.

Runes: A Handbook was originally conceived as a joint venture, to be written by Ray Page and me in collaboration. Ray was the doyen of runic studies and acknowledged as the foremost expert on English runes. Unfortunately infirmity prevented him from participating, and the work is surely the poorer for it. Certainly there would have been more questions and fewer answers had he been able to contribute his share.

In compiling this book I have received extensive help from others, primarily fellow runologists, who have patiently answered questions, supplied elusive pieces of information, and assisted in numerous other ways. Very special thanks must go to James Knirk of the University of Oslo and Henrik Williams of the University of Uppsala, both of whom read the complete book in typescript. They drew attention to sundry errors and infelicities, and made many suggestions about how the text might be improved. I am also grateful to the anonymous reader who offered comments on the work as a whole and on points of detail. Where practical, I have followed his/her advice. Among others who have provided special assistance of various kinds the following should be mentioned: Laila Kitzler Åhfeldt, Marit Åhlén, Staffan Fridell, Anne-Sofie Gräslund, Helmer Gustavson, Jan Ragnar Hagland, Lisbeth Imer, Judith Jesch, Magnus Källström, Svante Lagman, K. Jonas Nordby, Jan Owe, David Parsons, Lena Peterson, Þorgunnur Snædal, Guðrún Sveinbjarnardóttir; and the institutions and private individuals who provided illustrations or permitted them to be reproduced (acknowledgements detailed on pp. viii–xi).

The printing of *Runes: A Handbook* has been assisted by a grant from the Royal Gustavus Adolphus Academy for Swedish Folk Culture, Uppsala, Sweden, for which contribution I offer my grateful thanks.

London, February 2012

Michael P. Barnes

Abbreviations

acc.	accusative
dat.	dative
f.	feminine
gen.	genitive
Icel.	Icelandic
m.	masculine
n.	neuter
nom.	nominative
Nw.	Norwegian
OE	Old English
OHG	Old High German
ON	Old Norse
pl.	plural
pres.	present
r.	rune
rr.	runes
Scand.	Scandinavian
sg.	singular
subj.	subjunctive
*	(immediately preceding a word) hypothetical form
<	develops from
>	develops to

A general glossary, with explanations of other matters essential for a full understanding of *Runes: A Handbook*, will be found on pp. 218–20.

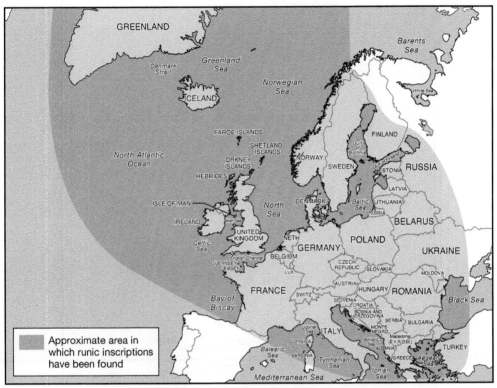

Map 1 The area of Europe in which runic inscriptions have been found
(This map should not be taken to imply that inscriptions have been found within
the borders of every country or island included in the shaded area.)

Map 2 The provinces of Scandinavia

1 Introduction

1.1 Rune and runic

This book is an introduction to runology: the study of runes and runic writing. The words "rune" and "runic" have many meanings, as a glance at the relevant entries in the *Oxford English Dictionary* will show. Here, though, the terms refer solely to a set of characters whose primary purpose is to record language. Runes, like roman, greek or cyrillic letters, are an alphabetic type of script: each character denotes one or more speech sounds (in contrast, for example, to writing systems whose symbols stand for complete words, such as the chinese, or for syllables, such as japanese hiragana or katakana). The word *horna* 'horn' thus appears in runes as ᚺᛟᚱᚾᚨ, where ᚺ stands for a sound similar to English *h*, ᛟ corresponds roughly to the *o*-sound of 'horn', ᚱ denotes a rolled *r*, ᛏ an *n*, and ᚨ an *a*-sound something like that in English *father* (hereafter phonetic or phonemic symbols will in the main be used to denote speech sounds; see pp. 221–2).

From this it follows that runes do *not* constitute a language in themselves as is sometimes supposed. In principle they may be used to write any language, although in practice they are best suited to the sound systems of the Germanic tongues (p. 218). It was for a type of Germanic ancestor language that the runes were originally invented, and by and large it is different manifestations of Germanic (e.g. Old English, Old Norse) that runes have recorded. Even so, a certain amount of runic writing from medieval Scandinavia presents texts in Latin, and occasionally runes are used to record Christian formulaic words or phrases in Greek and Hebrew (pp. 122–6). To "read runes" it is therefore necessary not only to recognise different runic characters and their sound value(s) but also to know something of the language in which an inscription is written.

The word "rune" has been the subject of much discussion. Although *run* is attested in Old English, the modern term seems to have been borrowed from seventeenth-century Scandinavian usage, where Latin *runa* and the native *runa*, *rune* are used of a character of the runic script. Old English *run* has connotations of 'mystery', 'secret', as do cognates in related languages, although the Old Norse plural *rúnar* generally denotes characters of the runic writing system. The Old English word for 'runic character' is *runstæf* 'rune-staff' 'runic letter'. Etymologists have tried to reconcile the sense of mystery or secret with that of writing by appealing to various verbs supposedly related to the Germanic root *run-* and denoting types of oral/aural communication. Some of these verbs, e.g. those meaning 'whisper' 'murmur', can be taken to imply a context of secret communication, and runic writing, which consists of symbols that denote sounds – so the thinking seems to go – might be used to convey such communication. Against this derivation it has been argued that across a variety of languages words denoting writing tend to indicate how the writing was originally done (by drawing, painting, scratching, cutting, etc.). In the light of this a new etymology has been proposed, which connects the root *run-* with words meaning 'dig' 'make furrows'. Semantically this seems more plausible.

1.2 Runic writing/runic inscriptions

Runes are an epigraphic script: they are found carved into stone, wood, metal, bone, and other solid materials. They are not normally written with ink on parchment or paper (but cf. p. 121). This means that the messages they carry are laconic; runic inscriptions do not preserve lengthy pieces of writing.

Unlike the roman, greek or cyrillic alphabets, runes are no longer in common use. While it is perfectly possible to compose a modern-day message in some variant of the runic alphabet, such activity is normally restricted to those with an antiquarian (or occasionally political) interest in the script. (A broad distinction may be made between the traditional use of runes by people who learnt them from an earlier generation, and learned use by people who gained their knowledge from books.) Traditional runic writing came to an end at different times in different places but – one or two outlying areas apart – it is probably fair to say that runes finally ceased to be an everyday script somewhen in the fifteenth century. The demise of traditional runic writing means that we are dealing with a finite corpus, and it is therefore possible to give approximate numbers of known runic inscriptions by country or region (within their modern borders). Sweden has the highest tally with about 3,500; Norway is next with some 1,600; then comes Denmark with around 850; Greenland has over 100, and England too if inscriptions in both the English and Scandinavian traditions are included; Iceland has just under 100; Germany (within its current borders) can muster over 80 and Orkney over 50; the Isle of Man has about 35, the Netherlands, Ireland and Scotland each around 20. Other areas, e.g. Shetland and the Faroe Islands, show fewer than ten inscriptions.

These are very crude figures and they mask several uncertainties, for example the fact that an inscription on a portable object may have been made far from the place it was found. Even stone inscriptions, which are more difficult to transport over long distances, cannot necessarily be ascribed to locals. The fifty-five or so runic texts from Orkney are a case in point: over half of these are almost certainly the work of Norwegians passing through the islands. Furthermore, the listing of totals for different countries and regions diverts attention from the enormous range of runic writing, which encompasses commemorative stones, charms, prayers, brief business letters, name tags, graffiti, and more. It is important to realise that the need for written communication in runes, as in other writing systems, varied according to time, place and situation, and as long as runes were in regular use they could be employed to set down whatever it was deemed necessary to record – subject to the limitations of space imposed by the epigraphic tradition. It should also be noted that the total number of runic inscriptions known to scholarship is constantly increasing as new finds are made.

We can be no more precise about the beginning of runic writing than the end. The oldest extant runic inscriptions that can be (reasonably) reliably dated are from AD 150–200. These are unlikely to be the very earliest, however, since they are spread over a wide area of northern and eastern Europe. Careful scholars would push the inception of runic writing back a hundred years or so beyond the earliest finds, to allow for the spread of the art. Yet some have argued for a date well into the BC era, basing their views on the shapes of individual runes and certain characteristics of the writing system. (See further chapter 2.)

1.3 Transliteration

Runic inscriptions are often presented in transliteration. That is to say, each rune is given an equivalent in a modern alphabet, most commonly the roman. Boldface type is the normal medium, though other systems are found (cf. p. 224). Thus the ᚺᛟᚱᚾᚨ quoted above may be rendered **horna**. (The roman equivalents generally used in this book are set out in 1.4; for a description of further conventions used in transliteration, see p. 224.)

The primary purpose of transliteration is to make runic inscriptions more accessible to those unfamiliar with the script, while preserving as many features as possible of the original text. In accordance with this, neither word division nor modern punctuation is introduced (though runic inscriptions themselves are often segmented in one way or another); line division is usually indicated by a symbol such as |, but sometimes the text may be reproduced line by line as in the original.

As far as individual characters go, what the transliterator seeks to reproduce are the distinctive runes of a particular rune-row (on the use of "rune-row" rather than "runic alphabet", cf. section 3.2; on different rune-rows, see 1.4). "Distinctive" in this context means contrasting. ᚠ **f**, for example, contrasts with ᚼ **s** in Scandinavian runic writing of the Viking Age, just as does 'f' with 's' in roman-alphabet writing. ᚠᛁᚠ **fik** gives the Scandinavian past tense verb form 'got' 'received', ᛋᛁᚠ **sik** a Scandinavian pronoun meaning 'self' ('himself' 'herself' 'themselves'). Similarly roman 'fun' denotes a different word in English from 'sun'. Viking-Age Scandinavian ᛋ and ', on the other hand, do not contrast in this way: either ᛋᛁᚠ or 'ᛁᚠ can be written and the word remains *sik* 'self'. Furthermore ᛋ and ' occupy the same place in the Viking-Age Scandinavian rune-row: they are both rune 11 (cf. 1.4, Figs 3 and 4). Likewise, 'fun', 'Fun' and '*fun*' all give the English word *fun*, and 'f' 'F' and '*f*' are variants of the sixth letter of the roman alphabet.

Sound value has less significance for transliteration. If the speech sounds denoted by runes were the main criterion, the reader would often not know which rune was being transliterated. ᚢ, for example, can denote as many as eight different sounds in Viking-Age Scandinavian. But if we were to use eight different roman equivalents according to the sound the rune was thought to represent, we would no longer be dealing with transliteration – the substituting of the letters of one script for another – but with phonetic transcription. And since /o(:)/, for example, is one of the values of ᚢ, and /y(:)/ another, but /o(:)/ is often written ᚭ and /y(:)/ ᛩ, there would be a great deal of confusion. Accordingly, ᚢ is transliterated **u**, whatever sound it is deemed to denote.

All this having been said, transliteration is first and foremost a practical tool and scholars tend to approach it in a pragmatic way. In accordance with this, roman equivalents are normally chosen that will indicate the approximate sound values of the runes being transliterated. Little is gained, for example, by rendering ᚠᚢᚦ **xyz** rather than **fuþ**, given that the first rune stands for [f] (or a sound close to it), the second (most often) for [u], and the third for [θ] (the sound of English *th* in **think**; see below). Also pragmatic is the marking of variant forms of a rune where this serves a particular purpose (for example **m** for older ᛖ and **m** for younger ᚤ, cf. pp. 61–2).

There are dangers inherent in transliteration, not least that the reader may come to regard the transliterated text as a facsimile of the original. Serious study of runes and runic writing requires examination of the inscriptions themselves. Where this is not possible, good photographs or drawings may provide a substitute. But it cannot be emphasised too strongly that runic inscriptions are much more than texts. The type of object bearing the inscription will often hold a clue to the interpretation of the message; size, shape and material can all influence layout; runes may owe their particular appearance, and words their spelling, to the condition of the surface into which the inscription is carved; and so on.

1.4 Rune-rows

In simplistic accounts runes are sometimes portrayed as a single, unvarying sequence of symbols. The reality is quite different. Rune forms changed over time, as did rune-rows. Sometimes change was gradual, sometimes (apparently) more abrupt and radical. It is common to distinguish four main types of rune-row: the older *fuþark* (*fuþark* after the first six characters: **f, u, þ, a, r, k**), the "Anglo-Frisian" *fuþorc*, the (Scandinavian) younger *fuþark*, and the (Scandinavian) so-called medieval *fuþork*. Finer distinctions are regularly and sometimes usefully made (see pp. 37–41, 61–4), but for those unfamiliar with runic writing this quadripartite division forms a convenient starting point.

The older *fuþark* was in use between roughly AD 100 (earlier according to some) and 700 in different parts of the Germanic world. It consists of twenty-four characters, and is preserved complete or in fragmentary form in eleven inscriptions. These early recordings of the runic alphabet show considerable homogeneity in the shape of individual runes, and, not least, the order in which they occur (which is quite different from that of the greek and roman alphabets). The fact that variation exists, however, means it is more helpful to the reader at this stage to present a model, rather than an actual, older *fuþark* – one based on typical forms and the most commonly attested order.

ᚠ ᚢ ᚦ ᚨ ᚱ ᚲ ᚷ ᚹ ᚺ ᚾ ᛁ ᛃ ᛂ ᛈ ᛉ ᛊ ᛏ ᛒ ᛖ ᛗ ᛚ ᛜ ᛟ ᛞ

f	u	þ	a	r	k	g	w	h	n	i	j	æ	p	z	s	t	b	e	m	l	ŋ	o	d
1	2	3	4	5	6	7	8	9	10	11	12	13	14	15	16	17	18	19	20	21	22	23	24

Fig. 1 The older *fuþark*

As indicated above, Þ denotes [θ], the consonant sound of English *think, method, path*. The reason it is transliterated þ is the use of this character in some kinds of roman-alphabet writing. Þ was adopted by scribes writing Old English because roman had no letter for [θ]. From England the usage spread to many parts of Scandinavia, and is still current in Iceland. The original value of ᛁ is quite unclear, and for that reason there is no agreement about how it should be transliterated; æ is a practical expedient, and should not be taken to imply the value [æ] (something like the vowel in English *cat*). The status of this rune is discussed in 2.4. ◊ seemingly stands for the final sound in southern English *sing*, the phonetic symbol for which is [ŋ], hence the transliteration ŋ. ŋ (or what has been interpreted as such) appears in a variety of forms, and some of these have been said to stand for [ŋ] + [g], as in northern English *sing*, or even for [iŋg]. There is, however, no unanimity on this point.

The "Anglo-Frisian" *fuþorc* (*fuþorc* from the [o(:)] value of the fourth rune and the use of 'c' in Old English manuscript writing for [k(:)]), found in Britain (chiefly England) and Frisia *c*. 450–1000 is marked by certain common innovations and an increase in the number of runes. There are differences between Anglo-Saxon (English) and Frisian usage (hence the inverted commas round "Anglo-Frisian"), as also between earlier and later Anglo-Saxon, but the following representation – again a model rune-row – can serve as a convenient starting point (the two final runes are not attested in inscriptions from Frisia).

ᚠ	ᚢ	ᚦ	ᚩ	ᚱ	ᚳ	ᚷ	ᚹ	ᚻ	ᚾ	ᛁ	ᛄ	ᛇ	ᛈ	ᛉ	ᛋ	ᛏ	ᛒ	ᛖ	ᛗ	ᛚ	ᛝ	ᛞ	ᛟ	ᚪ	ᚫ	ᚣ	ᛠ
f	u	þ	o	r	c	g	w	h	n	i	j	i	p	x	s	t	b	e	m	l	ŋ	d	œ	a	æ	y	ea
1	2	3	4	5	6	7	8	9	10	11	12	13	14	15	16	17	18	19	20	21	22	23	24	25	26	27	28

Fig. 2 The "Anglo-Frisian" *fuþorc*

The transliteration **i** for ᛁ reflects the fact that this rune sometimes stands for [i] (or at least a high front vowel, cf. p. 41) in early Anglo-Saxon inscriptions (see the commentary on Fig. 1 above). In the Anglo-Frisian tradition (cf. pp. 37–9) ᛟ denotes [ø] (as in French *peuple* 'people', German *schön* 'beautiful'); the ligature 'œ' is sometimes used for this sound as an alternative to 'ø' or 'ö', hence **œ**. ᛡ denotes [y], a vowel sound much as in French *tu* 'you', German *Bücher* 'books'; in this case the usual phonetic symbol has been chosen as the transliteration equivalent.

The younger *fuþark*, which appears in the North shortly after AD 700, and is a purely Scandinavian development, represents a drastic simplification of the older rune-row. It contains only sixteen runes, a reduction of a third, and the shapes of some of the characters are simplified (the tendency is for each rune to have a single vertical line and branches). The younger *fuþark* appears in several formats. The abandonment of eight runes is common to all and was therefore presumably the first stage in the development. The number of runes given a simpler shape and the extent of the simplification vary, seemingly the result of experimentation leading to different norms. The two (model) rune-rows given here show something of the variety.

ᚠᚢᚦᚨᚱᚲᚼᚾᛁᛅᛋᛏᛒᛘᛚᛦ

f u þ ã r k h n i a s t b m l ʀ

1 2 3 4 5 6 7 8 9 10 11 12 13 14 15 16

Fig. 3 A less simplified younger *fuþark*

ᚠᚼᚦᚨᚱᚲᛂᚽᛁᛄ'ᚿᚦᛐᛚ,

f u þ ã r k h n i a s t b m l ʀ

1 2 3 4 5 6 7 8 9 10 11 12 13 14 15 16

Fig. 4   A more simplified younger *fuþark*

ᚨ commonly denotes the nasal vowel [ã] as in French ***danse*** 'dance', hence ã (often written ą as an alternative); since ᚨ can sometimes also denote [a(:)], however, the generic term *fuþark* is normally used of this type of rune-row. ᛅ or ı stands for a voiced palatal spirant with sibilant quality that developed from Germanic /z/; ultimately this sound coalesced with /r/, and because it must for a time before that have had an *r*-like quality, it is regularly transliterated **ʀ**.

The so-called medieval *fuþork*, likewise a purely Northern phenomenon, is a version of the younger *fuþark* expanded (using diacritics and other devices, see chapter 9) to take better account of the sound systems of medieval Scandinavian. The expansion took place gradually between the late tenth century and about 1200. By the thirteenth century usage was reasonably uniform throughout the Scandinavian world, although local variation can be found. The row given below is very much a modern construct, made up of forms found at different times and in different places. Rune-row inscriptions of the sixteen-character *fuþark* type illustrated in Figs 3 and 4 are well attested. Medieval rune-writers, however, do not normally present complete inventories of the symbols they employ. There are many medieval inscriptions consisting of or including complete or partial rune-rows, but the runes depicted tend still to be the sixteen of the younger *fuþark*. Odd supplementary characters are sometimes added, but seldom more than one or two. The order in which the supplementary runes are presented here is the arbitrary choice of the author.

ᚠ	ᚢ	ᚦ	ᚭ	ᚱ	ᚲ	ᚼ	ᚾ	ᛁ	ᛆ	ᛌ/ᚼ	ᛐ	ᛒ	ᛦ	ᛚ	ᛅ	ᚠ	ᚦ	ᚧ	ᚱ	ᛂ	ᛐ	ᛌ/ᚼ	ᛐ	ᛒ	ᚴ	ᚦ
f	u	þ	o	r	k	h	n	i	a	s	t	b	m	l	y	f̈	þ̈	ü	k̈	ï	æ	c/z	ï̈	b̈	p	ø
1	2	3	4	5	6	7	8	9	10	11	12	13	14	15	16	17	18	19	20	21	22	23	24	25	26	27

Fig. 5 The medieval runes

The so-called "dotted" runes ᚠ, ᚦ, ᚼ, ᚱ, ᛐ, ᛁ, ᛒ are transliterated with dotted roman equivalents. This is a departure from normal practice, but the aim is to show that the characters concerned are derived from their plain counterparts. Traditional procedure is to render them **v, ð, y, g, e, d, p** respectively ([ð] denotes the consonant sound of ***then, father***, see further p. 222), but there are problems with that notation. Here we may note that ᛂ, for example, is not really an *e*-rune, but an *i*-rune marked to distinguish it in some way from plain ᛁ. A further problem affects ᚼ and ᛒ: the transliteration of the former as **y** and the latter as **p** means they cannot be distinguished from ᚼ and ᚴ respectively (unless we adopt some other notation for these). ᚯ not only denotes the mid front rounded vowel [ø] (as in French *peuple* 'people', German *schön* 'beautiful', see above), but is sometimes used for the low back rounded vowel [ɔ], as in English *hot*. This vowel, however, is more commonly written ᛆ (i.e. not distinguished from [o]). Some transliterate ᚯ as ǫ where it denotes [ɔ], but that is to confuse transliteration with phonetic transcription. Yet, an element of confusion has proved hard to avoid. ᚼ is by some medieval carvers used as the equivalent of roman 's', by others for roman 'c' or 'z'; and the same applies to ᛁ. Here, practice has often been to transliterate according to the perceived intention of the carver rather than, say, rendering every occurrence of ᚼ/ᛁ as **s**, or distinguishing between the two entirely on the basis of form, making ᚼ **s** and ᛁ **S** for example. This is not a very satisfactory solution, however, since it opens the door to arbitrary variation. (See further pp. 94–6.)

1.5 Runology and runologists

"Runology" is the term generally applied to the study of runes and runic writing, and its practitioners are known as runologists. These are umbrella terms, however, which can cover a multitude of sins. Unlike mathematics, history, geography and other established disciplines, runology has no core teachings, no universally agreed principles or standard methodology. There is as yet no modern textbook of runology, nor could it until recently be studied in school or university as a subject in its own right. The most prominent runologists were self-taught, scholars trained in related disciplines who developed an abiding interest in runes and runic writing. It is hardly surprising that they tended to approach the subject in different ways, reflecting their academic background and particular intellectual make-up. Language historians not unnaturally paid most attention to speech sounds, word forms and sentence structures, and to runes as a writing system. Archaeologists were more concerned with find reports, context, age, and, to a lesser extent, what an inscription said. Art historians emphasised such things as style and layout. Historians tended to see runic inscriptions as primary sources, though often drawing a sharp (but unwarranted) distinction between texts inscribed with runes into wood, bone, metal, etc. and those written with ink on parchment or paper (in whatever alphabet): some have been inclined to view only the latter as true "historical documents".

There has also been something of a divide between the imaginative and the sceptical runologist. In a field unconstrained by established principles or generally accepted methodology, the imaginative scholar can allow him-/ herself considerable freedom to speculate. The difficulty is that a proposal or idea that cannot be substantiated or falsified – or at least made more plausible than rival notions – does not normally have the power to persuade. Too often in runology one interpretation has been piled upon another, where in truth the evidence has been too slight to allow sensible conclusions to be drawn. This lack of self-discipline on the part of a number of serious runologists has permitted the proliferation of ideas among the general public that have little or no basis in fact. It is widely held, for example, that runes are magical symbols; that they have healing powers; or are signs by which the future can be predicted. While there is some evidence from particular times and places that certain people acquainted with runes believed one or more of these propositions, there is no indication that those who created the runic characters or the majority of those who used them ever thought in such terms (pp. 190–94, 207–8).

That runes are an alphabetic writing system cannot be emphasised too strongly. In this they are no different from the roman or other alphabets. Throughout their history their primary purpose has been to record language. Not surprisingly, runes might sometimes be used to write spells and magic formulae (as might any type of script), but such usage needs to be clearly distinguished from the idea that the runic characters themselves were imbued with magic powers.

Select reading list

Jansson, Sven B. F. 1987. *Runes in Sweden*. Stockholm: Gidlunds.

Knirk, James E. 2002. 'Runes: Origin, development of the futhark, functions, applications, and methodological considerations'. In: (Oskar Bandle *et al.*, eds) *The Nordic Languages: An International Handbook of the History of the North Germanic Languages* 1 (Handbücher zur Sprache- und Kommunikationswissenschaft 22:1). Berlin/New York: Walter de Gruyter, 634–48.

Moltke, Erik 1985. *Runes and their Origin: Denmark and Elsewhere.* Copenhagen: National Museum of Denmark.

Page, R. I. 1987 (and later printings). *Runes* (Reading the Past). London: British Museum.

Page, R. I. 1999. *An Introduction to English Runes* (2nd ed.). Woodbridge: Boydell Press.

Spurkland, Terje 2005. *Norwegian Runes and Runic Inscriptions*. Woodbridge: Boydell Press.

Williams, Henrik 2008. 'Runes'. In: (Stefan Brink and Neil Price, eds) *The Viking World*. London/New York: Routledge, 281–90.

[These are introductions to runes and runic writing, but they vary greatly in scope, degree of detail, and technical difficulty. Easiest for the beginner are Jansson 1987, Page 1987, Spurkland 2005 and Williams 2008, of which Page 1987 offers the best all-round account. Moltke 1985 deals with the origin of the runes and presents and discusses numerous Danish inscriptions.]

2 The origin of the runes

2.1 Questions

When, where, by whom and for what purpose or purposes the runes were created are questions to which many scholars – and a good few others besides – have tried to supply answers. The debate has generated as much heat as light, and we are still a long way from a generally accepted theory of runic origins. In the absence of a scholarly consensus, the safest procedure is to outline the main issues around which discussion has centred, separating what is more from what is less plausible. Runes have attracted people with varied interests and passions, and many claims that have been made about the origin and purpose of runic writing are based not on the dispassionate sifting of evidence but on preconceived ideas and flights of fancy. Esoteric approaches will be ignored in the following.

The questions "when?" "where?" "by whom?" and "for what purpose?" are so bound up with each other that it is not sensible to consider them in isolation. Indeed, the task of any well-integrated hypothesis about the origin of runic writing must be to make the answers to these four questions – as far as possible – accord with each other and with the known facts. A group of people with a reason to develop their own system of writing must be in the right place at the right time.

2.2 Four basic points

It is best to start with the known, and from there work towards that which is less well understood. There are four points on which most serious runologists would agree.

(1) Runic writing goes back to at least the second century of the Christian era. The earliest certain examples are dated by archaeologists to the period AD *c.* 150–200. One artefact put at AD 50 or a little earlier, the Meldorf fibula from northern Germany, has an inscription that may be runic but could also be roman. Since the early runic inscriptions are spread over a wide area, and because it would be something of a coincidence if the oldest extant examples were the very first to be made, it is common to place the creation of the runes at some time between the birth of Christ and the first half of the second century AD. New finds could of course push the date back some way, as would the Meldorf fibula could it be shown to be indubitably runic.

(2) The centre of the earliest documented runic activity is the area that comprises modern Denmark, southern Norway and southern Sweden. That is where the bulk of the oldest inscriptions have been found, although a small number have find spots in northern Germany and eastern Europe. All of these inscriptions are on portable objects, and may thus have been made far from the place where they were discovered. In the view of certain archaeologists, for example, many of those found in Denmark are carved on objects manufactured elsewhere in Scandinavia (though it is often uncertain whether object and

inscription are contemporaneous). This does not, however, alter the picture of southern Scandinavia as the cradle of runic writing.

(3) The runes are part of the Mediterranean (phoenician-greek-etruscan-roman) alphabetic writing tradition. They are based on the same principle and a number of runes are identical or virtually identical to characters in one or other, or several, of these alphabets (especially the roman and those of northern Italy, derived from the etruscan). They nevertheless show more than a little independence of the Mediterranean tradition (e.g. in the order in which characters are placed in the rune-row).

(4) The runes were almost certainly developed in an area in contact with but not part of the Roman Empire. At the beginning of the Christian era, this Empire extended as far as the present-day Netherlands in the west and well into present-day southern Germany in the south. In the Roman-occupied territories the roman alphabet was the norm, and tended to oust rival systems.

These four points offer us some guidance about the creation of the runic alphabet, but they are far from providing clear answers to the questions posed at the outset. We need to evaluate various proposals that have been made, and to try to understand the thinking behind them.

2.3 Context

The similarity between the runic and various Mediterranean writing systems cannot be due to chance. Since there is no evidence that the runes influenced the development of Mediterranean writing, it is a reasonable assumption that the Germanic script derives from one or more Mediterranean forerunners. For this to have happened, prolonged contact must be assumed between speakers of Germanic and one or more southern European tongues. Germanic speakers must have learnt other languages proficiently, and ultimately how to read and write them. They would have observed the difference between their own illiterate world and the literate culture they came face-to-face with in the south, and have noted the purposes for which script could be used and how this affected the running of society in general. Their meeting with literacy must have inspired them to imitation, to export the skill to their homelands. But they did not, as they might have done, simply adapt an existing alphabet to the needs of their native language. Instead they created one of their own. Any theory of runic origins that is to carry conviction has to take these considerations into account.

Three Mediterranean writing systems have been brought into the discussion: the greek, the etruscan and its north italic derivatives, and the roman.

In the early part of the twentieth century it was widely held that the runes were based on a cursive form of greek script, though with certain symbols modelled on roman letters. The context was the Black Sea area, where a group of Goths – East Germanic speakers – arrived in about AD 200 and may well have come into contact with greek writing. This hypothesis had eventually to be abandoned, not least for chronological reasons. If indubitably runic inscriptions exist dated to the second century AD, runes cannot have emerged from an encounter between Greek speakers and Goths at a later period. The

Black Sea is also geographically distant from southern Scandinavia where the bulk of the earliest runic inscriptions are found.

Belief in a third-century greek source gave way to the idea that the runes were based on the etruscan alphabet and/or north italic scripts derived from it. Certainly it is plausible that Germanic speakers were in the southern Alps and adjacent areas in the first century AD, and they may well have come into contact with one or more of these alphabets. What is questionable is whether small groups of mountain dwellers, speaking various different languages and rapidly coming under the domination of Roman culture, can have inspired anyone to create the runic alphabet. Germanic people in the southern Alps in the first century AD would first and foremost have come to appreciate the value of writing from its use in the expanding Roman Empire and would thus most likely have modelled their characters on the prestige alphabet of the day. There is the further problem that no runic inscriptions have been found in southern *Germania* dated earlier than the fifth century. If runic writing had begun in northern Italy and spread to Scandinavia, we should expect at least a sprinkling of inscriptions to have been left behind on the way north.

With these points in mind, it is no surprise that influential nineteenth-century runologists tended to view the roman as the source alphabet. And that is the position that many returned to during the second half of the twentieth century. Archaeology has revealed extensive contacts between the northern part of the Germanic world and the Roman Empire. There was thus ample opportunity for people of the North to observe a literate culture in action, and that may have led them to conclude that they too should have a writing system. At the same time, the geographical and political distance of northern *Germania* from the Roman world might explain why the roman alphabet was not adopted lock, stock and barrel and why the *fuþark* is relatively independent of the proposed model.

Opportunity is one thing, motivation another. Granted that there were Germanic speakers who mastered one or more Mediterranean languages, and that they learnt to operate within a literate culture, it is still not wholly clear why they felt the need for a writing system of their own. If the intention was to introduce full-blown literacy on, for example, the Roman model, with public notices, accounts, letters, literature, etc., very little came of it. The earliest inscriptions are laconic in the extreme, and appear to consist chiefly of names (see chapter 4). Possibly, as has been suggested, the aim was to imitate some of the outward manifestations of a literate culture. This could have been done to demonstrate and reinforce the high status of an elite vis-à-vis lower ranking members of Germanic society. An alternative or additional purpose might have been to proclaim independence of the Mediterranean world: to show that the roman (or whatever) alphabet and the Latin (or whatever) language were not essential prerequisites for written communication.

When considering motivation it is important to distinguish clearly between the earliest inscriptions and those that followed. Whatever the initial impetus, once the runes were in existence they could be used to write all manner of things. To take a pertinent example: even though a good many extant inscriptions in the older *fuþark* are on stone and appear to be of commemorative type, we would be wrong to assume that it was in order to create such monuments the runic alphabet was invented. No rune-stone can be shown to emanate from the period when runic writing was in its infancy.

2.4 Source alphabets, writing practices, and phonological systems

So far we have concentrated chiefly on the context in which the runes might have been created. A different matter is the relationship of the runic characters and runic writing in general with the proposed source. How far can individual runes be derived from particular letters? How closely do writing practices (such as direction of carving or word division) tally with those of the supposed model? A further, but separate, question concerns the relationship between the runes and language. What form or forms of early Germanic are written with runes, and what speech sounds do individual characters denote? The answers to these questions, which have concerned certain runologists far more than the contextual problems aired above, can cast a rather different light on the problem of runic origins.

Deriving individual runic shapes from Mediterranean models, let it be said at once, can be a frustrating exercise. This is because so much is in the eye of the beholder. To take but one example: ᚹ **w** has been derived from roman 'P', roman 'Q', greek ϒ (upsilon), archaic greek ϝ (digamma), and more besides. Nevertheless some derivations are more immediately plausible than others. There is an obvious correspondence between, say, roman 'B', 'H', 'R', and the runic counterparts ᛒ, ᚺ, ᚱ – not only in shape but also in sound value. Several other runes look very similar to roman capitals and denote roughly the same sound, e.g. ᚠ and 'F', ᚢ and 'V', ᛏ and 'T'. Some have claimed there are "rules" of runic form, such that, for example, branches never proceed exclusively from the base (hence ᚢ rather than a runic replica of 'V') and horizontal lines are avoided (hence ᚠ and ᛏ). While the rule about branches not proceeding exclusively from the base accords well enough with the evidence (though cf. inverted runes, p. 19), it is by no means clear that the creators of the *fuþark* eschewed horizontal lines, since an early form of **e** is ⊓ rather than (the commoner) ᛖ. Some runes exhibit a rather fainter likeness to possible roman originals, but that can in part have to do with the angular form in which they are commonly presented. ᚨ does not look very like 'A' at the best of times, but ᚦ and ᚲ can resemble 'D' and 'C' in their rounded forms ᚦ and ((see further 3.3). Some runes resemble roman letters but have a very different sound value, e.g. ᚷ, ᚹ, which look like 'X' and 'P' respectively but denote /g/ and /w/ (on ᚹ cf. above). Finally there are runes quite unlike any character of the roman alphabet, e.g. ᛃ, ᛈ, ᛞ (it has nevertheless been suggested these are based on 'G', 'K' and a combined right- and left-facing 'D' respectively).

All things considered, there is a much closer correspondence between runes and roman capitals than between runes and any form of classical greek script, notwithstanding the similarity between, say, ᛊ **s** and Σ (sigma) or ᛟ **o** and Ω (omega). Some have observed clearer points of likeness with characters of various north italic alphabets, and have suggested the creator(s) of the runes adopted characters from several (albeit closely related) alpine writing systems – a highly unusual procedure in alphabet history – or alternatively from a single system, which has yet to be discovered. But having made this leap of faith, proponents of the north italic theory still have to assume the inclusion of certain roman letters to make up the full complement of runes.

Too much weight has perhaps been placed on the shapes of individual runes and their supposed prototypes in other alphabets. In recent years it has been increasingly argued that the whole writing system must be taken into account when considering the origins of a particular script, not merely the characters that make it up. Following that line of thinking, archaic greek writing from around 400 BC has been identified as a likely source of the runes. Not only are there clear correspondences between individual characters. Runic writing, like the earliest greek (and archaic latin and etruscan, for that matter), may run from left to right or right to left, or boustrophedon (alternately left-right and right-left, like the ploughing of a field); in both systems nasals (p. 223) are frequently omitted before other consonants, so *landa-* 'land', for example, may appear in runic writing as **lada-** (cf. p. 25); in neither system are characters normally doubled (i.e. written twice in succession as the two 'n's in English *funny*; cf. p. 24); greek letters have names, as do runes (see 3.4); and so on. Not all of this evidence carries equal weight. Nevertheless the list of correspondences is long – and substantial enough.

Phonological arguments, too, have been adduced in support of the view that runic writing is considerably older than the oldest attested inscriptions. Twenty-two of the twenty-four runes appear to denote distinctive sounds of what is confidently assumed to have been the phonological system of most forms of Germanic around the beginning of the Christian era (see 3.5). This throws the spotlight on the two runes, ſ and ◇, which do not appear to justify their presence on phonological grounds. ◇ cannot in point of fact tell us anything about the age of the runes, since it stands either for [ŋ], which was a variant of /n/ that occurred immediately before [g] (as English *single* versus *sinful*), or for [ŋ] (or even [iŋ]) + [g] (a quicker alternative to writing (|) ♁Ж). ſ, on the other hand, does not seem to fulfil any obvious phonological or phonetic function at the time of the earliest runic inscriptions. It has therefore been suggested that it originally denoted [æ] (a vowel rather like that in English *cat*), which was arguably a distinctive sound in the earliest Germanic. This would take the creation of the runes well back into the BC era.

The evidence from writing practices and phonological systems must be given due consideration. Its precise significance is hard to gauge, however. Many of the features shared by runic and archaic greek writing occur elsewhere, and some or all of them could have arisen independently. The characters of the Irish ogam script, for example, are provided with names, yet there is little doubt ogam was invented by people familiar first and foremost with the roman alphabet. Variable direction of writing might be a manifestation of first steps in literacy, the product of experimentation, or the result of a conscious attempt to create distance from the roman model (as with the order of runes in the *fuþark*).

Nor can the mere presence of ∫ in the rune-row guarantee it originally represented /æ/. In certain inscriptions in the older *fuþark* and Anglo-Frisian *fuþorc* the character is used to denote [i(:)], and in some Anglo-Saxon inscriptions it may also stand for [ç] (see p. 41). However, none of these occurrences is dated earlier than the fifth century, and what they indicate first and foremost is the development of differing traditions about the value of ∫. Perhaps we are looking in the wrong area entirely. Conceivably, as some have claimed, ∫ and ◊ owe their place in the *fuþark* to a desire on the part of its creator(s) to achieve a total of precisely twenty-four runes. Why that should have been an important goal is not clear, but it is worth noting that when the Scandinavians later reduced the size of their rune-row (chapter 7) they dispensed with exactly one third of the stock of characters, leaving sixteen, which like twenty-four is a multiple of eight. Such pointers notwithstanding, the seemingly close correspondence between the characters of the older *fuþark* and the sound system it predominantly represented warns against viewing ∫ and ◊ as mere makeweights, added to achieve a desired number. (In this book ∫ is regularly transliterated æ, but that should not be taken to imply acceptance that [æ] was its original value. As noted in 1.3, transliteration indicates chiefly the distinctive shape of a character, not what sound or sounds it represented.)

Whatever the strengths and weaknesses of the arguments based on writing practices and phonology, they have to be set against the strong contextual evidence in favour of roman as the source alphabet. We may legitimately ask: were there sufficiently strong motivating factors around 400 BC – or at any time BC – for the creation of a Germanic system of writing? Why are there no inscriptions dated before the second half of the second century AD if runic writing came into existence several hundred years earlier? Neither question finds an obvious answer.

2.5 Conclusion

The upshot of the preceding discussion is that there can be no certainty when, where, by whom and for what purpose the runes were created. However, when dispassionately considered, the evidence points to the first century or two of the Christian era, to Denmark and southern Scandinavia, and to linguistically aware people of Germanic origin familiar with the Latin language and roman literacy, who saw an advantage in having a script of their own. Quite why they thought they needed a script is less clear, as are their reasons for developing a rune-row in preference to simply adopting the roman alphabet.

Select reading list

Derolez, R. 1998. *The Origin of the Runes: An Alternative Approach* (Academiae Analecta – Klasse der Letteren, Jaargang 60, 1). Brussels: Koninklijke Academie voor Wetenschappen, Letteren en Schone Kunsten van België. [A clear and informative general survey.]

Mees, Bernard 2000. 'The North Etruscan thesis of the origin of the runes', *Arkiv för nordisk filologi* 115, 33–82. [Dense and hard to follow in places, but represents a modern attempt to plead the "north etruscan" case.]

Moltke, Erik 1985. *Runes and their Origin: Denmark and Elsewhere.* Copenhagen: National Museum of Denmark, 21–73. [A detailed survey, which argues for roman capitals as the inspiration and trade as the motivating factor.]

Morris, Richard L. 1988. *Runic and Mediterranean Epigraphy* (*NOWELE* supplement 4). Odense: Odense University Press. [Presents the case for a BC origin and archaic greek as the source alphabet.]

Odenstedt, Bengt 1990. *On the Origin and Early History of the Runic Script* (Acta Academiae Regiae Gustavi Adolphi 59). Uppsala: Gustav Adolfs Akademien, 145–73. [Presents the case for classical roman capitals as the source alphabet.]

Williams, Henrik 1992. 'Which came first, ᛗ or ᚠ?', *Arkiv för nordisk filologi* 107, 192–205. [A detailed critique of Odenstedt's 1990 book.]

Williams, Henrik 2004. 'Reasons for runes'. In: (Stephen D. Houston, ed.) *The First Writing: Script Invention as History and Process.* Cambridge: Cambridge University Press, 262–73. [A brief, but wide-ranging discussion about the origin of the runes; it favours a derivation from classical roman script.]

Plate 1 The Kylver stone, Gotland, with its complete older *fuþark*

3 The older *fuþark*

3.1 Preamble

The subject matter of this chapter is rather broader than the title might suggest. Under consideration here are not only the characters of the older *fuþark* and their sound values, but also the languages and orthographic system(s) to be found in inscriptions written with this early type of rune-row. Analysis of what the inscriptions say, on the other hand, is relegated to chapter 4. In the discussion of individual rune forms, standardised representations are used unless otherwise stated (see 3.3).

3.2 The *fuþark* order

Although "alphabet" is sometimes used of a total set of runes, the synonyms "rune-row" and *fuþark* are more precise. The greek and roman letter-rows are properly called "alphabets" since their first two characters are *alpha* and *beta*, or 'a' and 'b'. The *fuþark*, in contrast, begins **f, u**; and it continues **þ, a, r, k**, not γ, δ, ε, ζ or 'c, d, e, f'. The order in which the runes are placed in their row is in fact totally different from that of the greek and roman alphabets, which maintain a sequence that ultimately derives from phoenician writing. Many hypotheses have been put forward to explain why the runes appear in the particular order they do, but none has gained general acceptance. We know the order from a number of *fuþark* (rune-row) inscriptions, dated (approximately in some cases) to the fifth and sixth centuries. There are eleven in all, though only four give the complete older *fuþark*, and of these just three have independent value since one appears on two bracteates (one-sided medallions) from the same die. Judging from these eleven inscriptions, the order of the runes was remarkably uniform, although minor variations are found. The Kylver stone from the Baltic island of Gotland (Plate 1), most notably, has ᚲᛊ for rr. 13–14 and ᛗᛉ for rr. 23–4, while the other rows that contain these characters have ᛊᚲ and ᛉᛗ. Whether the basic order we find in the fifth and sixth centuries was established from the start is unknown, but there is no good reason to think it was not.

In two of the complete rune-rows, on the Vadstena and Grumpan bracteates (from Öster- and Västergötland, Sweden, respectively), the *fuþark* is divided into three groups of eight. The significance of this is unclear, but in later Scandinavian tradition the tripartite division forms the basis of a common type of runic cryptography (see pp. 149–52). In Icelandic manuscripts from the seventeenth century on, the three groups are called *ættir*, which may be either plural of the word *ætt* 'family' or of the homonym *ætt* 'group of eight', related to the numeral *átta* 'eight'. How far back this designation goes is uncertain.

3.3 Rune forms

Discussion of the shapes of runes and the extent to which they can vary requires the introduction of a few technical terms. Those used in this book are ones commonly found in the English-speaking world.

Most runes are based on one or more vertical lines, and these are known as "verticals". The eleventh rune, | **i**, consists solely of a vertical. Extending diagonally (very occasionally horizontally) or in a curve from the vertical are "branches" (sometimes called "twigs"), as in, e.g., ᚠ **f** or ᚢ **u**, the first and second runes. Where a diagonal line leaves the vertical and rejoins it, as in ᚦ, the third rune, we talk of a bow. In the case of ᚱ, the fifth rune, we have a tail in addition to the (in older-*fuþark* inscriptions usually incomplete) bow. "Tail" is used here in preference to "branch" for clarity's sake (since a bow itself can be seen as consisting of two connecting branches). Some runes have no vertical, only diagonal lines, e.g. ᚷ, ᛃ, ᛉ. There is no agreement on the terminology to describe these, and ad-hoc solutions are adopted in the following as necessary.

vertical → | ↑ ← vertical + branches
vertical + bow → ᚦ   ᚱ ← vertical + bow and tail

Fig. 6 The essential components of most runes

In general discussions of runes and runic writing it is common to use standardised forms (as, for example in chapter 1, Figs 1–5). These are convenient abstractions: they facilitate consideration of the general as opposed to the specific, and are easier for font-makers and printers to deal with. But they do not reflect the reality. Runes, just as the handwritten letters of the roman alphabet, differ in shape from place to place, time to time, and person to person. Reference has already been made to the fact that branches may be straight or curved. They may also be longer or shorter, proceed – within a certain degree of tolerance – from higher or lower on the vertical; bows may be incomplete (ᚱ) or complete (ᚱ); and so on.

The distinction between straight and curved branches (e.g. ᚠ v. ᚠ) – and likewise angular and rounded bows (e.g. ᚦ v. ᚦ) – could be considered trivial but for the fact that many runologists have claimed that the straight and angular forms are the original ones. With circular reasoning they have argued (1) that the vertical, diagonal and angular lines seen in some of the earliest inscriptions reflect the fact that runes were designed to be carved in wood (at an angle to the grain and avoiding curves, which would have been difficult to cut); (2) that since wood was the primary material, the first runes must have had a shape suited to working in that medium: vertical, diagonal, angular, and with studied avoidance of horizontal and curving lines (horizontal liable to be confused with the grain). In much of the literature the "angular runes = wood, wood = angular runes" proposition has become axiomatic. But it is in truth no more than hypothesis. Most of the earliest inscriptions are found on metal and contain runes with curved as well as straight lines and rounded as well as angular bows (also the occasional **e** with a horizontal branch: ᛖ). It can of course be argued (and has been) that wood is a perishable material; that most of the older-*fuþark* inscriptions in wood have duly perished; and that therein lies the reason for the wealth of apparent counter-evidence. As a general principle, however, we are on safer ground arguing from what exists rather than what does not. Furthermore, there are a great number of medieval runic inscriptions in wood with beautifully rounded runes.

A further type of variation concerns orientation. Runic inscriptions run both left to right and right to left, and asymmetrical characters tend to face the direction of writing. Thus the word *alu*, arguably an early form of the word *ale*, is written ᚨᛚᚢ left to right and ᚢᛚᚨ right to left. Direction cannot of course be indicated by symmetrical runes such as ᚷ **g**, ᛉ **z**, ᛞ **d**; nor in fact by asymmetrical ᚺ **h**, ᚾ **n**, ᛃ **j**, ᛇ **æ**, since the choice between these and the variants ᚺ, ᚾ, ᛃ, ᛇ seems to be independent of an inscription's orientation. Occasionally runes are found that face the opposite way from the general direction (cf. ᚨ **a** and ᛒ **b** in the left-to-right Kylver rune-row, Plate 1). These are known as "retrograde or "reverse" runes. There are also characters which appear upside down, most notably **z**, which often has the form ᛦ (as in the Kylver row). Such runes are called "inverted".

Variation in runic shape can be idiosyncratic, but may also have local, regional, social or chronological significance. In the 1980s a small group of inscriptions came to light in Illerup, eastern Jutland, where the bow of ᚦ and ᚹ occurs on both sides of the vertical: ᚦ, ᚹ. Although it is far from clear these inscriptions were made in eastern Jutland, the use of ᚦ and ᚹ could reflect a short-lived local development somewhere in Scandinavia. It has also been suggested that the double-sided forms are only found on high-status objects, and that social as well as – or rather than – local variation may be at play. Of course it is also possible we are dealing with a chance embellishment that might affect any asymmetrical rune based on a single vertical, but the concentration in a particular group suggests something more significant than that. It is also worth noting in this connection how new finds can alter our conception of the runes and their development.

Clearly regional is the distinction between ᚺ and ᚻ. The double-branch form occurs almost entirely in the West Germanic world (primarily Anglo-Saxon England after about 650, Frisia and southern Germany). The single-branch variant is characteristic of Scandinavia, though it is also found in northern Germany and around the Continental North-Sea coast (also in Anglo-Saxon England before about 650). Unclear is whether both varieties existed from the start or whether one of them is a later innovation. ᚻ does not seem to be certainly attested before the fifth century, but against that must be set the fact that the bulk of the earliest inscriptions are found in Scandinavia.

That the shapes of some runes develop over time is uncontroversial. There is, however, considerable disagreement about specific forms: do they really reflect the period in which they were carved, or could they have been determined by the material used, by local traditions, the whim of the carver, or something other? And if the period is the decisive factor, can a rough date be given to it, or must we content ourselves with relative dating – concluding simply that form X is older than form Y? Different runologists supply different answers to these questions, though the extent of the disagreement can vary from rune to rune. Some runes retain the same basic appearance throughout the period of their use, e.g. ᚠ **f**, ᚷ **g**, ᛁ **i**, ᛚ **l**. Others show a clear pattern of development. That is especially true of ᚲ **k**, and ᛃ **j**, two of the three runes that were commonly of smaller size than the others (the third, ᛜ **ŋ**, is too poorly attested for any clear view to be formed about how its shape might have changed). There is an increasing tendency to give ᚲ and ᛃ full height, and ultimately to supply them with a vertical. As manifestations of **k** we find, for example, ᛉ, ᛃ, ᚴ, and of **j** ᛀ, ᚺ, ᛉ. Conservative runologists would probably go no further than to say that ᚲ or ᛃ are likely to indicate an early inscription, ᛉ, ᛃ or ᛀ, ᚺ a later, and ᚴ, ᛉ one carved towards the end of the older-*fuþark* period. Others have been willing to assign particular forms to periods within a given century. Recently an attempt has been made using archaeologically datable inscriptions to show that several runes, including **k** and **j**, do exhibit a clear pattern of development from one specific period to another. The relatively small number of inscriptions involved, however, still leaves a fair margin of uncertainty. At one time it was argued, for example, that ᚟ was an early form of **e** (notwithstanding the horizontal branch). This view was based partly on archaeological dating, partly on the general impression runologists had of inscriptions containing ᚟. Subsequently it was pointed out that most of these inscriptions were on metal, and that the type of surface, rather than age, might be the factor determining the shape of the branch. Now it has been shown that all ten occurrences of **e** datable to before AD *c.* 375 have the form ᚟. It is also noteworthy, however, that seven of the ten ᚟s are carved into metal, one into bone and just two (in the same inscription) into wood. The inference to be drawn is that ᚟ was an earlier form of **e** than ᛗ, but it is still possible our view is skewed by the large number of metal inscriptions making up the sample.

As well as exhibiting variation in form, runes may on occasion be joined together. Usually this affects just two, rather as roman 'æ' is made up of 'a' and 'e', but occasionally three or more can be merged into a single character. Such ligatures are known as "bind-runes". Examples are ᚼ, which is made up of ᚺ **h** and ᚨ **a**, and ᛗ, which consists of ᚟ **e** and ᛗ **m**.

Variation in runic form has implications for transliteration. How far does the runologist go in attempting to convey the potentially infinite variety of the original? Most would say it is enough to reproduce the distinctive units of the writing system (cf. pp. 3–4). Attempts to make finer distinctions (except for specific purposes) are likely to result in considerable complexity, with little practical gain at the end of the process. Those interested in the details of runic form had best examine the runes themselves, or failing that, good photographs or drawings. Commonly occurring characteristics can be (and usually are) noted in commentaries, e.g. right-to-left direction of writing, retrograde and inverted runes. More specific features may be pointed out as appropriate. Bind-runes are normally signified by placing a slur over the relevant roman characters, e.g. h͡a.

3.4 Rune names

Unlike the letters of the roman alphabet, runes had names (or, more precisely, designations, but "name" is the term commonly used). That is also true of greek letters, but whereas their names were inherited from Phoenician and thus had no meaning in Greek, those given to the runes were derived from Germanic common or proper nouns. It is not known whether the names go back to the beginnings of runic writing. The earliest direct evidence for them is in ninth- and tenth-century Continental and English manuscripts (cf. pp. 157, 159). These give the Anglo-Saxon and/or Scandinavian younger-*fuþark* runes together with the names by which they were then known to scribes. Since the younger *fuþark* contained just sixteen runes, there are eight for which we have only Anglo-Saxon designations. There is, however, enough of a correspondence between the sixteen rune names that survive in both traditions for us to believe that the nomenclature as a whole shares a common origin in the Germanic past. No rune names are known emanating from other parts of the Germanic world. The appellations given to the letters of a ?tenth-century version of the gothic alphabet (created not later than the fourth century for writing Gothic, an East Germanic language) are similar enough to suggest a connection, but the version concerned and the associated names bear all the signs of an antiquarian reworking, perhaps far removed from actual gothic letter names (if such ever existed).

Several attempts have been made to relate the rune names to postulated early Germanic belief systems, but none has proved persuasive. More striking is the key the names provide to sound value. In all but two cases the initial sound of the name gives the value of the rune. Thus ᚠ **f**, standing for /f/, is called in Old English *feoh*, in Old Norse *fé*, the Germanic ancestor form of which would have been **fehu* 'wealth' (the asterisk marks the form as reconstructed rather than actually attested); ᚢ **u**, standing for /u/, was *ur* in both languages (*úr* in normalised Old Norse spelling), though to the English this meant 'aurochs' (wild ox), to the Norwegians and Icelanders 'drizzle' (or perhaps 'slag' to the former); ᚦ **þ** was called *þorn* 'thorn' in Old English, *þurs* 'giant' in Old Norse, so we cannot be entirely sure what the earliest form of its name was, but in both cases the initial sound is [θ]. The rune names thus follow what is known as an acrophonic (initial sound) principle, and it is reasonable to suppose that the aim was they should function as a mnemonic device. In the two cases where the acrophonic principle is not applied there is good reason. ᛉ **z**, called in Old English *eolhx* (of uncertain meaning), and ᛜ **ŋ**, OE *Ing*, a proper name, denote sounds that never occurred at the beginning of a word in Germanic. There are some grounds for thinking their names may originally have been **alʒiz* and **ingwaz* respectively, in which case they each incorporated the relevant sound, but in final (**alʒiz*) and medial (**ingwaz*) position instead of initial.

Fig. 7 depicts the twenty-four runes of the older *fuþark* together with their assumed names, the latter reconstructed on the basis of later attestations. A macron over a vowel means it is long (vowel length, however, is not normally marked in older-*fuþark* inscriptions where these are presented as edited texts;

see p. 179). Serious uncertainty about a name or its meaning is indicated by a question mark.

ᚠ	f	*fehu*	'cattle' 'wealth'
ᚾ	u	*ūruz*	?'wild ox'
ᚦ	þ	?*þurisaz*	'giant' 'monster'
ᚨ	a	*ansuz*	'god'
ᚱ	r	*raiðō*	'riding' 'ride'
ᚲ	k	?*kauna*	'boil'
ᚷ	g	*gebō*	'gift'
ᚹ	w	*wunjō*	'joy'
ᚺ	h	*haȝalaz*	'hail'
ᚾ	n	*nauðiz*	'need' 'affliction'
ᛁ	i	*īsaz*	'ice'
ᛃ	j	*jāra*	'(good) year'
ᛇ	æ	?*ī(h)waz*	'yew'
ᛈ	p	?*perþō*	?
ᛉ	z	?*alȝiz*	?'elk'
ᛋ	s	*sōwilō*	'sun'
ᛏ	t	*tīwaz*	'the god Týr'
ᛒ	b	*berkana*	?'birchwood'
ᛖ	e	*ehwaz*	'horse'
ᛗ	m	*mannaz*	'man' 'human'
ᛚ	l	*laȝuz*	'water' 'liquid'
ᛝ	ŋ	*ingwaz*	'Ing [a proper name]'
ᛟ	o	*ōþala/*ōþila*	'inherited possession'
ᛞ	d	*daȝaz*	'day'

Fig. 7 The probable or possible older-*fuþark* rune names

Further discussion of the rune names and their meanings will be found in chapter 13.

3.5 The languages and orthographic system(s) of the older-*fuþark* inscriptions

The language of most of the inscriptions written in the older *fuþark* is remarkable for its uniformity. There are a few early texts that seem to reflect an East Germanic type of speech, a somewhat later group from southern Germany that are in an early type of German, and a small number of Scandinavian inscriptions, probably of the late sixth or seventh century, which bear witness to radical linguistic change in the North. These apart, the older-*fuþark* inscriptions present us with a form of language that has been called variously Primitive Scandinavian, North-West Germanic, "the Runic Language", and much else besides. Behind these differing appellations lie fundamental disagreements about the nature and status of the language concerned.

Since most of the older-*fuþark* inscriptions are found in Scandinavia, there has been a natural tendency to think they document an early form of Scandinavian (hence Primitive Scandinavian). Against that view it has been argued (a) that dispassionate examination reveals a language much closer to the common ancestor of all the Germanic tongues than to later Scandinavian, and (b) that this language represents an earlier stage of West Germanic just as much as of Scandinavian (hence North-West Germanic). The evidence is not wholly conclusive either way; it is worth noting, though, that a recent detailed study deems the idiom to have been "mildly Scandinavian". To avoid coming down on one side or the other, neutral terms like "the Runic Language" have been coined, though it has been maintained with fair justification that it is unsatisfactory to name a language after the system used to write it, and further that (depending on how precisely "the Runic Language" is defined) more than one type of Germanic idiom may be involved.

Rejecting all these points of view, some have claimed that the language in the bulk of older-*fuþark* inscriptions is not a reflection of actual speech at all but a supra-dialectal norm, invented and used by rune-carvers. It is hard to believe that people inhabiting, say, the south of Jutland ever spoke precisely like those on the Atlantic coast of Norway or that either used a type of language identical to that found on the Baltic coast of Sweden – so why otherwise should the language of the inscriptions be so uniform? On the other hand, there is no indication of a central authority of the kind one would think a prerequisite for the development of a written norm. The likelihood is perhaps that the extreme sparseness of the sources combined with a certain conservatism among rune-writers contrives to give an impression of linguistic homogeneity where in reality none existed – that beneath the apparently uniform surface lurks widespread speech variation.

Whatever the rights and wrongs of this debate, there has – surprisingly perhaps – been fairly general agreement about the phonological system underlying most of the older-*fuþark* inscriptions. It should be stressed, however, that we are dealing with a model rather than demonstrable reality – a model that owes much to the interpretation of the inscriptions themselves (with the danger of circularity that involves). However, as long as we are aware of the problems, the postulated system serves a practical purpose in that it allows us to attribute speech sounds to almost all of the twenty-four runes of the *fuþark*. It is worth reiterating, though, that this system may be rather different from the one for which the runes were originally devised (cf. pp. 13–14).

By common consent, the correspondence between rune and phoneme in most older-*fuþark* inscriptions is as shown in Fig. 8 (on [(i)ŋ(g)] – speech sounds not phonemes – see below).

ᛒ, ᛗ and ᚷ were often realised as [β], [ð], [ɣ] (commonly rendered ƀ, ð, ȝ where inscriptions are presented as edited texts, see p. 222); [b], [d], [g] tended to occur in initial position, when geminated, and immediately after nasal consonants, [β], [ð], [ɣ] elsewhere, i.e. each pair were positional variants (phonemes whose realisation varied according to the phonetic environment). The quality or qualities of ᚺ are uncertain: to begin with it probably chiefly denoted [x], but this must gradually have changed to [h] in most positions.

vowels:	/i/ ᛁ		/u/ ᚢ		
	/e/ ᛖ		/o/ ᛟ		
		/a/ ᚨ			
consonants:	/p/ ᛈ		/t/ ᛏ		/k/ ᚲ
	/b/ ᛒ		/d/ ᛞ		/g/ ᚷ
	/f/ ᚠ		/θ/ ᚦ		/h/ ᚺ
	/m/ ᛗ		/n/ ᚾ		[(i)ŋ(g)] ᛜ
		/s/ ᛊ		/z/ ᛉ	
		/l/ ᛚ		/r/ ᚱ	
		/w/ ᚹ		/j/ ᛃ	

Fig. 8 The phonemes (+ the sound(s) [(i)ŋ(g)]) denoted by the runes of the older *fuþark*

If the sound system outlined here is anything like the one actually used by those who carved the bulk of the older-*fuþark* inscriptions, it shows a remarkably close – almost one-to-one – correspondence between rune and phoneme. The relationship between speech and writing is quite unlike that in modern English, where, for example, the diphthong /ai/ may be written 'ie' as in *lie*, 'igh' as in *sigh*, 'y' as in *why*, and so on, and where there are homophones like *to*, *too* and *two* each with a different spelling. Only two runes, ᛇ and ᛜ, do not denote a distinctive speech sound (as discussed in 2.4). ᛇ rarely occurs in meaningful inscriptions, and where it does seems mostly to stand for /i(:)/, normally represented by ᛁ. ᛜ denotes either [ŋ] or [ŋg] (or possibly [iŋg]); [ŋ] is a positional variant of /n/, occurring before /g/, while [(i)ŋg] is a cluster of two consonants (or a vowel + two consonants), which could be, and sometimes was, written (ᛁ)ᚾᚷ.

In the writing of some languages letters may be doubled to indicate a long sound as opposed to a short. This is not a feature of runic orthography (except where influenced by roman-alphabet practice). Indeed, where one word ends and the next begins with the same rune, the requisite character may be written only once. Unambiguous examples are hard to find in older-*fuþark* inscriptions, but are common enough in Viking-Age Scandinavia. On the early ninth-century Rök stone from Östergötland, Sweden, for example, we read **uarinumnaʀ**, to be understood as *warin numnaʀ* 'were taken'.

The single marking of two identical sounds across a word boundary is made easier by the fact that in runic writing there is often no word separation. Older-*fuþark* inscriptions in particular can consist of a single unbroken sequence of runes. Where separators do occur (in the earliest times usually in the form of one or more points), they are not necessarily inserted between each word, although they may be. The Tune stone, from Østfold, south-eastern Norway, begins, for example: **ekwiwazafter·woduri|de**... 'I Wiwaz after Woðuriðaz...' (the point here perhaps highlighting the name which follows it). Word division is never marked by a space in older-*fuþark* inscriptions, though separate words are sometimes placed on different lines, or on different faces of an object. Points or other marks may be used not just as separators but also to signal the beginning or end of an inscription.

A further notable feature of runic orthography is the omission of runes denoting nasal consonants where these occur immediately before consonants with the same place of articulation (cf. p. 223). In older-*fuþark* inscriptions this affects in particular **m** before **b** (both bilabial), **n** before **d** (both dental), and **n** or **ŋ** before **g** (both velar), as in, for example, ᛉᚨᛃᛁᚱᚨᚹᚨᛞᚨᛚ **ladawarijaz** (written right to left) on the Tørvika A stone from Hordaland, south-western Norway, which by general consent gives the personal name *Landawarijaz* (consisting of the elements 'land' and 'guardian'). However, where we have a word or element that is less easily recognised, the practice can cause problems of interpretation. On the Stenstad stone from Telemark, southern Norway, we find the two-word sequence ᛁᚷᛁᛃᛟᚾᚺᛚᚨᛉ **igijonh͡alaz**. The second word, **h͡alaz** 'stone', is unproblematic; the first is taken as the genitive of a personal name, thus 'X's stone', a laconic memorial. The difficulty is to identify 'X's' name. It might begin *Ig-* or *Ing-*. Both have been suggested, but the arguments are inconclusive either way. This example draws attention once again to the marginal status of ᛜ **ŋ**, the twenty-second rune. Not only could [ŋg] be written ᚾᚷ **ng**, but also simply ᚷ **g**.

The fact that runes had names inspired carvers on occasion to use them as ideographs, that is, to stand for their name rather than the sound they normally represented. Clear examples in older-*fuþark* inscriptions are rare, but one certainly occurs on the Stentoften stone from Blekinge, south-eastern Sweden (probably seventh-century, at which time Blekinge is to be reckoned part of Denmark). There, near the beginning of a lengthy text, we read ᚺᛡᚦᚢᚹᛟᛚᛡᚠᛦᚷᛡᚠᛄ **hAþuwolAfzgAfj** 'Haþuwulfz [name consisting of the elements 'battle' and 'wolf'] gave a good year [i.e. a good harvest]'. ᛄ cannot here be interpreted as a rune for /j/, since /j/ on its own is not a Germanic word, and what is required to complete the sentence is a word that can function as the object of 'gave'. But if we deem ᛄ to stand for its name, **jāra* 'year' 'a good year', perfect sense is achieved (Haþuwulfz as king or ruler is being given credit for a good harvest). Some have argued that runes were regularly used not only in abbreviation of their names, but of any other word that began with the sound they represented. None of the examples that have been identified in older-*fuþark* inscriptions have carried total conviction; they are certainly less clear-cut than Stentoften's ᛄ (see further pp. 146–7).

Select reading list

Antonsen, Elmer H. 1975. *A Concise Grammar of the Older Runic Inscriptions*. Tübingen: Niemeyer, 1–14. [A fairly technical introduction to the older *fuþark*.]

Antonsen, Elmer H. 2002. *Runes and Germanic Linguistics* (Trends in Linguistics, Studies and Monographs 140). Berlin/New York: Mouton de Gruyter, 37–71. [A fairly technical introduction to the older *fuþark*, more recent and detailed than the preceding.]

Nielsen, Hans Frede 2000. *The Early Runic Language of Scandinavia: Studies in Germanic Dialect Geography*. Heidelberg: Universitätsverlag C. Winter. [An exhaustive study of the language of older-*fuþark* inscriptions of Scandinavia, showing how it relates to other north-western European forms of Germanic.]

Odenstedt, Bengt 1990. *On the Origin and Early History of the Runic Script* (Acta Academiae Regiae Gustavi Adolphi 59). Uppsala: Gustav Adolfs Akademien, 11–128. [A very detailed and fairly technical account of the individual runes of the older *fuþark*.]

Spurkland, Terje 2005. *Norwegian Runes and Runic Inscriptions*. Woodbridge: Boydell Press, 5–19. [An introduction to the older *fuþark* for the general reader.]

4 Inscriptions in the older *fuþark*

4.1 Problems

At the latest count there are a little short of 400 inscriptions known in the twenty-four-character older *fuþark*. Many are only partly legible, either because of wear or damage or because characters are used that do not coincide with those we expect on the basis of our experience. Some inscriptions consist of or contain sequences of runes that do not record language, or perhaps record it in encrypted or abbreviated guise. Prime examples of the former are those that present the older *fuþark* complete or in part. A possible example of the latter is the sequence **aaaaaaaazzznnn*bmuttt** (* marking a character made unreadable by damage) on the Lindholmen amulet (AD *c.* 375–575) from Skåne (now south-western Sweden). Since there is nothing here resembling a Germanic word (despite a claim to the contrary), we conclude that no straightforward linguistic message was intended. Possibly, as has been suggested, some at least of the runes in this part of the inscription stand for their names, giving **ansuz* eight times, ?**alʒiz* three times, and so on. But should this interpretation indeed be correct, we have no real notion of the purpose of such repetition – notwithstanding the various ideas that have been floated.

Even when confronted with a reasonably well-preserved inscription sporting a sequence of runes interpretable as one or more Germanic words, we may often be very far from understanding what the carver intended to communicate. The extremely laconic nature of the texts puts us at a disadvantage, but even more so our ignorance of the society from which they spring. Archaeology can tell us something; there are occasional accounts from outside observers of the Germanic world; and there is the testimony of the inscriptions themselves. But these sources only bring us a little way towards determining the kind of things Germanic peoples of the older-*fuþark* period would have thought worth inscribing.

By way of comparison, let us imagine a world some 2,000 years hence in which the only written records of our present-day English-speaking civilisation consist of around 400 extremely brief texts. Little is known of this civilisation otherwise, though its language can be reconstructed in part. One of the texts, on an uninformative piece of material, says simply: *wordperfect*. How is this to be understood? Is it one word or more? Is it a name? Can it be analysed as noun + adjective with the meaning 'perfect word'? If so, does it have religious connotations? Or is *perfect* a verb (with the stress on the last syllable)? In that case, can we interpret it as a kind of injunction: 'write well so that others can read what you write'? Let us further imagine the text is poorly preserved. Some, thinking to see an 's' before the initial 'w', read *swordperfect* and – uncertain of the date of the inscription or ignorant of the giant strides made by the nineteenth- and twentieth-century armaments industry – try to connect the text with a weapon-maker or with the site of a postulated battle. Others, reading *wortperfect*, judge the inscription to refer in some way to intoxicating liquor, and place it in the context of cult practices involving mental stimulants. Ultimately none of them have it right because knowledge of computers and their associated software programmes has been lost.

This comparison may seem far-fetched, but consideration of the inscription on the Reistad stone (probably from before AD 500), Vest-Agder, southern Norway, shows it to have some force. The inscription is in three lines and is normally read:

> iuþingaz
> ekwakraz:unnam
> wraita

iuþingaz and **wakraz** are interpreted as personal names (of disputed meaning); **ek** is the pronoun 'I' (cf. German *ich*, Latin *ego*). So far there is broad agreement. One scholar reads **idringaz** rather than **iuþingaz**, but still recognises a personal name here (which he translates 'of memorable lineage'). **unnam|wraita**, on the other hand, has been understood in two completely different ways: (1) to mean something like 'undertook the writing', or (2) as 'took the land'. **unnam** has also been read **unnamz**, whereupon it metamorphoses from a verb into an adjective qualifying **wakraz**, and **wraita** becomes the verb: 'I Wakraz, the untakeable, wrote [this]'. The only point the three interpretations of this part of the inscription agree on is that the sequence **nam** is somehow to be connected with a verb meaning 'take' (cf. German *nehmen*). Beyond that they go their separate ways.

The problem here, as commonly where runic inscriptions are subject to rival interpretations, is to identify grounds for preferring one interpretation to another. To determine the most likely *reading* runologists can do no better than examine the inscription at issue for themselves and record what they think to see, but in the case of a very worn surface or one with cuts and gashes, or natural lines and ridges (as on the Reistad stone), certainty may be hard to achieve. The reading ultimately proposed and the text derived from it must convince as a word, phrase or sentence of a language belonging to the place and time in which the inscription is located. That is far from straightforward in the case of many older-*fuþark* inscriptions, since knowledge of early forms of Germanic is limited, allowing considerable scope for imaginative reconstruction. Finally the text should offer plausible sense, and with regard to the older runic writings we come back to the dilemma outlined at the outset: our ignorance of early Germanic society, particularly in the first six or seven centuries of the Christian era, and the resulting uncertainty about what rune-writers might have thought it important to record. Ignorance and uncertainty allow scholars freedom to speculate and some have exploited this to the full. They also make it difficult to dismiss out of hand even some apparently quite fanciful interpretations.

In the light of this, the continuing lack of consensus about the reading and interpretation of the Reistad inscription is no surprise. Close examination of the stone suggests that **iuþingaz** and **unnam** are more likely readings than **idringaz** and **unnamz**. It is impossible, however, to decide on the basis of the Reistad text alone whether **ekwakraz:unnam|wraita** means 'I Wakraz undertook the writing' or 'I Wakraz took the land' – or indeed something else. What we need is comparative evidence, and that comes first and foremost from other runic inscriptions of the early period.

4.2 Solutions

A good deal of early runic writing can be tolerably well interpreted, at least on a superficial level. That is to say, runologists can often agree about the word or words used, about the grammatical forms, and the plain meaning of the text – if not the intention behind it.

By general consent one of the oldest extant runic inscriptions is that found on the lance-head from Øvre Stabu, Oppland, eastern Norway. It is dated to the second half of the second century of the Christian era. The runes read **raunijaz**, which gives us a word apparently meaning 'tester' or 'prober' (ON *reynir*). Many other pieces of military equipment have been found with single-word runic inscriptions, which fact, together with the apparent sense of the words, has led to the view that these are likely to be names. Since Germanic peoples (at different times and places) are known to have named their weapons, and since 'tester' seems appropriate to a lance (whose purpose or desired attribute is to probe the enemies' defences), **raunijaz** has been commonly accepted as applying to the Øvre Stabu lance-head itself. In other cases a name may refer not to an individual weapon, but to a group. Three lance-heads from about AD 200–250, two found in Illerup, eastern Jutland, and one in Vimose on the neighbouring island of Fyn, all bear the text **wagnijo**, interpreted as 'rider' 'traveller'. On two of the lance-heads the runes are cut, but on the third they are stamped. Both the recurrence of the name and the stamping technique employed indicate mass production, and from that it has been deduced that **wagnijo** is to be seen as a product name or trademark rather than specific to a particular lance. But is the purpose of the trademark to indicate a characteristic of the weapons, or to identify the maker (or the owner of the weapon smithy) by placing his (or just conceivably her) name on the products? While 'prober' seems a reasonable designation for a lance, 'rider' is less appropriate, for lances were not thrown through the air like spears, but used in close combat. And we know that makers or manufacturers did sometimes identify themselves on objects they produced, for we have several two-word inscriptions consisting of a name followed by a verb meaning 'made', e.g. **niþijo|tawide** 'Niþijo [a man's name of uncertain meaning] made' on a mount for a shield-grip from Illerup (AD *c.* 200–250), or **hagiradaz:tawide**: 'Haჳiraðaz [a man's name consisting of the elements 'beneficial' and 'advisor'] made' on a wooden box from Garbølle, Zealand (before AD 400). Where we find what appears to be a personal name, and nothing more, there is also the possibility it refers to the owner of the object on which it appears. Another shield-grip mount from Illerup (*c.* 200–250), for example, carries the inscription **swarta**. This is probably a nickname derived from an adjective meaning 'dark' or 'black' (cf. English *swarthy*), referring perhaps to the dark skin or black hair of the owner of the shield – if not to the general appearance of one who works in a smithy.

Older-*fuþark* inscriptions carved on stone can also consist of one or two words only, but are sometimes a little or considerably longer (cf. Reistad above). Single-word stone inscriptions, like their counterparts on loose objects, mostly exhibit the nominative grammatical case. From this and from the lexical composition of the words concerned it has been concluded that here too we are dealing with names, but exclusively the names of people. The intention behind such laconic inscriptions is not immediately apparent, but comparison with the wider corpus offers pointers. The Amla stone (of uncertain date) from Sogn og Fjordane, western Norway, says:]*izhaiwidazþar, in edited and amended form, ...*iz hlaiwiðaz þar*, '[?name with the nominative ending *-iz*] buried here'. The perhaps fifth-century Kjølevik stone (Plate 2; see further 15.2), Rogaland, south-western Norway, is more informative still, proclaiming in three lines (written right to left):

> **hadulaikaz**
> **ekhagustadaz**
> **ﬂaaiwidomaguminino**

Edited and translated, that is: *Haðulaikaz. Ek ?Haʒustaldaz hlaiwiðo maʒu minino* 'Haðulaikaz [a man's name consisting of the elements 'battle' and 'play']. I ?Haʒustaldaz [perhaps a man's name, but of uncertain identification and meaning; cf. pp. 181–3] buried my son' (some prefer to interpret the first name as *Handulaikaz*, 'hand' + 'play', but that need not concern us here). On the basis of these and other lengthier stone inscriptions it is possible to surmise that single names in the nominative may fulfil the same role as **hadulaikaz** apparently does on the Kjølevik stone, announcing the identity of a deceased relative, and that such inscriptions could thus be of commemorative type. This surmise is strengthened by the occurrence of a number of older-*fuþark* stone inscriptions with what appear to be personal names in the genitive (possessive) case, followed by a word meaning 'grave', 'stone' or 'monument'. The Bø stone (of uncertain date), Rogaland, south-western Norway, with its **hnab(u)dashlaiwa** 'Hnabuða's [a man's name perhaps derived from a verb meaning 'maim'] grave' may serve as an example.

Comparative evidence thus suggests that the Reistad stone, discussed above, is most likely to be of commemorative type: Iuþingaz is the deceased and Wakraz the carver, or at least the commissioner, of the monument. No other stone inscriptions of the older-*fuþark* period appear to record the taking of land, and for that reason it must be judged unlikely that Reistad documents such an act – though we do not have enough evidence to exclude this interpretation entirely. And we certainly cannot assume all stone inscriptions in the older *fuþark* to be of commemorative type. The seventh-century Stentoften stone, Blekinge (now south-eastern Sweden), sports a text over twenty words long that does not appear to be primarily commemorative, if at all. At the other end of the scale, the Elgesem stone (of uncertain date), Vestfold, south-eastern Norway, says simply **alu**, by many scholars (but by no means all) interpreted as an early form of the word *ale*.

This last inscription would stand as a total aberration, were it not for the existence of a number of loose objects bearing the same word. By and large

Plate 2 The Kjølevik stone, Rogaland, Norway

the objects concerned are bracteates, and in most cases **alu** appears on its own (Plate 3 shows an example). These gold medallions, from the period AD *c.* 450–550, also sport other single words whose meaning seems relatively clear but whose purpose is not immediately obvious. We find **e͡hwu** 'mare', **hagalu** 'hail-stones', **laukaz** 'leek', **laþu** 'invitation', all of which also appear in longer inscriptions on bracteates and/or other loose objects (the first, though, in rather uncertain form, the second as the singular **hagala** 'hail'). On the grounds that the words concerned can be placed in a context of belief and worship (there is evidence of Germanic veneration of the horse and cult practices involving the leek, for example), and that bracteates may have functioned as amulets, these minimal runic texts have been connected with the world of the supernatural. In the case of the frequently occurring **alu** a link has been made to the use of intoxicating substances in religious practices, known from different parts of the world (this interpretation is of course dependent on **alu**'s being a word for 'ale').

Plate 3 The Bjørnerud bracteate, Vestfold, Norway, displaying the word **alu**
(running right to left at a 90° angle to the head)

The typological approach exemplified here has merit, but it should be noted that many bracteates carry texts which, to us at least, are incomprehensible, while a couple sport older *fuþark*s that include various otherwise undocumented rune forms. To explain such occurrences the concept of the illiterate metalworker has been developed. Germanic bracteate production began in imitation of Roman coins and medallions, and these required a legend. What is suggested is that many Germanic metalworkers simply copied patterns of writing on to their bracteates from models (supplied, perhaps, in some cases by customers not always highly skilled in runic writing themselves), which they understood only imperfectly or not at all.

These two views of bracteate legends are not of course mutually exclusive. While there is no reason to suppose all metalworkers were literate, there were clearly enough who were (or who were overseen by a literate person) to ensure that some bracteates carried meaningful texts; and certain of those texts may have reflected cult practices. Much, though, depends on how bracteates functioned. There is disagreement about whether they were first and foremost amulets or served more as adornments of one kind or another, or perhaps symbols of allegiance. Their function may of course have changed over time, and possibly they had different uses in different areas.

While the bulk of older-*fuþark* inscriptions from Scandinavia are found on military equipment, stones and bracteates, those from Germany occur chiefly on brooches and other personal objects. Most of the German runic finds are from the sixth century and are concentrated in the south-western part of the country. The finds consist almost exclusively of grave goods – objects of value buried with their owners – and a great many come from female graves. The inscriptions predominantly record personal names, but there are also references to the writing of runes; some carvers express wishes, and the term of endearment **leub** or **leob** 'dear' appears several times. Individually the German inscriptions can be hard to interpret satisfactorily. In particular, there are often problems understanding how two or more names relate to each other. The Weimar 3 (buckle) inscription from Thüringen, can serve as an illustrative example. It has two sequences of runes: **ida:bigina:hahwar:** and **:awimund:isd:...eo...iduni** (... indicates illegible and uncountable runes; in contrast to the rest of the inscription **iduni** runs right to left, or upside-down). This, it has been suggested, is to be understood: 'Ida [owns this]. Bigina [and] Hahwar [?give it ?wish good fortune]. Awimund is ?dear to Ida'. As can be seen, much in the interpretation of the first sequence is expansion, and the postulated relationship between the three persons involved, whose names are all in the nominative (subject) case, is based partly on more explicit inscriptions of the same type, partly on general assumptions about what the presence of more than one name in the nominative on a buckle is likely to imply. The interpretation of the second sequence is hindered by the illegibility of the central section. Some have seen in **...eo...** the remains of the adjective *liub* 'dear', while others have averred that more than four runes must originally have stood here, and a reading **leob** is therefore unlikely.

The German inscriptions come to a fairly abrupt end around the beginning of the seventh century, and this has been connected with the increasing influence of Christianity and a resulting change in burial customs, whereby the dead were no longer buried with a selection of worldly possessions. There are of course unanswered questions here. Were the runic messages carved as part of the inhumation ceremony, or did the objects laid in the graves already bear a runic text? In the first case the introduction of new burial customs explains the sudden disappearance of this type of inscription, in the second it does not. There is no reason why people should not have continued to carve runes on brooches and the like after the introduction of Christianity if the practice was unconnected with pagan burial customs. Some have suggested that the Church sought to suppress runes, which it regarded as a script with pagan connotations, but the evidence for this is slight, and it is certainly not true of Anglo-Saxon England or Scandinavia. More likely it is the chance of preservation that gives a false impression. What appears to be a rapid rise and decline in runic activity in southern Germany may at least in part have to do with circumstances favourable to the survival of a particular type of runic artefact. The custom of placing goods in graves secured neat collections of personal objects – some rune-inscribed, some not – for the archaeologist to dig up. Weapons with runic inscriptions are another case in point. Many of these come from large deposits of military hardware in bogs and lakes, generally interpreted as offerings by the victors (the weapons have often been deliberately broken). Had it not been for this custom, and soil conditions suitable to the preservation of metals, it is unclear whether we would today think one of the chief uses of runic script was for marking names on weapons.

An estimate that has become famous in runological circles runs as follows. If there were as few as ten rune-carvers at any given time, and if these carvers made as few as ten inscriptions a year, some 40,000 inscriptions must have been produced between AD 200 and 600. Of these we have less than 1%. The likelihood is of course that the number greatly exceeds 40,000. Thus, what the chance of survival has left us may give a very misleading impression of the totality of runic activity in the older-*fuþark* period. Although we have to base our conclusions on what exists rather than what might have existed, we should constantly bear in mind that the vast majority of older-*fuþark* inscriptions have assuredly perished and what we are left with is a mere sample. That sample may well be unrepresentative, and new finds could radically alter our view of the uses to which runic writing was put in the first six centuries or so of its existence.

4.3 Summary

With the above caveat firmly in mind, the following conclusions seem warranted on the basis of current evidence. Runic writing in the period AD *c.* 175–700 was marginal to society. There is no evidence of its use in administration, in public discourse, or for the recording of events – as was the case with roman script in the Roman Empire. Runes appear to have served different purposes at different times and in different places, as customs or fashions came and went.

Inscriptions on military equipment – chiefly names – dominate the earliest period of runic writing, and this use of the script is documented from several parts of the Germanic world: Scandinavia, northern Germany, eastern Europe. Runes are also found on weaponry from England, the Netherlands and southern Germany, but in these areas the relevant inscriptions are dated after AD 400.

The raising of rune-stones, apparently chiefly for commemorative purposes, is a phenomenon found in the period up to AD 650–700 solely on the Scandinavian peninsula. Most of the early rune-stones are hard to date because of the lack of a clear archaeological context. Attempts have been made to allot them to different periods on the basis of language and/or rune forms (cf. pp. 19–20), but very different conclusions have been reached, and according to some runologists most early rune-stones can only be classified as "belonging to the older-*fuþark* period". The rune-stone can perhaps be seen as a type of public document, but it is unclear how many people were able to read the texts the stones carried. Nor is it known what inspired the Scandinavians to set up such monuments, although the fusion of runic writing with an earlier tradition of raising uninscribed memorial stones has been mooted.

Rune-inscribed gold bracteates are concentrated within a limited period (AD *c.* 450–550). In origin they are clearly imitations of Roman models. Possibly production began after the collapse of the Roman Empire, which may have made it hard to obtain the genuine article from the south. Bracteates are high-status objects, and were presumably manufactured in centres of power and wealth. The majority have been found in Scandinavia, and it is likely a good many were made there, but of course the find spot of a portable object does not necessarily reveal anything about its place of origin. Some bracteates have been discovered in large deposits, certain of them possibly sacrificial offerings, others individually in graves. The rapid cessation of bracteate production around the middle of the sixth century has been put down to changes in society, but the relevant changes have proved hard to identify.

Personal adornments with runes provide a thin thread of continuity in the early centuries of runic writing. These come from all over the Germanic world and do not appear to belong to any particular period. The concentration in southern Germany during the sixth century has doubtless to do with the practice of burying personal objects with the dead, a practice which flourished there at the time. Equally large numbers of rune-inscribed adornments may have existed elsewhere and at other periods. These could have perished (or not been discovered) because they did not find their way into graves and from there into the hands of archaeologists.

Pieces of military equipment, stone monuments, bracteates and personal adornments do not by any means make up the sum total of rune-inscribed objects in the older *fuþark* (or its early derivatives, see chapter 5). We find containers (urns and a pail), tools or parts thereof (planes, handles, items of weaving equipment and a possible hide-scraper), household objects (combs, boxes, a spoon and a footstool), worked and unworked pieces of bone, yew sticks, amber beads, a Christian liturgical object, coins, a bronze figure, a marble column (from Breza, Bosnia, inscribed with an incomplete *fuþark* inscription – an apparent graffito), and last but not least the magnificent gold horn from Gallehus, southern Jutland (one of a pair – now destroyed, but preserved in drawings – the second of which bore no runes; cf. pp. 194–5). The raw materials involved are equally diverse, comprising, in addition to the precious and non-precious metals, wood, bone and amber already mentioned, antler, ivory and pottery. The texts on these objects also vary widely: many are (to us) incomprehensible; among those we think to understand we find a spread of personal names (often of uncertain significance, but in at least some cases probably referring to owners, alternatively givers and/or recipients), the odd maker's signature (cf. 'Haȝiraðaz made', p. 29), occasional designations of the object on which the runes stand (e.g. **kobu** 'comb' on the eighth-century Tornweerd antler comb from near Groningen, Holland), coin legends giving in many cases the moneyer's name, rune-writers' formulas (e.g. 'Bliþguþ wrote runes' on the Neudingen-Baar 2 weaving-stave inscription, Baden-Württemberg, Germany), and the "cult" word *alu* (pp. 30, 32, 43–4). These heterogeneous inscriptions are too scattered in time and place and disparate in type to form the basis of conclusions about trends and developments in the uses of runic writing. The runic coins of the older-*fuþark* period appear to emanate chiefly from the North Sea coastal area later occupied by medieval Frisia (they are usually classed as Frisian, cf. chapters 5 and 6), though a few have an English provenance; all are dated after the middle of the sixth century. Combs are also relatively common in the Frisian corpus. Beyond that it is hard to go.

Select reading list

Antonsen, Elmer H. 1975. *A Concise Grammar of the Older Runic Inscriptions.* Tübingen: Niemeyer, 29–89. [A basic corpus of inscriptions in the older *fuþark* that "lend themselves to linguistic interpretation"; English translations and etymologies are given, but the reader should be aware that these are based on the author's interpretations, some of which other runologists disagree with.]

Antonsen, Elmer H. 2002. *Runes and Germanic Linguistics.* Berlin/New York: de Gruyter, 169–235. [On the nature and typology of inscriptions in the older *fuþark*; the author argues forcefully that they are secular rather than "sacral" or magical.]

Looijenga, Tineke 2003. *Texts and Contexts of the Oldest Runic Inscriptions.* Leiden/Boston: Brill.

Spurkland, Terje 2005. *Norwegian Runes and Runic Inscriptions.* Woodbridge: Boydell Press, 20–53. [Offers detailed discussion of a selection of inscriptions in the older *fuþark*, chiefly Norwegian.]

5 The development of runes in Anglo-Saxon England and Frisia

5.1 Anglo-Frisian innovations

Writing systems are not immutable. They change over time. Classical roman capitals are very different from archaic roman letters; Anglo-Saxon scribes writing in the roman alphabet used one type of script for Latin, another, derived from Ireland, for the vernacular; modern roman typefaces are quite unlike black letter (German *Fraktur*). It is thus no surprise to learn that the older *fuþark* too was subject to change and variation. In many areas runic writing seems to have been abandoned before significant developments to the system could take place. Where runes persisted in use – in Anglo-Saxon England, Frisia, and, above all, Scandinavia, the *fuþark* was reshaped. The Scandinavian experience is detailed in chapter 7. Here attention is directed at England and Frisia. (Whereas England is a reasonably well-defined concept, Frisia is less so. The geographical area referred to is northern coastal Holland and the adjoining part of Germany, but it is unclear whether this was a politically or linguistically distinct entity during the period runes were in use there. "Frisia" and "Frisian" are adopted in this account for convenience but should be understood chiefly as geographical terms.)

Runic inscriptions appear in England in the fifth century (one or two of the early examples may, however, be imports). The date is unsurprising. The Anglo-Saxon invasion of the country occurred in the fifth century, and the Germanic tribes who settled there presumably brought the runic script with them. We would not expect the pre-Anglo-Saxon, Romano-Celtic, population to have used what was a purely Germanic form of writing. In Frisia use of runes also seems to go back to the fifth century, though there the tradition could in theory be older. Concrete evidence is slight, however, and scholars do not always agree on the criteria for classifying an inscription as Frisian (see p. 52).

The English runic corpus up to roughly the last decades of the seventh century comprises some fifteen to twenty inscriptions (excluding coins; a precise figure is hard to achieve because of uncertainties about provenance, date, and the nature of some of the symbols concerned, see p. 42). The runes used in most of these early texts are indistinguishable from those in older-*fuþark* inscriptions from other parts of the Germanic world. However, in a few of them two new characters appear: ᚪ and ᚫ. The former (as part of the

ᚠ	ᚢ	ᚦ	ᚩ	ᚱ	ᚳ	ᚷ	ᚹ	ᚻ	ᚾ	ᛁ	ᛄ	ᛇ	ᛈ	ᛉ	ᛋ	ᛏ	ᛒ	ᛖ	ᛗ	ᛚ	ᛝ	ᛞ	ᛟ	ᚪ	ᚫ	ᚣ	ᛠ
f	u	þ	o	r	c	g	w	h	n	i	j	ï	p	x	s	t	b	e	m	l	ŋ	d	œ	a	æ	y	ea
1	2	3	4	5	6	7	8	9	10	11	12	13	14	15	16	17	18	19	20	21	22	23	24	25	26	27	28

Fig. 9 The "Anglo-Frisian" *fuþorc* (repeated from p. 5 for convenience)

bind-rune ᚷ) occurs on the Undley bracteate from Suffolk, which has been dated to the second half of the fifth century, perhaps around 475. If this date is correct (it is based on the bracteate's pictorial features), it makes it possibly the oldest of all the English runic finds. That might be taken to imply that ᚩ was not invented in England but brought over by settlers from the Continent. The supposition gains some support from the appearance on Frisian coins from around 600 of the related innovation ᚪ, although that character is also found on the Harford Farm brooch from Norfolk, dated stylistically and according to the fineness of its gold to the first half of the seventh century. ᚪ is also well attested in Frisia, but the only datable objects from there that bear this rune have been placed in the eighth century. Neither ᚩ nor ᚪ has so far been found outside England or Frisia.

Much effort has been expended on trying to determine where ᚩ and ᚪ originated, but, chiefly because of the paucity of evidence, no consensus has been reached. The two new runes – patently variations on older-*fuþark* ᚠ **a** – were fashioned in reaction to changes that took place in the vowel systems of the developing Old English and Frisian. In both, the sequence /ans/ became first /ãːs/ and ultimately /oːs/. The dates of these changes cannot be precisely determined, either in Old English or Frisian. When they occurred, they affected the fourth rune, the earliest form of whose name was almost certainly **ansuz*. The name will have changed first to **āsuz* and then **osuz* – or perhaps to *ās*(*s*) then *os*(*s*) (depending on when the unstressed vowel of the second syllable was lost and the final consonant shortened). In accordance with the acrophonic principle (cf. p. 21) the fourth rune could no longer easily denote /a/; the likelihood is it stood for /ã/ for a time before finally becoming an *o*-rune. Harder to explain is why its shape was changed from ᚪ to ᚩ. The ᚪ-form continued to be part of the rune-row, but was (in Old English, at least) renamed *æsc* 'ash' and used to denote /æ/, a new vowel sound (much as in modern English *ash, fat*) into which /a/ developed in many Old English and Frisian words. The /a/-phoneme did not disappear entirely, however, and new instances also developed (not least because of the monophthongisation /ai/ > /aː/ in Old English), so there was still a need for an *a*-rune. This was provided by the invention of ᚪ, called in England *ac* 'oak' (< **aik*). A further change affected ᛟ, whose name, **ōþila*, was subject to *i*-mutation (cf. p. 219). Mutation changed the name to *œþil*, and thereafter – again in accordance with the acrophonic principle – ᛟ denoted /ø/, a vowel sound much like that in French *peuple* 'people' or German *schön* 'beautiful'.

Although the changes to the English and Frisian rune-rows constitute a neat enough solution to the problems presented by developments in the vowel system, much in the process is unclear – not least the order in which the phonological and graphic changes took place. It seems possible that /ans/ > /āːs/ > /oːs/ before /a/ > /æ/, but we have no way of knowing whether graphic followed phonological innovation immediately, nor whether graphic innovations were implemented everywhere simultaneously. In the absence of a central administration, it is likely it took time for the new system to settle in.

This system, where ᚩ denotes /o/, ᚪ /a/, ᚪ /æ/ and ᛟ /ø/, is Anglo-Frisian

(ᛟ /ø/ is inferred for Frisia but not unambiguously documented). From the surviving Old English epigraphic and, especially, manuscript *fuþorc*s (no Frisian counterparts have so far been discovered), we know that, in England at least, the new characters and values became recognised elements of the rune-row: ᚩ was rune no. 4, ᛟ no. 24, ᚪ no. 25, and ᚫ no. 26. The fourth and twenty-fourth runes thus keep their place (based on an older-*fuþark* order **do** rather than **od** for runes 23 and 24, cf. p. 17), while ᚪ **a** and ᚫ **æ** are added to the end of the row. ᚩ undergoes a change of both shape and value, to be sure, but can be counted the continuation of older-*fuþark* ᚨ insofar as its name is *os*, the reflex of earlier **ansuz*. Although the rationale behind the system is opaque, it seems reasonable to conclude that importance was accorded to the names of the runes and the link they provided to sound value. The case of **ansuz/os* has just been mentioned. The twenty-fourth rune, **ōþila*, is similarly affected by a change of name and corresponding change of value (while retaining its place in the row). ᚪ and ᚫ are given names from which their value can be deduced. The acrophonic principle is maintained throughout.

5.2 English innovations

Further developments occur in the Old English rune-row, which are not seen in Frisian inscriptions. This could be because of the small size of the Frisian corpus, but a more plausible explanation is that we are dealing with later, purely English innovations. A persuasive (but by no means irrefutable) case has been made for a conscious reform of the rune-row in England towards the end of the seventh century. This, it is argued, was inspired by the newly established Christian Church, and entailed both the introduction of new runic characters and a standardisation of those already in use.

Principal among the innovations – whatever their inspiration – are ᛦ and ᛠ, runes for /y/ and the diphthong /æa/ respectively. Like /ø/, /y/ was a product of *i*-mutation (cf., e.g., OE *mys* 'mice' from earlier **musiz*); its sound approximates to that of the 'u' in French *tu* 'you' or the 'ü' in German *Bücher* 'books'. As a recent arrival in the language, /y/ did not have a rune assigned to it, and it is understandable – at least in the light of the Anglo-Frisian tradition of *fuþorc* expansion – that one was invented. The shape of ᛦ would seem to reflect the realisation of its creator(s) that /y/ contained elements of /u/ and /i/, for the new rune is a ᚢ encasing what appears to be a small ᛁ. The name given to the character, *yr*, is most readily explained as an adaptation of *ur*, the name of ᚢ; *yr* is of uncertain meaning in Old English, if indeed it has a meaning at all. Why a rune was created for /æa/ is harder to understand. Other diphthongs in Old English were written with two separate vowel runes (as was /æa/ on occasion), and there is no obvious reason why a special character should have been provided for /æa/. Because it denotes a diphthong, ᛠ (name *ear*, of uncertain meaning) is often transliterated **ea**, with or without a slur beneath the letters. **ea** without a slur goes against the principle that each rune should have a single roman equivalent, while a slur beneath may easily be taken as indicating a bind-rune (normally marked by a slur above, cf. p. 224), which ᛠ is not. In this account **ea** is adopted as a pragmatic compromise.

Other runic innovations in England appear more locally based, and are thus unlikely to have been part of a general reform. They may have resulted from experimentation, inspired by the various additional forms that had already been embraced. ᚸ on the eighth-century Ruthwell (Dumfries and Galloway) and Bewcastle (Cumbria) stone crosses distinguishes a velar variant of /g/ from its palatal counterpart (cf. that modern English *gold* and *gilded* have different /g/s, the former more velar, the latter more palatal – according to the quality of the immediately following vowel; see further p. 223). Not only /g/ is thus affected. Several inscriptions from the north of England use ᛣ for velar /k/ in distinction to ᚳ **c**, which stands for the palatal variant (cf. modern English *cart* versus *kit*; at some point in the development of Old English, palatal /g/ and /k/ became /j/ and /tʃ/ respectively – like the initial consonants of modern English *yet* and *chip* – but it is unclear exactly when this happened or where it began). The Ruthwell cross also has a distinct rune for a /k/ that immediately precedes an *i*-mutated vowel, a position in which velar /k/ is nevertheless to be expected: the initial consonant of the word *cyning* 'king', for example (modern English *king*, not **ching*), is rendered ᚸ rather than ᛣ. The significance of this spelling is not well understood; conceivably it reflects a local pronunciation of the day, or perhaps ᚸ is to be seen as a variant of ᛣ, its form based on ᚸ. ᚸ and ᛣ, the former almost certainly developed from ᚷ **g**, the latter from ᚳ **c**, appear in some manuscript rune-rows, where they may also have names: ᛣ *calc* '?chalk' '?cup' '?sandal', ᚸ *gar* 'spear'. ᚸ is so far known only from the Ruthwell cross, and thus no name is recorded.

One of the strongest pieces of evidence for a reform of the English rune-row comes from changes of form affecting **c**, **h**, **s**. Before the eighth century **c** appears as ᛣ, ᚲ, and ᚾ, **h** as ᚺ, and **s** as ᚦ, ᛋ, and ᛋ. In inscriptions after *c.* 700 we find that **c** is regularly ᚳ, **h** is ᚻ and **s** is ᚻ, or, less commonly, ᚱ. **c** – together with **j** and **ŋ** originally smaller than the other runes (cf. p. 20) – is provided with a full-length vertical. The double-branch form of **h** was presumably already known in England as a variant of ᚺ even though it does not occur in any of the early English inscriptions so far discovered; ᚻ is well attested on the Continent (cf. p. 19). ᚻ is perhaps a development of ᛋ, in which what may be seen as a "split" vertical replaces three diagonal lines. The rarer ᚱ has (like ᚳ **c**) gained a full-length vertical, but it is hard to see how it is related to any of the earlier forms of **s**, unless the branch be viewed as one of the strokes of ᛋ or its more complex variants.

The shape of **ŋ** is also radically altered, but we do not have any examples of this rune from England in the first two-and-a-half centuries or so of Anglo-Saxon settlement. In several of its earliest manifestations (chiefly Scandinavian) the twenty-second rune appears as ᛜ or something very like it. The ᛝ that is found in later English inscriptions is not known from anywhere else and is thus presumably an English invention. It is perhaps made up of ᛜ with branches at either end bringing it up to full height.

The *j*-rune in post-seventh century English tradition takes the forms ᛄ and ᛡ. The latter also becomes the common way of writing the original twelfth rune in seventh- and eight-century Scandinavia (cf. p. 61). ᛄ might be a development of ᛇ, where the two interlocking angles come together to form a lozenge and a vertical is driven through the middle. The relationship between ᚩ and ᚪ, and of ᚩ to older *fuþark* ᚬ, is harder to visualise, as it is to understand the connection (if any) between English and Scandinavian ᚩ. It is just possible English ᚩ is not derived from ᚬ at all, but a bind of ᚷ **g** and ᛁ **i**, invented by a person or persons in whose pronunciation original [gi-] had become [ji-] (cf. above), but this assumes a good deal of sophistication on the part of the inventor.

Two runes, ᛁ and ᛦ, keep their form and place in the rune-row but are given fresh sound values. The original value of ᛁ is unknown (cf. pp. 13–14), but whatever sound this was, it had in all probability disappeared from the developing English, since carvers use the thirteenth rune for /i/, /j/, [ç] and [x] (for /i/ already in a fifth-century inscription, cf. p. 42). The sound originally denoted by ᛦ was [z], which seems to have developed into a fricative (p. 223) with sibilant quality before coalescing with /r/. Like ᛁ, ᛦ thus became otiose. That it was later used to denote the equivalent of roman 'x' – useful in the writing of Latin but not Old English – strongly suggests learned, i.e. Church, involvement.

All of the various English innovations considered here might of course be the outcome of gradual evolution rather than deliberate reform. However, the apparently rapid disappearance of certain older forms and usages after the end of the seventh century and the adoption of several new ones, as it seems wherever English runes were written, argues quite strongly in favour of a reform scenario, even if a limited one.

The Frisian and English rune-rows did not develop further. In both areas runic writing died out relatively early, in Frisia apparently in the ninth century, in England around AD 1000 or a little later. Possible reasons for the demise of the script are suggested on pp. 50, 53.

Select reading list

Page, R. I. 1999. *An Introduction to English Runes* (2nd ed.). Woodbridge: Boydell Press, 16–48. [On the route or routes by which runes came to England, and their subsequent development.]

Page, R. I. 2010. 'The position of Old English runes in the runic tradition'. In: (John Ole Askedal *et al.*, eds) *Zentrale Probleme bei der Erforschung der älteren Runen: Akten einer internationalen Tagung an der Norwegischen Akademie der Wissenschaften* (Osloer Beiträge zur Germanistik 41). Frankfurt a/M: Peter Lang, 137–50.

Parsons, David N. 1999. *Recasting the Runes: The Reform of the Anglo-Saxon Futhorc* (Runrön 14). Uppsala: Institutionen för nordiska språk, Uppsala universitet. [Argues for a reform of the Anglo-Saxon *fuþorc* in the seventh century; offers in addition a detailed account of the development of runic writing in Anglo-Saxon England.]

Looijenga, Tineke 2003. *Texts and Contexts of the Oldest Runic Inscriptions.* Leiden/Boston: Brill, 299–328. [Deals chiefly with runic material deemed to be Frisian, but takes the form of a presentation and discussion of the runes, language and content of inscriptions "in or from the Netherlands".]

6 The English and Frisian inscriptions

6.1 The English inscriptions

According to one of the leading authorities, English runes were used epigraphically for three main purposes: practical and general; monumental; magical. There is a danger of over-simplification in such a rough-and-ready division. Moreover, while the monumental use of runes is relatively easy to define and recognise, the "general" and "magical" inscription can be harder to capture. "General" quickly becomes the default category into which everything is placed that cannot be classified as something else, while "magical" requires (a) a definition of magic, (b) a way of showing that magical intent, however defined, is present. Nevertheless, some kind of rudimentary categorisation is a helpful starting point for an examination of the Old English inscriptions. The reader can judge how valid it is in the light of the evidence.

The three types of inscription identified have an uneven distribution. Runic monuments – almost entirely commemorative stones – are found in the north of England and the extreme south of Scotland (following the current border), with a couple of outliers in the Isle of Man and the south, and they all belong to the period after *c.* 700. Rune-inscribed non-stone objects, mostly portable, come from both north and south (though not the south-west) and span the whole period of English runic usage.

Inscriptions dated before *c.* 675 – coins apart – are few and far between. Sixteen or so have been fairly confidently identified, almost all from the eastern half of England. They are found on brooches, bracteates, bits of weaponry, utensils, cremation urns, and a bone. Some of the inscriptions are hard to read because of damage or the use of ambiguous or unexpected runic shapes. Most have defied interpretation, in spite of the many ingenious attempts made to suggest possible meanings.

Straightforward enough is the text on the probably mid-seventh century Harford Farm brooch (from outside Norwich, Norfolk). The brooch shows an obvious repair and is inscribed ᛚᚢᛞᚪ:ᚷᛁᛒᛟᛏᚫᛋᛁᚷᛁᛚᚫ **luda:gibœtæsigilæ**, early OE *Luda gibœttæ sigilæ* 'Luda mended the brooch' (meanings of personal names or name elements are hereafter only given where their explication may throw light on a person or inscription; most names will gradually have lost their literal sense and become opaque to those who used them). This provides a good example of the "practical" use of runes. Comprehensible, too, under the now generally accepted interpretation, is the sequence ᚱᚫᛁᚻᚪᚾ **raïhan**, carved into the astragalus (ankle-bone) of a roe deer. The bone was also found near Norwich (Caistor-by-Norwich), during the excavation of an Anglo-Saxon cemetery. It lay in a fifth-century cremation urn together with a large number of pieces apparently belonging to some kind of board game. **raïhan** (transliterated thus rather than **ræïhæn** because of the early date and the seemingly archaic linguistic form of the word; cf. pp. 3–4, 37–9) does not obviously refer to a game, however, but seems to identify the bone itself. The runes are taken to give *raihan*, an early genitive or dative form of later OE *raha, ra* 'roe deer' and meaning 'of a roe deer' or 'from a roe deer'. This type of inscription, defining the material or the object the runes are carved upon, is not common in the English corpus, but is well attested in Scandinavian tradition, particularly in the Middle Ages.

More typical of early English runic inscriptions is the one that adorns the fifth- or sixth-century Lovedon Hill (Lincolnshire) cremation urn. The runes, cut into the clay before firing, are clumsy to the point that uncertainty arises about parts of the reading (see Fig. 10). The first five characters are fairly clearly **siþæb** (though some prefer an **a** transliteration for the fourth rune ᚠ, see above). Rune 6 appears also to be **æ** (or **a**), though in view of the double-cutting of the vertical and double-cutting elsewhere in the inscription it has also been taken as a malformed **l**. Rune 7 is **d**. Thereafter two verticals seem to form a separation mark. There follows as r. 8 a character that might be either **w** or **þ**, then perhaps an **i** leaning heavily to the right, **k** (transliterated thus rather than **c** because of the age of the object), and **w** – rr. 9–11. Thereupon comes a further apparent separation mark (almost identical in form to the previous one), and after that a confused assemblage that might perhaps be a malformed single-branch **h** (r. 12, if rune it is) followed by **l** (r. 13). The inscription ends with two shapes: the first could be **æ** (**a**) or **l**, the second is not obviously identifiable as a rune. So much for the reading. The interpretation is no less precarious. The initial seven-rune sequence is taken as a personal name, *Siþab(a)ld/Siþaba(l)d, Siþabad*, or some such – the meaning of the first element being perhaps 'journey' and of the second 'bold' or 'battle'. However rr. 8–11 and the material after the assumed second separation mark are read, no obvious sense emerges. Neither **wikw** nor **þikw** suggests an OE word, and the *hlaf* 'bread' and *hlæw* 'grave' that have been proposed for the final four characters fail to convince because of the uncertainty of the reading and (in the case of *hlaf*, at least) the lack of a persuasive context.

Fig. 10 The Lovedon Hill runes

Insofar as we can draw conclusions about the types to which the early English inscriptions might belong, "practical" and "general" thus seem to be represented – notwithstanding certain problems of reading and interpretation. It has also been suggested that magical purposes lie behind some of them. Stamped several times upon three cremation urns (fifth or sixth century) from Spong Hill, Norfolk, are the unusual looking characters to be seen in Plate 4. Current thinking favours the transliteration **alu**, the assumption being that the branches of each rune are doubled (cf. p. 19). If this reading is correct it places the "cult" word *alu* (pp. 30, 32) in the context of death and

Plate 4   A cremation urn from Spong Hill, Norfolk,
with probable "doubled" runes, giving the word **alu**

burial, whatever that may imply. The Lovedon Hill cremation urn runes have
also been taken as evidence of magical intent. The rough and uncertain shapes
they exhibit have to some suggested that their importance derived not from
the visual impression they made, or the message they carried, but from their
mere presence on the urn. This is a point of some importance, for if it could
be substantiated it would supply evidence that runes were believed to be more
than just alphabetic characters – in one particular rune-writing milieu, at least.
The difficulty is to move from supposition to conviction. There are, after all,
several reasons why an inscription might be botched: incompetence, haste,
poor materials or tools all spring to mind. (See further below on "magical"
English inscriptions.)

Far removed from the world of magic, and severely practical in purpose,
is the use of runes in coin legends. In England runic coins begin in the early
seventh century and continue well into the ninth. They thus span the late
seventh-century dividing line, following which runic usage appears to change
and become more standardised (see pp. 39–41). Unfortunately, none of the
runes that occur on coins of the 600s are diagnostic either of early usage or
the postulated new standard. Indeed, seventh-century English coins of any

sort are rare, those with runic legends rarer still, and the legends themselves extremely brief and sometimes garbled. Until the appearance of the moneyer's name ᚲᚠᛗᚠ **pada** (together with non-runic legends) on a mixed gold and silver penny issue, probably from Kent and dated *c.* 660–685, we find only problematic sequences of runes. These occur on gold coins (some of which may in fact have been intended as adornments rather than money) and are in imitation of the lettering on Roman prototypes. Such legends may in fact never have had a meaning, but simply been placed on the coin to make it look authentic. The next runic issue after the **pada** coins are late seventh- and early eighth-century silver pennies from Kent and East Anglia, which, like Pada's pieces, give the name of the moneyer in runes (though in contrast to Pada's, no further legend). Particularly common are the coinages of Epa and Wigræd, whose names often appear in garbled form. Towards the end of the eighth century a larger, so-called "broad penny" was introduced in southern England. Unlike the earlier coins, which were struck by independent moneyers, the broad pennies were a regal coinage. They show the name of the king on the obverse, that of the moneyer on the reverse. The king's name is normally written with roman letters, the moneyer's name may be in roman or runic, or a mixture of both (in the case of a few characters, notably B/B, R/R, there can be doubt about whether runic or roman is intended). In the north of England copper coins were issued in the ninth century by the kings of Northumbria. Some of those produced in the middle years of the century have the name of the moneyer in runes or mixed roman and runic (e.g. ᛈᛁᛚᛏᚱᛗᚺ **wiitred**, ᛈᛁᚺᛏᚱᚱ **wihTrr**, VIHᛏRED VIHtRED for *Wihtred*); the king's name is always in roman.

The practical use of runes in England after *c.* 700 is by no means limited to coin legends. Makers' signatures, owners' names, and prayers for makers are all represented – perhaps prayers for owners too. The ninth-century Manchester gold ring, part runic part roman, records: +ᚠDREDMECAHEAᛏREDMECᚠᚷROᚣ, *Ædred mec ah, Eanred mec agrof* 'Ædred owns me, Eanred inscribed me'. The Mortain casket (of a variety of materials, and of uncertain date, but patently Christian), found and preserved in Normandy but of English, possibly Mercian, manufacture, states: **+goodhelpe:æadan|þiiosneciismeelgewar|ahtæ**, *God helpe Æadan þiosne cismel gewarahtæ* 'God help Æada [who] made this *cismel*' (*cismel*, otherwise unknown, possibly a corruption of Latin *crismal* 'container for the host'). The casket also carries Latin texts in roman letters. The incomplete Whitby (bone) comb inscription, probably to be associated with a nearby monastery founded in 657 and destroyed in the latter half of the ninth century, runs: **d(æ)usmæus godaluwalu dohelipæcy[**, *Dæus mæus, God aluwaludo helipæ Cy-* 'My God! God Almighty help Cy-'. The first three runes are damaged but the reading is reasonably secure; the spaces occur where the rivets are placed; the end of the inscription is lost. God is invoked with the Latin *Deus meus*, while in the Old English continuation He is asked to help someone the first element of whose name was probably *Cyne-*. What is unclear is the relationship of this person to the comb. Cyne- could be the maker, the owner, or someone else.

Perhaps of a "general" rather than strictly practical nature are those inscriptions that identify the object that bears them (as, apparently, **raïhan** above). A few of these can be found in the later Anglo-Saxon corpus, for example the Wheatley Hill (Durham) silver-gilt finger-ring, possibly of the late eighth century, which is now taken to read **(h)ringich͡att(æ)**, *hring ic hatæ* 'I am called a ring' (the first and last runes are largely obscured).

Another type of inscription that hovers between the practical and the general is that which comments on an accompanying image or images. Here we may instance the runes on St Cuthbert's coffin, one of only two extant examples of English runic writing carved in wood. In fact the St Cuthbert inscriptions are in a mixture of runic and roman, a not uncommon feature of English epigraphy as has already been shown. The coffin, which was made in Lindisfarne in 698, and whose remains are now preserved in Durham Cathedral, displays apostles, evangelists, archangels, and the Virgin Mary with the Christ child. Some of the surviving figures have their names delineated in runes or roman letters, or a mixture, and we may surmise that originally all were accompanied by an explanatory label of this kind. Most notably, Christ is identified by the regular abbreviation (ᛁ)ᚻ(ᚴ) ᛉᛈᚴ **(i)h(s) xps** (the first and third runes cannot be made out in their entirety but may be safely inferred from the context). This shows a carver thoroughly at home in roman script for he is in fact transliterating from roman to runic: *ihs xps* (giving *Iesus Christus*) incorporates the greek letters H *eta* (for /eː/), X *chi* (for /x/), and P *rho* (for /r/) in romanised form, and these are faithfully reproduced in runes as though they were the roman letters 'h', 'x', 'p'.

Another famous Anglo-Saxon runic inscription – or rather series of inscriptions – that offers commentary on accompanying sculptures is found on the Franks, or Auzon, casket. Dated to the early 700s and made chiefly of whalebone, the casket, almost certainly of northern English origin, at some point found its way to France. Most of it is now preserved in the British Museum; one side, discovered later, came to the Bargello Museum, Florence. The iconography and inscriptions of this piece are too complex to be gone into here. Suffice to say, the casket carries a number of texts, mostly runic but sometimes roman, mostly in Old English but occasionally in Latin, commenting on depictions of Roman and Germanic myth, Roman history, and the Christian story. There is also a poem on the origin of the whalebone.

One further type of runic activity, part practical part general, stems from the Englishman abroad. At two Italian sites (one at Monte Sant' Angelo on the east coast, one in Rome) English travellers, possibly pilgrims, have carved their names, some in roman some in runes. Runic graffiti of this type have not so far been found in England itself, but are well represented in medieval Scandinavia (cf. pp. 116–17, 119–20).

The monumental use of runes, unattested in England before *c.* 700, dominates – or appears to dominate – the scene in the following two centuries. In total thirty-seven Anglo-Saxon rune-stones are known, as compared with a roughly similar number for all other types of post-700 English runic artefact. One reason the stone monuments loom so large may be that stone survives better than other materials. They also tend to be solid and imposing, and many of them contain relatively lengthy inscriptions. Some are patently commemorative, and most can be interpreted as memorials of one kind or another. The simplest carry a single name, the more detailed are arranged around a formula stating who caused the monument to be put up and for whom. One or two have inscriptions of considerably greater complexity. The English rune-stones are difficult to date at all closely, but they are firmly rooted in the Christian era; indeed, almost all were found in association with churches or other religious institutions or sites.

The Maughold 1 slab, Isle of Man, bears a cross, encircled by two framing lines. Between the lines almost immediately above the cross stands the name ᛒᛚᚪᚷᚳᛗᚩᚾ **blagcmon**, OE *Blacmon* (*blac* 'dark' 'swarthy' + *mon*, a variant of *mann* 'man', probably originally a nickname). The shape of the slab suggests it was intended as a headstone for a grave. Much smaller than Maughold 1 are the so-called "name-stones" from Lindisfarne (Northumberland), Hartlepool (Cleveland), and Monkwearmouth (Tyne and Wear). These carry a cross set within a border. The cross divides the surface into quadrants. Below the cross arm, and interrupted by the shaft, is a name. A second name may stand above the arm. Sometimes the inscriptions are runic, sometimes roman, sometimes a mixture of both. Where two names are recorded, as on the damaged Monkwearmouth 2 stone, it is likely one represents the commemorated, the other the commemorator, although Lindisfarne 1 gives the name *Osgyþ* twice, once in runes and once in roman (Plate 5). This might be a double reference to the same person, or refer to two different people with the same name, perhaps mother and daughter.

The belief that name-stones with two names proclaim commemorated and commemorator is strengthened by the occurrence on larger runic monuments of a formula that does so explicitly. In its simplest form this consists of the following: name of commemorator + verb meaning 'raised' 'set up' + preposition 'after' 'in memory of' + name of deceased. Thornhill 2 (West Yorkshire), for example, reads **+eadred|seteæfte|eateinne**, *Eadred sette æfter Eadþegne* 'Eadred set up after Eadþegn'. Fuller versions of the formula add the word *becun* 'monument' (modern English *beacon*) as object of 'set up', and can include supplementary information such as the relationship of the commemorator with the commemorated. In addition there may be a prayer for the soul of the departed.

Much more elaborate than any of the above is the Bewcastle cross inscription (Cumbria), dated – on shifting grounds – to different parts of the eighth or early ninth century. Unfortunately the cross is so worn and damaged that little is now legible. There was once an extensive runic text, together with sculptured images and decoration. From what can be made out, the inscription was at least in part of commemorative type, for it includes the suggestive word **setton** 'set up [pl.]', preceded by **þissigb*c***, apparently *þis sigbecn* 'this victory monument', and followed by what are taken to be personal names (identifying the raisers or commissioners of the monument). There also seems to be an injunction to pray for the soul of some person or persons. In addition there were explanatory labels as on St Cuthbert's coffin: above a panel depicting Christ is the inscription **g(e)ssus|kristtus** 'Jesus Christ'.

Plate 5 The Lindisfarne 1 name-stone, with *Osgyþ* in runes and roman

Related to Bewcastle in style and geography – and probably also date – is the Ruthwell cross (Dumfries and Galloway). At roughly 5.5 m high it is the tallest of the English runic monuments. Ruthwell is much better preserved than Bewcastle, having clearly spent much of its existence under cover. However, it suffered considerable breakage in the seventeenth century when it was thrown down by reformers. As far as can be ascertained, Ruthwell carried no commemorative text. Some of its inscriptions belong, like those on St Cuthbert's coffin and the Auzon casket, to the type that identifies and/

or comments on accompanying images. In addition, there is part of an Old English poem known as the *Dream of the Rood*. While most of the writing on the cross is runic, some is roman.

Further brief consideration must finally be given to "magical" inscriptions. As indicated at the outset, these are not easy to identify. We might define magic loosely as an action designed to harness the power of the supernatural, which of course presupposes belief in the supernatural and in an ability to use it for particular purposes. The task is then to find Anglo-Saxon runic inscriptions that satisfy this definition. From the pre-700 corpus Spong Hill and Lovedon Hill were mentioned as possible candidates. The difficulty with accepting either of these as magical is the lack of positive evidence. If we agree that Spong Hill really does say *alu*, it belongs in a category to which cult as well as magic significance has been ascribed (see pp. 30, 32). And should the inscribing of *alu* indeed be an attempt to harness supernatural powers, we are surely right in supposing that the magic resided chiefly or solely in the word itself, not in the runic characters of which it was made up.

Uncertainties likewise afflict the four English inscriptions from the post-700 period that have been assigned – tentatively by some, more confidently by others – to the magical category. The ?ninth-century gold amulet rings from Bramham Moor (West Yorkshire) and Kingmoor (Cumbria) have an identical text, which begins **ærkriu**, strongly reminiscent of the sequence *ærcrio* or *aer crio* that appears in two versions of an Old English charm for staunching blood. **ærkriu** does not make obvious sense (though it has been suggested it derives from an Irish phrase meaning 'against blood'), nor do the runes that follow. The inscriptions have been described as "magical gibberish". What appears to be a variant, or corrupt, version of the text appears on a third (agate) ring, undated, from Linstock Castle (Cumbria), and – even further removed – as part of the inscription on a runic stick from medieval Bergen, Norway (cf. pp. 106–7). There is a strong suggestion in these four artefacts of magical purpose, provided the connection between **ærkriu** and *ærcrio/aer crio* is accepted. But we cannot know precisely what the maker or makers of the rings/stick (or alternatively their commissioner(s)) had in mind, and ultimately we have to fall back on supposition. What does seem clear, as in the case of *alu* above, is that any magic involved had to do with the text. The suggestion that the runes themselves lent additional force to the working of the charm is pure speculation. The final inscription in this quartet is the tenth-century Thames scramasax (single-edged short sword). This has engraved upon it the personal name **beagnoþ**, perhaps the owner's, though possibly the maker's, together with a twenty-eight character *fuþorc* containing one or two unusual forms, and with rr. 20–23 in unexpected order. Magic has been mooted here on the grounds that no other reason for the presence of the *fuþorc* on the blade suggests itself. Its function could, however, have been decorative. The maker or commissioner may simply have been following an old tradition of inscribing runes upon weapons (cf. p. 29). The *fuþorc* itself, like many of those from medieval Scandinavian towns, reveals lack of familiarity with the latter part of the rune-row. Which suggests a carver with a less than certain grasp of his script – not a good starting-point for a runic magician.

The epigraphic evidence for sorcery as an important function of runic writing in England must be judged slight, and the evidence for the use of runes themselves as magic symbols virtually non-existent. Old English literature contains one or two possible references to runes as characters imbued with magic, but these have been interpreted in different ways and their value is uncertain.

In conclusion, a few general observations may be made about Anglo-Saxon runic writing. Its original purpose or purposes are as hard to gauge as are the reason or reasons why runes were invented in the first place. There is little in the English inscriptions dated before *c.* 700 that suggests a pressing need for a writing system, whether for practical or other uses. However, the adoption of runes for coin legends in the seventh century, and their widespread appearance on coins for over 200 years, indicates that they came to be viewed by some at least as a script with practical applications. Roman characters occur on seventh-century coins too, and this introduces a roughly 400-year period during which the two writing systems were employed side-by-side – except in the writing of manuscripts, which was almost exclusively the province of the roman alphabet (on manuscript runes, see chapter 13). The precise relationship between runic and roman in England is unclear: it probably varied from one part of the country to another, and changed over time. What is beyond doubt, however, is that the two scripts did not lead totally separate lives. Elements of Anglo-Saxon runic writing seem to derive from knowledge of roman, e.g. the doubling of characters to indicate long or repeated consonants (and seemingly for other purposes too), the occasional ornamentation of runes with serifs, the use of the fifteenth rune ᛉ to represent roman 'x', whose value could have been rendered **cs**. Conversely, when the roman alphabet was employed for writing Old English, runic þ was borrowed for /θ/, which did not occur in Latin, and ƿ for /w/, which existed only as a variant of /u/ in that language (see further p. 153). Many inscriptions – and coin legends – mix runic and roman, as we have seen. Furthermore, the distribution of runic and roman inscriptions in the period *c.* 700–900 is quite similar (cf. Map 3). Clearly, many people were literate in both scripts. There is not enough evidence, however, to show why runes continued to be used in parallel with roman letters, nor what governed the choice between the two in particular contexts. On coins the names of rulers tend to be in roman, those of moneyers in runes, though this is by no means an absolute rule. Coin legends apart, tendencies of any kind in the choice of script are hard to discern.

Unclear, too, is for how long runic writing persisted in England. The Whithorn 1 gravestone (Dumfries and Galloway) is dated to the end of the tenth or beginning of the eleventh century, and thereafter Anglo-Saxon runic epigraphy seems to come to an end. Some have associated its final demise with the Norman Conquest, but the fact that the last known inscriptions and the Conquest coincide roughly in time does not of course demonstrate a causal relationship.

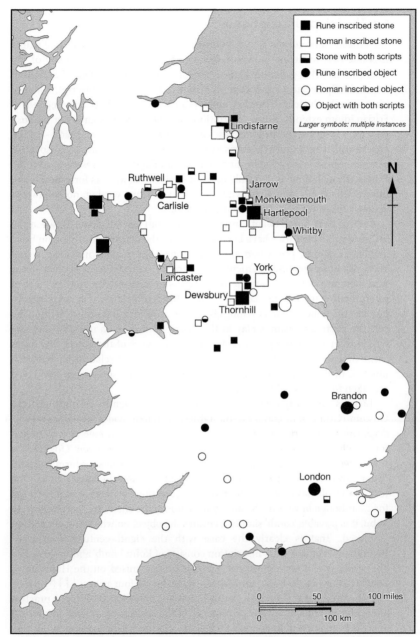

■	Rune inscribed stone
□	Roman inscribed stone
⬒	Stone with both scripts
●	Rune inscribed object
○	Roman inscribed object
◐	Object with both scripts

Larger symbols: multiple instances

N

Lindisfarne

Ruthwell

Jarrow

Carlisle

Monkwearmouth

Hartlepool

Whitby

Lancaster

York

Dewsbury

Thornhill

Brandon

London

Map 3 The distribution of runic and roman inscriptions in England *c.* 700–900

6.2 The Frisian inscriptions

The Frisian runic corpus is much harder to get to grips with than the English. It is not easy to define; however defined, it is relatively small; many of the inscriptions lack a generally agreed interpretation. The problem of definition arises chiefly because knowledge of Frisian is based on manuscript evidence starting in the thirteenth century, and it is unclear how far back an independent Frisian idiom extends. Runic inscriptions are classed as Frisian either because they were found – and in some cases are believed to have been made – in the area in which medieval Frisia was located (cf. p. 37), or because – irrespective of where found – they display linguistic or runological features deemed to be Frisian (though none is certainly or exclusively so, as witness for example the innovations ᚠ **o**, ᚠ **a**, shared with Anglo-Saxon runic writing; no epigraphic Frisian rune-row has so far been discovered).

On this basis some twenty inscriptions or coin legends dated between the fifth and ninth centuries have been assigned to the corpus (occurring on bone and antler combs, yew-wood and whalebone objects, gold and silver coins). There is, however, disagreement about the Frisian status of several items. And there are doubts about the runic status or authenticity of a few as well. Interpretation tends to be slanted towards the identification of personal names because these more than anything else are what runologists expect to find. The role the postulated names play in the inscriptions is often unclear. They are mostly interpreted as signifying the maker or owner of the object that bears them, though in one or two cases some other function or relationship has been mooted. In the absence of recognisable regal issues personal names on coins are taken to be those of moneyers.

There is one fairly certain maker's formula: the eighth- or ninth-century Oostum (Groningen) comb's **deda habuku** 'Habuku made', which, as well as displaying Anglo-Frisian ᚠ **a**, sports what have been interpreted as ornamental forms of **h** and **b** with three branches and three bows respectively. Oostum has further writing. On the other side of the comb from the maker's formula stand ?three symbols that have been variously read, followed by **kabu** 'comb'. The text as a whole has been interpreted as a dedication: 'Habuka made the comb for …', although in view of the uncertain status of the characters accompanying **kabu**, it is possible 'comb' simply identifies the object on which the inscription is placed. That is clearly the case with the eighth-century Toornwerd (Groningen) comb, whose inscription consists of **kobu** 'comb' and nothing else. The same type of inscription can perhaps be recognised on the Hamwih, or Southampton, cattle-bone, unworked except for its four runes: ᚲᚠᛏᚠ – to be transliterated **catæ** if English, **katæ** if Frisian, following traditional practice. There are few clues about the provenance of the inscription or what purpose, if any, the bone served. In favour of a Frisian origin it has been pointed out that Hamwih was a port with trading links to Frisia, that the ᚠ variant of ᚠ appears to be Frisian, and that the Old Frisian language had a word *kate* 'knuckle-bone'.

Although the Frisian runic corpus is more puzzling than the English, it is perhaps no more so than the group of English inscriptions made before the establishment of Christian culture and roman writing (neither of which phenomena appear to have reached Frisia during the period runes were in use). What is baffling in both cases is the purpose in adopting and perpetuating a writing system for the occasional and trivial uses to which it seems to have been put. Of course, the chance of survival may be skewing our view of the Frisian as of other runic traditions. The majority of runic objects found in Frisia come from *terpen* – artificial mounds built for human habitation in a region subject to regular inundations by the sea. These were commercially exploited for soil between the late nineteenth century and the 1930s, a process which revealed numerous antiquities, including runic inscriptions. Possibly Frisia had a more widespread and practical use of runes than the *terp* finds suggest, but there is little evidence for it beyond perhaps the few runic coins and/or medallions that have been classified as Frisian, some of which seem to pre-date the earliest English coinage.

The sporadic and trifling nature of the tradition may be what ultimately led to the disappearance of runic writing from Frisia. There is at least no better explanation in the current state of our knowledge.

Select reading list

Page, R. I. 1996. 'On the baffling nature of Frisian runes'. In: (Tineke Looijenga and Arend Quak, eds) *Frisian Runes and Neighbouring Traditions* (Amsterdamer Beiträge zur älteren Germanistik 45). Amsterdam/Atlanta: Rodopi, 131–50. [In spite of its title, this paper discusses Frisian runic *inscriptions.*]

Page, R. I. 1999. *An Introduction to English Runes* (2nd ed.). Woodbridge: Boydell Press, 16–37, 96–185. [Offers a detailed presentation and discussion of the Anglo-Saxon runic corpus.]

Parsons, David N. 1999. *Recasting the Runes: The Reform of the Anglo-Saxon Futhorc* (Runrön 14). Uppsala: Institutionen för nordiska språk, Uppsala universitet, 40–72. [Examines in detail the earliest Anglo-Saxon inscriptions.]

Looijenga, Tineke 1996. 'Checklist Frisian runic inscriptions'. In: (Tineke Looijenga and Arend Quak, eds) *Frisian Runes and Neighbouring Traditions* (Amsterdamer Beiträge zur älteren Germanistik 45). Amsterdam/Atlanta: Rodopi, 91–108. [Gives a brief presentation of the Frisian runic corpus.]

Looijenga, Tineke 2003. *Texts and Contexts of the Oldest Runic Inscriptions.* Leiden/Boston: Brill, 299–328. [See the reading list at the end of chapter 5.]

7 The development of runes in Scandinavia

7.1 Introduction

English and Frisian rune-writers, as we have seen, expanded the twenty-four character rune-row to cater for sound changes that affected the forms of Germanic spoken in England and Frisia. During the sixth and seventh centuries the sound system of Scandinavian Germanic also underwent changes. The result was a greatly increased number of vowels and altered functions for many consonants. Unlike their English and Frisian brethren, however, the Scandinavians reduced the size of the rune-row, jettisoning a full eight of the twenty-four characters they had inherited. This has seemed to most runologists a remarkable occurrence, and a great deal of effort has gone into finding a plausible explanation. The outcome has been a number of hypotheses, none of which has gained general acceptance.

7.2 The reduction of the *fuþark*: evolution or design?

Fig. 11 sets out the older *fuþark* in three groups of eight (p. 17), with those runes that were lost placed in square brackets.

ᚠ ᚢ ᚦ ᚨ ᚱ ᚲ [ᚷ ᚹ]:ᚺ ᚾ ᛁ ᛃ [ᛇ ᛈ] ᛉ ᛊ: ᛏ ᛒ [ᛗ] ᛗ ᛚ [ᛜ ᛞ ᛟ]

Fig. 11 The Scandinavian reduction of the older *fuþark*

Contemplating this row, scholars have focused their attention on different aspects. Some have noted that the reduction left sixteen runes, which, like twenty-four, is a multiple of eight. Others have observed that the abandoned runes tend to come towards or at the end of each group. It has also been claimed that the lost characters have on the whole more complex shapes than those which survived. Many have sought to relate the contraction of the rune-row to the sound changes that affected the developing Scandinavian, but they have disagreed about the precise causal link between the two. One influential hypothesis shows how phonological developments are likely to have affected the initial sound in the names of several runes, and suggests (in accordance with the acrophonic principle, p. 21) that this would have meant the runes concerned could no longer be used with their original values.

The reason none of these approaches to the problem has been generally accepted is the weakness (in some cases the non-existence) of supporting evidence and the force of various counter arguments.

It is undeniable that sixteen and twenty-four are both multiples of eight, but in itself that does not get us very far. There would need to be independent evidence that eight and multiples thereof were considered crucially important numbers by rune-writers of the relevant period, and that has not been forthcoming (though see p. 17). Even if such evidence existed, little would have been explained: why reduce the number of runes in the row from one multiple of eight to another?

That the abandoned runes come towards or at the end of each of the three groups is only partly true. And the significance of the observation is hard to gauge. The occurrence of a large number of uncompleted *fuþark* inscriptions from the Scandinavian Middle Ages suggests that some carvers of that era were better acquainted with the beginning of the rune-row than the end, but it is difficult to connect this uncertainty with the loss of eight runes from different parts of the row hundreds of years earlier. The idea that the last two runes of the first group of eight, rr. 5–6 of the second group, and rr. 3 and 6–8 of the third were dropped because carvers simply forgot about them or were ignorant of their existence lacks supporting evidence and must be judged far-fetched.

Some of the abandoned runes undeniably have complex shapes: ᛗ with two verticals connected by diagonals is considerably more intricate than ᛁ or ᚱ, for example. On the other hand ᚦ and ᛈ are of precisely equal complexity. The proposal is not, however, that runes were jettisoned simply because they came to be considered too complex, but that where it was felt a single rune could serve for two or more related speech sounds, a more cumbersome fellow that might equally well have represented those sounds was the one chosen for elimination. The dental stops /d/ and /t/, for example, were distinguished principally by the presence or absence of voice (the use of the vocal cords): /d/ (voiced) was represented by ᛗ, /t/ (unvoiced) by ᛏ; so – the reasoning goes – the more complex ᛗ was abandoned and ᛏ thereafter used for /t/ and /d/ alike. ᛟ stood for /o/, ᚢ for /u/, both of them rounded vowels (i.e. pronounced with lip-rounding); ᛟ was given up, leaving the simpler ᚢ to denote /o/ and /u/, and indeed all rounded vowels. The procedure or development postulated here leaves several questions unanswered, first and foremost why a reduction in the number of runes was considered desirable in the first place. The answer often given is that it made the learning and (with fewer complex shapes) the carving of the characters easier and quicker. But that is only partly true. There were fewer runes to learn, to be sure, but the carver still had to produce complex shapes such as ᚱ, ᚺ, ᛒ, ᛗ. And some relatively straightforward runes like ᛈ and ᛚ were also lost. The easing of graphical complexity can hardly rank as a principal cause of the reduction of the older *fuþark* in Scandinavia, if indeed it played a role at all.

Because of the unsatisfactory nature of other explanations, most scholars have assumed there must be a connection between the sound changes that took place in Scandinavian in the sixth and seventh centuries and the reductive changes in the writing system, first clearly documented in the early 700s. The difficulty has been to establish a *plausible* connection. Detailed and subtle arguments have been deployed, and it would lead too far to enter into them here in any detail. In rough outline the position is as follows.

By 700, the five-vowel system depicted on p. 24 had been augmented by /y/, /ø/, /æ/ and /ɔ/, all of which arose through the process known as mutation (p. 219). The nine vowels of early Viking-Age Scandinavian might be long or short, nasal (as in French *danse* 'dance', for example) or oral. The consonant system had changed too, in that /f/, /θ/, /h/ now only occurred in initial position in a word, together with /p/, /t/, /k/ and /b/, /d/, /g/, while in other positions /p/, /t/, /k/ contrasted almost exclusively with [β], [ð], [ɣ]. In addition, /j/ and /w/ had ceased to be distinctive speech sounds, becoming variants of /i/ and /u/. The runes lost from the *fuþark* were: X, which stood for /g/, ᚹ, which stood for /w/, ᛚ (of uncertain value), ᚲ /p/, ᛗ /e/, ◇ [(i)ŋ(g)], ᛉ /o/, ᛗ /d/. The problem that faces those seeking to establish a connection between the phonological changes on the one hand and the graphic developments on the other is this: why, in response to a vast increase in the number of vowels, altered relationships between the labial, dental and velar consonants (p. 223), and the reduction of /j/ and /w/ to variants of /i/ and /u/, were eight runes lost, and in particular the eight just listed? Initially the juxtaposition of the two happenings does not suggest an obvious causal relationship.

The inclusion of further details may shed a bit more light. Three of the abandoned runes were very restricted in their use. Although ᛚ may well have had a fixed sound value at the inception of runic writing, it seems to have become surplus to requirements early on (see pp. 13, 41); ◇ stood for [ŋ] or [ŋg], perhaps even [iŋg], which could be written ᛏ, (ᛏ)X and I(ᛏ)X respectively; ᚲ denoted /p/, which was a rare sound in Germanic. None of these three runes is much attested in Scandinavia, indeed ᚲ had not until late 2009 been found there in other than rune-row inscriptions. ᚹ may have gone out of use after /w/ lost its status as a distinctive speech sound; once [w] became a variant of /u/ it would have been natural enough to start writing it ᚾ – the norm in later Scandinavian tradition.

The disappearance of X, ᛗ, ᛉ, and ᛗ is harder to account for. One hypothesis has it that the sixteen-character *fuþark* reflected the pronunciation of unstressed syllables in Viking-Age Scandinavian. In these, it is affirmed, a fundamentally three-vowel system, /a/, /i/, /u/, prevailed, while in the case of certain consonants there was only a two-way contrast between unvoiced stop and voiced spirant (see above): /t/ and [ð] occurred, for example, but not /θ/ or /d/ (cf. that *bátar* 'boats' and *báðar* 'both [nom./acc. f.]' are Old Norse words, whereas **báþar* and **bádar* are impossible). According to this hypothesis ᛗ /e/ and ᛉ /o/ had become otiose, while of the members of each of the three original three-rune series: labial ᚠ /f/, ᚲ /p/, ᛒ /b/, dental ᚦ /θ/, ᛏ /t/, ᛗ /d/, and velar ᚺ /h/, ᚲ /k/, X /g/, only two were needed, one representing an unvoiced stop (for which ᛒ, ᛏ, ᚴ were chosen; on the form ᚴ, see 7.4), one a voiced spirant (for which ᚠ, ᚦ and, oddly, ᚴ were preferred). Ingenious as this proposal is, it fails to convince. Crucially, too much essential information resides in initial syllables for them to be dismissed from consideration (it is the distinction between /t/ and /d/, for example, that separates *tœma* '[to] empty' from *dœma* '[to] judge', and that between /k/ and /g/ which differentiates words such as *krǫf* 'demand' and *grǫf* 'ditch' 'grave'). Another difficulty is that ᚴ is found for both unvoiced stop /k/ (as in **auk** 'and', ON *ok*) and voiced spirant [ɣ] (as in **mak** 'male relation by marriage', ON *mág* [acc.]), whereas, following the logic of the hypothesis, one would have expected a different character for the latter – ᚺ being the most likely candidate among the runes that survived. There are further problems too complex to consider here, such as whether there really were just three unstressed vowels at the beginning of the eighth century.

Most of the theories that offer a purely phonological explanation for the reduction of the *fuþark* come up against difficulties of this kind. It is in an attempt to find a way around them that the rune names have been brought into the discussion. Some runologists have pointed out that of the eight runes that were lost, four, or perhaps five, had names the initial sound of which would have altered as a result of the changes that affected Scandinavian in the period *c.* 500–700. A note of caution must be sounded here: we do not have the original rune names, and our reconstructions are in some cases based on rather tenuous evidence (see pp. 157, 159–61). Nevertheless, there is a reasonable to strong possibility that the names of four of the lost runes changed in the following way:

ᚹ **wunjō > *yn*
ᛇ **ī(h)waz > *ýʀ*
ᛖ **ehwaz > *jóʀ*
ᛜ **ingwaz > *yngʀ/*ingʀ*

ᛟ may have been called **ōþila* (cf. OE *œþil* 'land' 'ancestral property' with *i*-mutation) or **ōþala* (cf. ON *óðal* 'inherited property'), or both (or yet something other). There is thus the possibility its initial /o:/ developed to /ø:/ in (at least parts of) Scandinavia as well as England.

If the acrophonic principle had been strictly applied none of ᚹ, ᛇ, ᛖ, ᛜ could have preserved their original values (nor ᛟ if its name became **œðil* in Scandinavia), while there would have been a surfeit of runes denoting /y/. What is uncertain is how essential the connection was deemed to be between the initial sound of a rune name and the phonetic value the rune represented. Its importance has been questioned on the grounds that rune-carvers could have operated perfectly well without this mnemonic aid. Nevertheless the Anglo-Frisian (pp. 37–9) and Scandinavian evidence indicates that when the initial sound of a rune name altered, the phonetic value of the rune altered with it. The Scandinavian evidence comprises the following (assuming our reconstruction of early runic nomenclature to be correct): (1) the original twelfth rune, whose name **jāra* developed to **ár(a)* and whose value changed from /j/ to /a/; (2) the fourth rune, whose name **ansuz* developed to **ǭss/*ā̃ss* and then to *óss* and whose value altered correspondingly from /a/ to /ã/ and then to /o/; (3) the original fifteenth rune, which, as well as denoting /ʀ/ (< /z/), may stand not only for /y/ (because its name, in western Scandinavia at least, came to be *ýr*) but also for /e/ and /æ/ (because in certain areas of eastern Scandinavia, according to some, it came to be called **eʀ*, **æʀ*, or **ælgʀ*); (4) the younger seventh rune, *hagall*, which seems occasionally to be used to denote /a/ in parts of Sweden where the loss of initial /h-/ was common. In the light of these (and the Anglo-Frisian) examples it is hard to argue there was not a connection between rune name and phonetic value. Perhaps we are dealing with a well-established convention rather than a crutch for rune-carvers to lean on – although the rune-writing novice may often have been thankful for a mnemonic tool of this kind.

The "rune-name hypothesis", whatever importance is attached to it, cannot on its own explain the reduction of the *fuþark* in Scandinavia from twenty-four to sixteen runes. It does not account for the disappearance of ᚷ **g** and ᛗ **d**, whose probable original names, **gebō* and **daȝaz*, would have retained the initial consonant in later incarnations (cf. ON *gjǫf, dagr*). Nor does it encompass ᚲ **p**: whatever the original name of this rune, it almost certainly began with /p/, and that initial phoneme would have remained unchanged.

A false conceit seems to underlie most attempts to account for the loss of ᚷ, ᚹ, ᛁ, ᚲ, ᛗ, ◇, ᚨ, ᛗ from Scandinavian runic writing. It is that there must be a single explanation for the whole process. In reality a number of different factors may have been at work. ᛁ and ◇, as noted above, appear to have been little used and are likely to have become marginal characters. They may well have continued as part of the rune-row, but eventually, perhaps following changes to the initial sound of their names, they must have been deemed excess to requirements. ᚹ suffered in two ways: the initial /w/ was lost from its name (as regularly in Scandinavian immediately before a rounded vowel, cf., e.g., English *word*, Icelandic *orð*, English *wolf*, Swedish *ulv*), and it ceased to denote a distinctive speech sound (after /w/ became a variant of /u/). ᛗ was subject to the drastic name change **ehwaz > *jóʀ*; if the acrophonic principle – or acrophonic convention, perhaps – was to be maintained, the rune could hardly continue to denote /e/. The initial sound in the name of ᚨ may have altered too, but only if (or where) its earlier name was **ōþila*, and for that there is no evidence from Scandinavia (cf. above). Leaving ᚨ aside, we are left with ᚷ, ᚲ and ᛗ, whose loss cannot (in part at least) be explained by the effect of phonological change on their names. ᚲ, like ᛁ and ◇, was little used, and indeed in the probably sixth-century Vadstena bracteate rune-row (Östergötland, south-eastern Sweden), it appears to have been replaced by ᛒ – **p** has the form ᛜ and **b** ᛜ in the bracteate's right-to-left running text. This single piece of evidence cannot however be taken to mean that ᚲ was on its way out of the *fuþark* as early as the sixth century. Perhaps, rather, there was uncertainty about its form.

The fate of ᚷ, ᚲ, and ᛗ raises an important question: to what extent was the reduction of the *fuþark* in Scandinavia the outcome of a deliberate decision? Most who have addressed the topic have considered it so, describing the process as a "reform". But it has been argued recently that this is a misnomer: that the sixteen-character *fuþark* is instead the end result of a gradual wasting-away of elements of the system. Scandinavian runic writing, it is maintained, was fundamentally conservative, its conservatism attributable to lack of contact with the outside world and in particular with roman-alphabet writing. In contrast, the argument continues, stands the Anglo-Frisian *fuþorc/k*, which was expanded in a systematic way to take account of significant sound changes (in Anglo-Saxon England with the active involvement of the Church following the introduction of Christianity in the seventh century; cf. chapter 5). In Scandinavia no new runes were invented to cater for the new phonemes that arose, with the result that the existing characters became multifunctional, ᚿ,

for example, ultimately standing for /u/, /o/, /y/, /ø/, [w] (and occasionally /ɔ/ and a couple of diphthongs besides). This multifunctionality made it easier to regard as superfluous runes whose names had suffered deleterious change to their initial sound, and to begin to think of others as expendable. Those in the former category were gradually dropped from the *fuþark*, those in the latter were used less and less and were likewise finally excluded from the rune-row altogether.

While there is something to be said in favour of this line of thinking, it leaves certain questions unanswered. For one or other, or several, of the reasons offered above ᚹ, ᛁ, ᚲ, ᛗ, ◇, and perhaps ᛉ, may have come to seem superfluous. It is less clear why ᚷ and ᛗ should have been considered expendable by the generality of rune-writers and gradually gone out of use. There are suggestions the distinction between /t/ and /d/ and /k/ and /g/ was neutralised in some positions (e.g. gen. *dags* [daxs] 'day's', where the /g/ variant [ɣ] is assumed to be unvoiced to the /k/ variant [x] by the following [s]). But what was gained by spelling, say, *dag* 'day [acc.]' **tak** rather than **dag** (with the risk of confusion with *tak* 'take!') – other than the employment of fewer runes and slightly simpler shapes? And though it is true that ᛁ and ᚲ seem to be little used by Scandinavian rune-carvers and ◇ only for a short period (except, in each case, in representations of the *fuþark*), ᚷ, ᚹ, ᛗ, ᛉ, and ᛗ are all very much part of the system until about 700, whereupon they fairly rapidly vanish from runic writing in the North. We must of course bear in mind that the impression of rapid change lent by our meagre sources could be false, but on the basis of the evidence currently available some kind of conscious reform looks more probable than gradual attrition.

Reform or no reform, it is a mystery how the same eight runes could be universally abandoned throughout a society that seemingly lacked the central authority or bureaucracy to implement change on a broad scale. And it remains a puzzle why ᚷ and ᛗ were eliminated or lost. It is worth noting, however, that those (and they are many) who have viewed the reduction of the *fuþark* as an incomprehensible impoverishment of the writing system have considered the development very much from the point of view of the reader, not least the modern reader. For those who wrote runes, however, the new system must have been quicker to learn, and have offered economy of carving effort. And many of the inscriptions made in the Viking Age were stereotypical enough for the reader to be able to overcome any imperfections in the orthography (cf. chapter 8). It is unlikely, though, that the increasing popularity of formulaic commemorative inscriptions is what provided the impetus for the reduction of the rune-row. Apart from anything else, the arrival of this type of inscription seems to postdate the emergence of the new system.

7.3 The younger *fuþark*: a new, phonetically multifunctional writing system

The sixteen-character rune-row is known as the younger *fuþark*. This is to distinguish it from its twenty-four character predecessor, designated "older". The younger *fuþark* contained the following runes (here given in transliteration for convenience; for the actual forms, cf. 7.4):

f	u	þ	ã	r	k	h	n	i	a	s	t	b	m	l	ʀ
1	2	3	4	5	6	7	8	9	10	11	12	13	14	15	16

Fig. 12 The runes of the younger *fuþark* (transliterated)

Whether the characters were arranged in precisely this order from the start is unknown, but it is the one found in all extant Scandinavian Viking-Age inscriptions that present the complete row. It follows the older-*fuþark* order of the relevant runes except in the case of ᛦ/ᛉ z, which is moved to the end of the row (and now transliterated ʀ to reflect the increasingly *r*-like quality of the sound denoted). The tenth rune of the younger *fuþark*, **a**, is not the continuation of the original fourth rune, *ansuz, but the reflex of original **j** (cf. its name change *jāra > *ár* and corresponding change in value /j/ > /a/).

The parsimony of the younger *fuþark* meant that the multifunctionality discussed in 7.2 was rife. Fig. 13 sets out the principal values that can be attributed to each of the sixteen runes in the period *c.* 700–1000 (some of the values were phonemic, some phonetic, but phonetic notation is used here for the sake of uniformity; vowel and consonant length is ignored).

f	[f] [β]
u	[u] [o] [y] [ø] [w]
þ	[θ] [ð]
ã	[ã]
r	[r]
k	[k] [g] [ɣ] ([ŋk] [ŋg])
h	[h] [x]
n	[n]
i	[i] [e]
a	[a] [æ] [ɔ]
s	[s]
t	[t] [d] ([nt] [nd])
b	[b] [p] ([mb] [mp])
m	[m]
l	[l]
ʀ	[ʀ] (see p. 6)

Fig. 13 The runes of the younger *fuþark* (transliterated) and their principal phonetic values

With the runic inventory so drastically reduced, the fit between speech and writing altered radically. It is not least in the sounds and phonemes denoted by particular runes that we recognise whether an inscription is written in the older or the younger *fuþark*. From Ribe in southern Jutland comes a runic text carved into part of a human skull. It is dated to the period *c.* 725–760. Fifteen different runes are used in the inscription. Some have argued (largely because the actual forms of the runes are indistinguishable from those used in seventh-century older-*fuþark* inscriptions) that the carver may have had a larger inventory of characters at his disposal – possibly the full twenty-four – but that is rather beside the point. The question of whether the new writing system preceded the loss of runes from the *fuþark* is separate, and inscrutable. We have no way of knowing how many runes the Ribe carver was familiar with, but we can observe that he writes **hialb** for *hjalp* 'help!', **uþin** for *Oðinn* '[the god] Óðinn' and **tuirk** for *dverg* 'dwarf'. With **i** for [j], **b** for [p], **u** for [o], **þ** for [ð], **t** for [d], **i** for [e], and **k** for [ɣ] the carver is clearly employing the younger-*fuþark* system.

7.4 The younger *fuþark*: variety of form

The difficulty some have had in distinguishing consistently between older- and younger-*fuþark* inscriptions stems in large part from confusion of form and function of the kind just illustrated. In England, as we have seen, certain runes changed shape. That was also a feature of Scandinavian runic writing. But the changing shape of individual characters is a different matter from the reduction of the *fuþark* from twenty-four to sixteen runes and the adoption of a new writing system. In older-*fuþark* inscriptions of the seventh century, **k** tends to appear as ᚴ, **j** > **a** as ᛡ, **s** as ᛋ and **ʀ** as ᛦ, contrasting with earlier ᚲ, ᛃ, ᛊ, ᛉ respectively. In the oldest inscriptions in the younger *fuþark* **ã** has the form ᚨ, **h** ᚺ, **a** ᛡ, and **m** ᛗ; later, ᚬ **ã**, ᚼ **h**, ᛅ **a**, ᛉ or ᛘ **m** are common forms. There is no indication, however, that any of these developments is directly related to the loss of eight runes from the row. The relatively few eighth-century Scandinavian inscriptions known (assuming our datings can be relied upon), suggest that the earliest younger-*fuþark* carvers used the surviving sixteen runes in their inherited forms (Fig. 14).

ᚠ	ᚢ	ᚦ	ᚨ	ᚱ	ᚴ	ᚺ	ᚾ	ᛁ	ᛡ	ᛋ	ᛏ	ᛒ	ᛗ	ᛚ	ᛦ
f	**u**	**þ**	**ã**	**r**	**k**	**h**	**n**	**i**	**a**	**s**	**t**	**b**	**m**	**l**	**ʀ**
1	2	3	4	5	6	7	8	9	10	11	12	13	14	15	16

Fig. 14 The runes of the earliest younger-*fuþark* inscriptions (ᚺ, ᛡ, ᛗ are often transliterated H, A, M to distinguish them from later ᚼ **h**, ᛅ **a**, ᛉ/ᛘ **m**; p. 4)

Subsequently, there seems to have been a good deal of experimentation with simpler forms, leading to divergent results. It is a commonplace that two variants of the younger *fuþark* developed, one less simplified and called (by modern scholars) "long-branch", one more simplified and known as "short-twig". Model rune-rows illustrating the two types are given on p. 6, and are repeated here for convenience as Figs 15–16 (Fig. 15 slightly adapted).

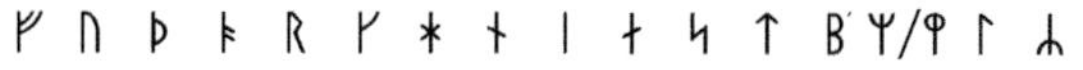

ᚠ ᚢ ᚦ ᚬ ᚱ ᚴ ᚼ ᚾ ᛁ ᛅ ᛋ ᛏ ᛒ ᛘ/ᛙ ᛚ ᛦ
f u þ ã r k h n i a s t b m l ʀ
1　2　3　4　5　6　7　8　9　10　11　12　13　14　15　16

Fig. 15 The less simplified "long-branch" younger *fuþark*

ᚠ ᚢ ᚦ ᚭ ᚱ ᚴ ᚼ ᚽ ᛁ ᛆ ᛌ ᛐ ᚦ ᛙ ᛚ ᛁ
f u þ ã r k h n i a s t b m l ʀ
1　2　3　4　5　6　7　8　9　10　11　12　13　14　15　16

Fig. 16 The more simplified "short-twig" younger *fuþark*

Based on the geographical distribution of inscriptions with "long-branch" and "short-twig" runes it has been concluded that the former were to begin with primarily a Danish phenomenon (by some called "Danish" or "normal" runes), while the latter (also known as "Swedish-Norwegian" or "Rök" runes – the latter designation after the Rök stone from Östergötland, south-eastern Sweden) belonged in Norway and Sweden. In the eleventh century, however, the long-branch type became dominant in Sweden (almost ubiquitous on rune-stones), while in Norway elements from both rows were used. (Fig. 17 shows the selection made by many Norwegian carvers.)

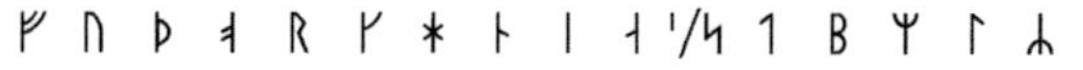

ᚠ ᚢ ᚦ ᚭ ᚱ ᚴ ᚼ ᚽ ᛁ ᚭ/ᚼ ᛐ ᛒ ᚤ ᛚ ᛅ
f u þ o r k h n i a s t b m l y
1　2　3　4　5　6　7　8　9　10　11　12　13　14　15　16

Fig. 17 The Norwegian so-called "mixed" *fuþark*
(on the transliteration of ᚭ as **o** and ᛅ as **y**, see pp. 93–4)

Not all have accepted that choice of younger-*fuþark* variant depended on a carver's place of origin or work. Some have seen the "long-branch" and "short-twig" rows as functional variants first and foremost: the former with its fuller forms was for use on stone monuments, while the latter was typically the preserve of everyday communication. However, those championing this view face the problem that few runic inscriptions from the Viking Age appear to be everyday communications (as many from the Scandinavian Middle Ages undoubtedly are, cf. chapter 10). Possibly, as has been argued, the wood on which such messages would mostly have been carved has perished. It is nevertheless remarkable, if Viking-Age Scandinavians communicated regularly by runic stick, that virtually none of the sticks have survived – or at least yet been discovered.

To some extent arguments about who used which variant of the younger *fuþark* are artificial. As noted above, Figs 15–16 present *model* rune-rows (and so, to a degree, do Figs 14 and 17). That is to say, a selection of forms has been put together as representative of common usage. Behind this neat compartmentalisation lies a rather messier reality. The position can be outlined as follows.

In the first 200 years or so of younger-*fuþark* usage, Denmark (within the medieval boundaries, which take in Skåne and Blekinge, now southern Sweden) shows evidence of variety and change. Not only do we see the runes of Fig. 14 giving way to those of Fig. 15, there are also inscriptions with the simpler runes of Fig. 16 or a mixture of simpler and more elaborate types. By the tenth century, however, the Danes seem to weary of variety and change and almost to a man opt for the long-branch characters of Fig. 15.

Early and mid-Viking Age Sweden is characterised by much greater variety and experimentation than Denmark. Variations on the simplified characters of Fig. 16 are many, e.g. ⊦ **a**, ⊺ **t**, ⊣ **b**, ⊺ **l**. We also find several of the forms that eventually became common or standard in Denmark, e.g. ✳ **h**, ✝ **n**, ✝ **a**, ⵦ **m**. Towards the end of the tenth century variety and experimentation give way to homogeneity. Long-branch characters (Fig. 15), apparently spreading from the south and east, become the norm. The homogeneity, though, is never as absolute as in Denmark, and the simpler forms ⊦ **n**, ⊣ **a**, ˈ **s**, ⊺ **t**, ⊬ **b**, ı **R** continue to occur – some occasionally, some more frequently – as alternatives to their more elaborate counterparts.

There are considerably fewer inscriptions preserved from Viking-Age Norway than Denmark or Sweden, but enough to document the use of a wide range of runic forms, and to indicate that the homogeneity sometimes characteristic of the other two areas never became part of Norwegian tradition. Variety of form is also found in the Scandinavian inscriptions of the British Isles, the products of settlers and their descendants.

7.5 Summary

On the basis of the evidence presented above, the following conclusions seem warranted. The younger *fuþark* was the outcome of a process (in part, at least, probably a conscious reform) that led to a reduction in the number of runes. However and wherever this development started, progressed and finished, the new *fuþark* was rapidly adopted throughout the whole of Scandinavia, and by the beginning of the eighth century all, or virtually all, rune-carvers were using the same sixteen runes – a remarkable example of unity in the apparent absence of a central authority to promote it. But that was as far as the unity went. When it came to the realisation of many of the sixteen runes, a much more open policy prevailed. Some carvers experimented with runic form, simplifying many characters. Others resisted change, or were unaware of it. Different traditions developed. In certain areas carvers adopted a single set of forms, while in others they had a stock of runic characters from which they might help themselves to a – carefully chosen or arbitrary – selection.

7.6 The staveless runes

Runic simplification reached its zenith with the staveless runes, so called because they mostly lack the "stave" (Scandinavian *stav*), i.e. the vertical, that characterises virtually all the graphs of other types of younger *fuþark*. These minimal characters do not appear to come from the period of experimentation that followed the emergence of the sixteen-rune *fuþark*; they are more probably a product of the late tenth or the eleventh century. Staveless runes occur in a handful of stone inscriptions from Hälsingland and Södermanland (central-eastern and south-eastern Sweden respectively), on three portable objects from Uppland (south-eastern Sweden), and on a runic stick from Bergen, western Norway. They also feature as occasional elements on a few rune-stones from Medelpad (central-eastern Sweden). On all but the stones from Hälsingland the staveless characters appear in company with runes of other (younger-*fuþark*) types. The Bergen stick contains a sequence of consonant runes with common medieval forms (for which an intricate interpretation has recently been suggested), some rune-like symbols, and an incomplete staveless rune-row, its final characters lost through damage. The shapes of the staveless runes can vary considerably. Fig. 18 presents those found on (or in one case to be inferred from) the Hälsingland stones.

f	u	þ	ã	r	k	h	n	i	a	s	t	b	m	l	ʀ
1	2	3	4	5	6	7	8	9	10	11	12	13	14	15	16

Fig. 18 The staveless runes of the Hälsingland stones
(ã is not documented but is inferred for systematic reasons;
a staveless r. 4 occurs only on the Bergen stick, and then in the form)

   It is hard to judge the purpose or function of these reduced runic characters. From their distribution they would appear to belong in Sweden (the Bergen stick looks to have been carved by someone with a general or antiquarian interest in runic script; p. 121). They may have been developed in the Uppland-Södermanland region and from there have spread north to Hälsingland, but that is far from assured. If constructed for a practical purpose at all, speed of writing seems the most obvious, though it is then odd to find the type preserved chiefly on commemorative stones. Going by the very small number of staveless inscriptions that exist, it would appear that this radical simplification never became popular, and it is not hard to see why. While quick to carve, staveless runes can be very laborious to read: so much depends on relative height, and it does not take much for, say, ⁻ **a,** ⁻ **t** and ⁻ **b** to become confused. The staveless experiment seems to have been short-lived, and to have had little impact on the development of mainstream runic writing in Scandinavia.

Select reading list

Barnes, Michael P. 1987. 'The origins of the younger *fuþark* – a reappraisal'. In: *Runor och runinskrifter: Föredrag vid Riksantikvarieämbetets och Vitterhetsakademiens symposium 8–11 september 1985* (Kungl. Vitterhets Historie och Antikvitets Akademien: Konferenser 15). Stockholm: Almqvist & Wiksell International, 29–45. [A general discussion of the problems surrounding the origin of the younger *fuþark*.]

Barnes, Michael P. 2006. 'Standardised *fuþark*s: a useful tool or a delusion?' In: (Marie Stoklund *et al.*, eds) *Runes and their Secrets: Studies in Runology*. Copenhagen: Museum Tusculanum Press, University of Copenhagen, 11–29. [Discussion of how the presentation of *fuþark*s in printed works can obscure the diversity of runic form, with particular reference to the younger *fuþark*.]

Barnes, Michael P. 2009. 'The origins of the younger *fuþark*: a review of recent and less recent research', *NOWELE* 56/57, 123–42. [Brings the discussion in the 1987 paper up to date.]

Fridell, Staffan 2011. 'Graphic variation and change in the younger fuþark', *NOWELE* 60/61, 69–88. [Argues that a number of developmental tendencies to be seen in the history of western alphabets can shed light on the graphic variation found in the younger *fuþark*.]

Liestøl, Aslak 1981. 'The Viking runes: the transition from the older to the younger *fuþark*', *Saga-Book* 20:4, 247–66. [Emphasises particularly the part played by the rune names in the transition from the older to the younger *fuþark*.]

Peterson, Lena 1994. 'The graphemic system of the staveless runes'. In: (James E. Knirk, ed.) *Proceedings of the Third International Symposium on Runes and Runic Inscriptions, Grindaheim, Norway, 8–12 August 1990* (Runrön 9). Uppsala: Institutionen för nordiska språk, Uppsala universitet, 223–52. [A detailed discussion of the distinctive features of the staveless runes.]

Schulte, Michael 2006. 'The transformation of the older fuþark: number magic, runographic or linguistic principles?', *Arkiv för nordisk filologi* 121, 41–74. [Discusses the change from the older to the younger *fuþark* and argues for a gradual transition rather than a conscious act of reform.]

Schulte, Michael 2009. 'The Scandinavian runic reform: a sound notion or a research dogma?', *NOWELE* 56/57, 107–21. [Argues strongly against the notion that the younger *fuþark* was the product of a reform.]

8 Scandinavian inscriptions of the Viking Age

8.1 The Viking-Age rune-stone

The term "Viking Age" is here used loosely, to denote the period *c.* 700–1050, extending to *c.* 1100–1130 in Sweden. One type of runic artefact in particular characterises this period in Scandinavia: the commemorative rune-stone. It predominates through sheer weight of numbers (rough figures including fragments and inscriptions known only from drawings are: Denmark 220; Norway 60, Sweden 2,600; plus some 50 from outside Scandinavia); it is also by and large more imposing than other types of inscription, and tends to have longer and more informative texts. Rune-stones are generally free-standing. Most were probably laid on the ground to be carved, and then raised up and embedded in the earth when completed. A small number of commemorative inscriptions are carved into bedrock.

8.2 Dating and the typology of rune-stones

Rune-stones are generally hard to date with any precision. There is seldom an archaeological context, and in its absence typological dating is employed. A few commemorative stones refer to persons and/or events known from other sources, and in favourable circumstances their genesis can be narrowed down to a particular decade or two. The runographic, linguistic and (if any) artistic features they display, and not least their layout, are then used as a point of reference in the dating of other rune-stones. Features are judged "earlier", "contemporary with" or "later" than those on the datable stones. This methodology is helpful as far as it goes, but suffers from drawbacks. Most significantly, typology can position one inscription relative to another, but can offer little in the way of positive datings (no more, at least, than the crudest date ranges). Primarily that is because ways of laying out a runic text, rune usage, language and artistic style can vary from place to place and carver to carver. An inscription with typologically "earlier" features could well have been made later than one in which the typology appears more recent.

The principal features used to classify a rune-stone as "earlier" are (1) unembellished layout (little or no ornamentation, lack of the framing lines between which runes are commonly set); (2) absence or only sporadic use of word-division; (3) older rune forms (in "long-branch" inscriptions the occurrence in particular of ᚠ, ᚬ **a**, ᚼ, ᛘ); (4) older linguistic forms; (5) vocabulary and/or formulas of apparently archaic type; (6) pre-Christian context. Individually these features do not necessarily weigh heavily, but the appearance of several of them together is usually suggestive. The typological features used to classify a rune-stone as "later" are in most cases the reverse of those just given: (1) intricate layout; (2) regular word-division (often in the form of small crosses); (3) later rune forms (in particular the occurrence of dotted runes, cf. chapter 9); (4) later linguistic forms; (5) vocabulary and/or formulas of standard type; (6) Christian context. In addition to the application of these general criteria, a finer chronology of (what are broadly considered) eleventh-century stones has been attempted for Sweden, based on styles of ornamentation. (See further p. 209.)

Although typological classification of this kind cannot reveal the age of individual rune-stones, it can offer reasonable guidance to general trends and developments. We are probably also safe in assigning most rune-stones to approximate periods. On that basis it has been concluded that relatively few were raised during the first 200 years or so of the Viking Age. After *c.* 900 the practice takes off in Jutland, and for the next 100–150 years commemorative stones are commissioned and produced at a steady rate in various parts of Denmark. The age of the rune-stone in Sweden is roughly the eleventh century, with large numbers emanating from some areas, fewer or virtually none (apparently) from others. Norway, which has the greatest concentration of pre-Viking Age rune-stones, can only muster a few from the Viking Age itself. It is difficult to say whether there was a continuous tradition of rune-stone raising in Norway, or whether the custom died out and was reintroduced, but either way the Norwegians seem never to have joined the scramble to erect runic monuments in which their Scandinavian neighbours were for a time involved.

The Viking-Age rune-stones that connect most closely in wording and layout with those of the preceding period come from the Danish area. This is odd insofar as no older-*fuþark* stones have so far been discovered in that part of Scandinavia (except in the outlying Blekinge, now south-eastern Sweden), but the circumstance can perhaps be explained by the age of the inscriptions concerned. Just as some older-*fuþark* monuments, the earliest (probably eighth-century) Danish stones exhibit either a personal name on its own in the nominative case or one in the genitive followed by *stæinn* 'stone' or a word for 'monument' – e.g. **hairulfʀ** 'Hærulfʀ' on the Øster Løgum stone, **āiriks:kubl** 'Æirikʀ's monument' in the right-to-left Starup inscription, both from southern Jutland. The two inscriptions run upwards. Øster Løgum places the runes fairly centrally on the stone and encloses them between framing lines; Starup has them along the edge and unframed.

By no means all the typologically early Danish rune-stone inscriptions are as laconic as these. The Snoldelev stone from Zealand goes into some detail about the man commemorated: **kun:uʌltstʌin:sunaʀ:|ruнalts:þulaʀ:āsal нauku(m)** (where **ʌ** transliterates **ⵜ** and **н** Ⴌ, cf. p. 61), edited and translated: *Gunnvalds stæinn, sunaʀ Hroalds, þulaʀ ā Salhaugum* 'Gunnvaldʀ's stone, son of Hroaldʀ, þulʀ at Salhaugaʀ'. Unfortunately we have no real idea what a *þulʀ* was. ON *þulr* seems to refer to someone steeped in ancient lore, while the ON verb *þylja* can mean 'recite' 'chant', so: 'reciter of ancient lore'? But how justified we are in using medieval Norwegian/Icelandic usage to interpret a Viking-Age Danish rune-stone is unclear. Snoldelev has prominent framing lines, but the following features suggest it is an early inscription: (a) the formula 'X's stone'; (b) **ⵜ** for /a/ and Ⴌ for /h/ (p. 61); (c) the apparent retention of initial /h-/ in Hroalds, even though the rune concerned appears to be in the wrong place (/hr-/ > /r-/ is an early Viking-Age development in Danish); (d) the lack of a separator to divide the sequence **uAltstAin** and the use of a single **s** for the final consonant of *Gunnvalds* and the initial consonant of *stæinn* (p. 24).

The Flemløse 1 stone from Fyn, rather than simply identifying itself as the dead person's monument, proclaims: 'After HrolfR stands this stone' (and goes on to say something of HrolfR, the commissioners, and the rune-carver). This *memorial* formula is distinctly uncommon and is found only in a few inscriptions that otherwise show every appearance of belonging to the early part of the Viking Age. The formula that soon becomes standard throughout Scandinavia is 'NN raised this stone after MM' (or variants thereof), which pushes the raiser or commissioner very firmly into the foreground. That sets off the vast majority of Viking-Age commemorative rune-stones from those of earlier and later periods, where attention by and large is focused on the deceased.

Although Denmark, Norway and Sweden (and the Scandinavian colonies where rune-stones have been found) share the basic "raiser formula", big differences of practice otherwise can be observed between countries, and also regions. These concern layout, rune-forms (cf. 7.4, 7.6), language, content, ornamentation, type or shape of stone, status of carver. Some differences are more immediately obvious than others. There is for example a fundamental divergence in the layout of Danish, Norwegian and Swedish Viking-Age rune-stones (with some overlap in border areas). Danish carvers tend to place their runes on the broad face of the stone; they are set between framing lines, and run both upwards and downwards (Plate 6). Norwegian carvers prefer the narrow edge, and their runes almost always run upwards (Plate 7). Swedish carvers, especially in the east of the country, have a predilection for "curly worms", known more formally as zoomorphic bands – stylised serpents, which twist and turn their way across the broad face of the stone (Plate 8). Many areas clearly had professional carvers, who specialised in the production of runic monuments. Demand in eastern Sweden seems to have led to the establishment of workshops, where runic apprentices could learn their trade. We do not have direct evidence of this, but laser scanning of stone surfaces has indicated that several people of varying competence may have been at work on some stones, even where "signed" by what appears to be an individual carver (cf. pp. 166–7). Furthermore, many unsigned monuments exhibit features characteristic of named carvers, and it has been surmised that these could be from workshops in which a master had imposed his preferred style.

Plate 6 *(above)* The Mejlby stone, northern Jutland, showing the typical Danish rune-stone layout

Plate 7 *(right)* The Oddernes stone, Vest-Agder, Norway, showing the typical Norwegian rune-stone layout

Plate 8 The Ågersta stone, Uppland, Sweden, showing the typical eastern Swedish rune-stone layout

8.3 Content

Most Viking-Age rune-stones have what has been called an "obligatory" formula. Chiefly that is the one referred to above, which identifies the raiser(s) or commissioner(s) of the stone, states that he, she or they raised it or caused it to be raised, names the person or persons in whose memory the stone stands and his, her or their relationship to the raiser(s)/commissioner(s). A characteristic example is provided by the Helland 3 inscription from Rogaland, south-western Norway (suggested dating, based on the stone's ornamentation, early eleventh century): **þurmuþr:risti:stin:þãnã|aft:þrunt: sunsin** 'Þormóðr raised this stone after Þróndr, his son'. Sometimes, as in this case, an inscription may consist of the obligatory formula alone. Very often, however, there is additional material, which can also be of a formulaic kind. It is common, for example, to describe the deceased as a 'very good warrior/ farmer/husband', or to indicate their position or status in some other way. In overtly Christian monuments, of which there are many from the latter part of the Viking Age, a prayer for the soul of the departed is often included: **kuþhialbionthans**, *Guð hjalpi ǫnd hans* 'God help his soul', which concludes one of the two Täby tä inscriptions, Uppland, Sweden (eleventh century), may serve as a typical example. It is where the additional material is less formulaic that the rune-stones can offer fascinating glimpses of Viking-Age society. Although extremely brief and fragmentary, the information to be gleaned from them is first-hand, and thus of prime importance. Written sources for Viking-Age Scandinavia come otherwise from foreign observers or from Danish, Icelandic or Norwegian writers of the twelfth century and later.

It is possible to categorise the various insights the rune-stones provide, although scholars have divided up the material in different ways, and categories can sometimes overlap. Broadly speaking, we have references to: politics (power struggles, conquests, major invasions); religion (heathendom, the conversion, Christianity); travel (for warlike, trading, or religious purposes); status or position in society (titles and/or appellations); inheritance; rune-writing (rune-writers' signatures, the interpreting of inscriptions, and their painting). In addition, something may be learnt about literature and myth: there is a great deal of verse – of types known from medieval Iceland and Norway – and now and again we find what appear to be literary allusions. Some stones bear images as well as an inscription. There are various depictions of what are almost certainly figures and motifs from Germanic poetry and myth. Christian iconography – besides the extremely common cross – is also represented.

The most striking example of a rune-stone with political themes is probably Jelling 2 from north-eastern Jutland. The inscription is as follows (in transliteration, edited as a text, and in translation; for the runes themselves, see Plate 9, which shows Face A, and Plate 16 below, which shows Face C).

Plate 9 Face A of the Jelling 2 stone from northern Jutland, showing the main part of the inscription

Face A   **haraltr:kunukʀ:baþ:kaurua**
          kubl:þausi:aft:kurmfaþursin
          aukaft:þāurui:muþur:sina:sa
          haraltr(:)ias:sāʀ:uan:tanmaurk
Face B   **ala:auknuruiak**
Face C   **aukt(a)ni(karþi)kristnā**

Haraldr kunungʀ bað gørva kumbl þøsi aft Gorm, faður sin, ok aft Þorvi,
moður sina. Sa Haraldr æs sæʀ vann Danmǫrk alla ok Norvæg ok dani
gærði kristnā.

'King Haraldr ordered [people] to make these monuments after Gormʀ,
his father, and after Þorvi, his mother. That Haraldr who won for himself
all Denmark, and Norway, and made the Danes Christian.'

Here King Haraldr ("Blacktooth") claims to have made himself master of
all Denmark and of Norway. These are among the earliest occurrences of
the designations "Denmark" and "Norway", and the way they are used in
the inscription implies that by the time of Haraldr's reign (*c.* 958–85) both
countries had become recognised entities. Haraldr further claims to have
made the Danes Christian, by which must be meant that he had declared
Christianity the official religion of the country. This is thus as much a political
as a religious statement. Because of its references to historical persons and
events, Jelling 2 is one of the few rune-stones for which a reasonably precise
date can be given. There has been much argument about details, but it is clear
that the inscription must post-date Haraldr's own conversion (*c.* 965), and is
likely to pre-date the defeats he appears to have suffered first at Hedeby (near
modern Schleswig) and then in Norway (*c.* 973–4). Some have argued that
the runes on the Jelling 2 stone were inscribed in two phases – the memorial
inscription soon after the death of King Gormʀ (whom Þorvi predeceased),
the rest in the 970s or even the 980s, perhaps after Haraldr's (or more properly
his son Svæinn Forkbeard's) reconquest of Hedeby in 983.

There are only two other references on rune-stones to an official act of
conversion. Sweden's most northerly stone, from Frösön, Jämtland, states that
a certain Austmaðr had Jämtland christianised. We are not dealing here with a
royal decree as in the Danish case, but with a decision by some local chieftain.
Who Austmaðr was is unknown. In the Viking Age Jämtland was a Norwegian
province (becoming Swedish only in 1645), but probably far enough away
from Norwegian centres of power for the inhabitants to be able to exercise
a good deal of autonomy. If, as some have suggested, the Frösö stone is from
the early eleventh century, Jämtland's conversion could have been an offshoot
of the introduction of Christianity in Norway by the kings Óláfr Tryggvason
(995–1000) and Óláfr Haraldsson (1015–28), later St Óláfr. On the other
hand, current opinion favours a dating 1050–1080, and the inscription itself
is of eastern Swedish type, which is conceivably reflected in the name of its
raiser, the literal meaning of *Austmaðr* being 'eastman' 'easterner' (often
applied to Norwegians in Iceland in the Icelandic sagas, but here perhaps to
someone from east of Jämtland). The Kuli stone from Møre, north-western

Plate 10 The Kuli stone, Møre og Romsdal, north-western Norway

Norway (Plate 10), speaks of christianisation in a different way. Following a fairly routine raiser formula, the inscription proclaims: 'Twelve winters had Christianity been in Norway'. There is no way of knowing for sure when the Kuli stone was inscribed and set up, but there are archaeological indications it may have happened in the mid-1030s (a causeway passing by the original site of the stone has been dated dendrochronologically to 1034). That would take "Christianity in Norway" back to the early 1020s, when Óláfr Haraldsson's missionary campaign had been in progress for some years. It is unclear, however, what act or event the raisers of the Kuli stone considered marked the introduction of Christianity in Norway, though some have argued for the assembly at Moster, Hordaland, at which Christian laws were adopted for the western part of the country. The precise date of this meeting is uncertain, but those who have examined the question most closely have suggested 1020, 1022 or 1024. If a connection between rune-stone, causeway and assembly is accepted, 1022 becomes the most likely year.

The more mundane Christian rune-stone may identify itself through the inclusion of prayers, as noted above, but other Christian features are also common. Many inscriptions refer to the building of 'bridges' (often causeways across marshy land or shallow water), and some to the clearing of pathways. Such activities were manifestly promoted as pious acts (commemorative stone raisers will often state that they performed them for the soul of the deceased), presumably because they improved communication and thereby assisted the work of the Church – of missionaries in particular. A few stones touch on the construction of churches and other buildings of an apparently religious character. There are also inscriptions that refer to a person's dying 'in white clothes', probably the baptismal robes worn by a convert at baptism and for a week thereafter. The implication in these cases is that the deceased was baptised when close to death. And there is the occasional stone that mentions a journey to Jerusalem, most likely a pilgrimage, while several speak of *Grikkjar* or *Grikkland* 'Greece' or more probably 'Byzantium', a recognised stage on the way from Scandinavia to the Holy Land.

There are, of course, many Viking-Age rune-stones which make no reference to Christianity. As we have seen, the new religion was not adopted in Denmark until the 960s and in Norway not until the early eleventh century. The christianisation of Sweden is more difficult to date (and the area was not politically united during the conversion period): many individual families seem to have begun turning to the new faith shortly before the year 1000, but it probably only became the official religion of a unified country towards the end of the eleventh century. The Viking Age was thus 200 or 300 years old before Christianity gained a dominant position in Scandinavia. There are nevertheless remarkably few Scandinavian rune-stones that are overtly pagan; commonly they provide no clues at all to the religious affiliation of their raisers. Of those that reveal their heathen character through wording, ornamentation or context, only a small number specifically refer to a Norse god.

A prime example of a heathen rune-stone is Glavendrup, from the island of Fyn, Denmark (Plate 11). Its lengthy and detailed commemorative text concludes with the invocation **þur:uiki:þasi:runaʀ** 'Þorr hallow these runes'.

Plate 11 Faces B and C of the Glavendrup stone, Fyn, Denmark.
Far right can be seen ᚦᚢᚱ:ᚢᛁᚴᛁ:ᚦᛆᛋᛁ:ᚱᚢᛌᛆᛌ, 'Þorr hallow these runes'.

There follows a warning against tampering with the stone, to which there are several parallels, all seemingly from heathen contexts. And if that were not enough, the runic monument is accompanied by a ship-setting – a series of standing stones laid out in the shape of a ship – a practice going back to early Iron-Age times and presumably reflecting a belief that the dead had to make a voyage in the after-life. The heathen character of a stone like Glavendrup does not of course guarantee it is older than any that proclaim a Christian affiliation. Individuals, particularly powerful ones, may have remained true to their old religion despite pressure to convert, whether from king or community. Glavendrup is conventionally dated to the period around 900, but need not be so old.

Numerous rune-stones document travel abroad. Popular destinations seem to have been the eastern Baltic, Russia and England, as well as Byzantium, although other areas also feature. The purpose of these journeys is seldom made entirely clear. Some who went to England appear to have taken part in large-scale invasions. There are inscriptions in memory of men who were 'with Knutr', presumably participants in the expedition mounted by Canute the Great in 1015 to seize the English throne (which he held until his death in 1035). A number of those who ended their lives in Byzantium will have been Varangians – Scandinavian mercenaries in the service of the Byzantine emperor – rather than pilgrims on their way to the Holy Land. Many who undertook expeditions abroad were clearly adventurers in search of booty. There are close on thirty stones, mostly from the Mälar region of eastern Sweden, commemorating men who went on an expedition with "Ingvarr". The stones agree the expedition was to the east, but that the participants met their end in the south, in "Særkland". Exactly where Særkland lay is disputed, but many have interpreted the name as 'Saracens' land' and assumed it to refer to the lands of the Abassid caliphate, centred on modern Iraq (recently a more general sense, "Arabia", has been suggested). The warlike nature of this and similar expeditions is underlined in many of the inscriptions. The concluding part of Gripsholm (Plate 12), one of the "Ingvarr stones", runs: *Þæir foru drængila, fiarri at gulli, auk austarla ærni gafu. Dou sunnarla, a Særklandi* 'They went manfully, far after gold, and in the east gave [food] to the eagle [i.e. despatched enemies in battle]. They died in the south, in Særkland'. The date of the Ingvarr stones is likely to be soon after 1041. In that year the Icelandic annals record the death of *Yngvarr hinn víðfǫrli* 'Yngvarr the Far-Travelled', an event equated with the disaster that – on the evidence of the inscriptions – struck Ingvarr and most or all of his followers somewhere "in the south". (The nickname 'Far-Travelled' is applied to an Yngvarr whose exploits on an expedition to the east are recounted in the fantastical Icelandic tale, *Yngvars saga víðfǫrla*, and who has been identified with the Ingvarr of the rune-stones).

Travel abroad was doubtless for trading purposes as well as plunder, although there are few if any rune-stones that make this explicit. The Mervalla stone, Södermanland, eastern Sweden, states of the Svæinn in whose memory it was raised: *Hann oft siglt til Sæimgala dyrum knærri um Domisnæs* 'He often sailed to Sæimgaliʀ with a much-prized ship around Domisnæs'.

Plate 12 The Gripsholm stone, Södermanland, Sweden. The word **þaiʀ** 'they'
was initially forgotten and is placed outside the main design.

The regularity of his voyages, the destination – almost certainly the Dvina estuary and the Zemgale plains in Latvia – and the type of boat, the heavy *knǫrr* often used by merchants, all point to trade rather than sporadic raiding. That trade formed an integral part of late Viking-Age Scandinavian life is confirmed by several references to *gildaʀ* 'guild-brothers', demonstrating the existence of guilds, mutual-help organisations for merchants.

A number of Viking-Age rune-stones contain what are, or appear to be, titles. These offer insights into the structure of Viking-Age society, but many occur only once and most just a few times, which can make their precise meaning difficult to determine. *Drotning* 'lady [wife of a *dróttinn*, see below]', *goði* '?priest', *hemþegi* 'member of the household' 'retainer', *landhirðiʀ* 'steward [of an estate]' and *þulʀ* '?reciter' are among the designations applied to those commemorated on Danish stones, while in Sweden we find *jarl* 'earl', *liðs forungi* 'leader of a host', *stallari* 'marshal' and *vikinga vǫrðr* 'guard against "Vikings"' or perhaps 'guard on behalf of "Vikings"'. Common to both Denmark and Sweden are *bryti* 'overseer', *felagi* 'comrade' 'partner', *konungʀ* 'king', *styrimaðr* 'ship's captain' and *þegn* 'thane' '?warrior'; to Norway and Sweden *skald* 'poet', and to all three Scandinavian countries *drengr* 'young warrior' and *dróttinn* 'lord'. How many of these words can be considered recognised titles, and how many are mere descriptive terms is unclear; the dividing-line between the two cannot always be sharply drawn – at least, not from a modern perspective. Judging from later Icelandic sources, a Viking-Age *skald* might be a poet employed by a king or nobleman, but could simply be a person known as a maker of verse. *Goði* and *þulʀ* occur in heathen contexts: a *goði* was presumably a heathen priest of some sort (cf. *goð* '[heathen] gods', and the Icelandic *goðar*, who although they ultimately became secular chieftains appear before the advent of Christianity to have had a religious function), while a *þulʀ* may have had the task of reciting pagan liturgy and/or ancient lore (cf. p. 67). Several of the titles/terms belong to the world of warfare. Some, such as *liðs forungi*, *stallari* (the latter a recognised medieval rank), speak for themselves. *Hemþegi* (literally 'one who receives a home') describes a man who in return for his keep gave military service to a king or chieftain. Titles such as *konungʀ*, *dróttinn*, *bryti* denote descending positions of rank in a hierarchy of power and administration. *Drengr* and *þegn* have been much discussed: current thinking seems to be that a *drengr* was often a 'young warrior', while a *þegn* might be a man in the service of a chieftain or simply an independent farmer. *Felagi*, from the contexts in which it appears, can refer either to a comrade in arms or a partner in trade. What late Viking-Age Scandinavians conceived a *Vikingr* to be is wholly unclear.

A case has been argued that one of the functions of commemorative rune-stones – perhaps the most important – was to document rights of inheritance. That, it is claimed, is why the obligatory raiser formula places such emphasis on the precise relationship of the deceased to the commissioner(s) of an inscription. Not all have found the case persuasive. A variety of reasons can be identified for the raising of rune-stones, the more important of which are discussed below. Furthermore, a few stones identify themselves beyond doubt as inheritance documents, and there is a striking difference between these and

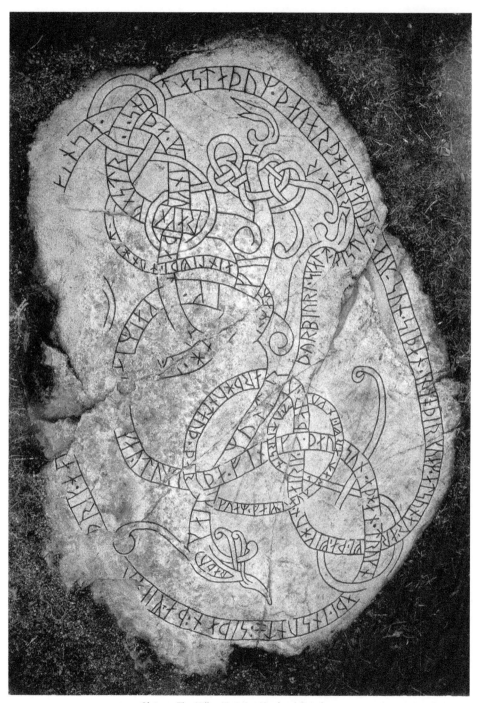

Plate 13 The Hillersjö stone, Uppland, Sweden

the generality. The Hillersjö stone (Uppland, Sweden; Plate 13), for example, lists a series of marriages, births and deaths with the clear aim of documenting the right of one GæiRlaug, through her deceased children and grandchildren, to the farm Hillersjö. The inscription is carved not on a raised stone but into bedrock very close to the modern farm buildings, and twice specifically refers to GæiRlaug's inheritance: *En moðiR kvam at sunaR arfi* 'But the mother took inheritance after her son', *Þar kvam GæiRlaug at arfi Ingu, dottur sinnaR* 'Then GæiRlaug took inheritance after Inga, her daughter'. Interestingly enough, the lines of inheritance documented on the Hillersjö stone correspond exactly to those set out in the provincial law of Uppland, codified in 1296 – almost three centuries later.

A good many rune-stones are "signed", that is, they conclude with what is ostensibly the name of the carver (but see pp. 166–7) and a verb denoting the carving activity, e.g. *AveR faði* 'AveR made' (Helnæs: Fyn, Denmark), *Skógr barði* 'Skógr hit [i.e. hammered]' (Skollevoll: Vest-Agder, Norway), *Þorkell ræist runaR* 'Þorkell cut [the] runes' (Högby: Östergötland, Sweden). Occasionally the painting or colouring of an inscription may be mentioned. This seems to have been a common practice, and a number of rune-stones or rune-stone fragments have been found with traces of their original colouring preserved. Indeed, the verb *fa*, used on the Helnæs stone, originally meant '[to] paint', but seems as early as older-*fuþark* times to have had its meaning extended to the carving of runic inscriptions – an indication that the tradition of colouring goes back a long way. On one of the two Gerstaberg stones from Ytterjärna, Södermanland, Sweden, the carving is attributed to one individual, the colouring to another: *Æsbern risti auk Ulfr stæindi* 'Æsbern carved and Ulfr "stained"'. References are also found to the reading/interpreting of inscriptions. Often this takes the form of an injunction, as in the Hillersjö inscription (above), which begins *Rað þu* 'Interpret!', but the approach can be less direct, as in the Ågersta stone's (Uppland, Sweden) *Raði ?drængR þaR rynn se runum þæim sum Balli risti* 'Let the ?man who may be "rune-skilled" interpret the runes that Balli carved' (Plate 8; see further p. 117).

This last passage is written in verse, as is the concluding section of the Gripsholm inscription, cited above. The type of verse concerned is called in Icelandic *fornyrðislag* 'old story metre', and is the one found in most of the Eddaic lays, anonymous verse (preserved in Iceland) dealing with pagan mythology and legendary heroes of the Germanic past. Simplifying somewhat, we may say that the metre is based on alliteration between one or more stressed words in the odd lines and the first stressed word of the even. Thus in the Gripsholm stanza we find *foru–fjarri, austarla–ærni* (alliteration may be between any vowels), *sunnarla–Særklandi*. Ågersta does not conform to the pattern quite so well in that *runum* in line 3 finds its alliterative partner in *risti*, the second stressed word of line 4. With a relatively unsophisticated metre of this kind, it is sometimes difficult to be sure whether verse is intended or not. The Dynna inscription from Hadeland, south-eastern Norway, raised by Gunnvǫr after her daughter Ásríðr, ends: *Sú vas mær hannarst á Haðalandi* 'She was the most dextrous maid in Haðaland'. This can be taken either as a couple of lines of rudimentary *fornyrðislag* or as "highly-wrought artistic

Plate 14 Face A of the Rök stone, Östergötland, Sweden

prose", as the opening of the Rök inscription (Östergötland, Sweden) has been described: *Aft Væmoð standa runaʀ þaʀ, en Varinn faði, faðiʀ aft fæigjan sunu* 'after Væmoðʀ stand these runes, but Varinn made [them], a father after a dead son' (Plate 14). The Rök stone also sports a complete *fornyrðislag* stanza, by far the earliest preserved if we are right in dating this artefact to the early 800s. As commonly read and interpreted, Rök offers several other, tantalising, glimpses of early Viking-Age literature with its apparent allusions to myths and stories now lost to us.

Most of the verse preserved on rune-stones is found within the boundaries of medieval Sweden. Norway has scarcely an example, while some of the most striking of the (few) Danish instances are found in Skåne (Swedish since 1658). On the island of Öland, just off the coast of south-eastern Sweden, stands the Karlevi stone. It bears a lengthy runic inscription, which includes a complete stanza in *dróttkvætt* 'court poetry metre'. *Dróttkvætt* is vastly more complex than *fornyrðislag*, and was used by Norwegian and above all Icelandic skaldic poets (named individuals who composed poems and occasional verse, often in honour of a king or chieftain; p. 109). The importance of the Karlevi stanza lies in the fact that we have it as it was originally written down (the Norwegian and Icelandic material – the odd medieval runic example apart – comes to us through the hands of numerous manuscript copyists). The stanza also offers evidence that skaldic form was known and used in eastern Scandinavia, although the nationality and linguistic affiliation of those involved in raising the Karlevi monument is a matter of dispute: while the monument itself is located in Sweden, its language appears to be West Scandinavian, its rune-forms of Danish type.

Karlevi is devoid of ornament. The runes are set between framing lines and run vertically, up and down the surface, in the manner of many Danish Viking-Age rune-stone inscriptions. On Swedish stones, as we have seen, the runes are typically placed in zoomorphic bands. A common practice is for the inscription to begin in the lower left corner of the composition, especially when the head of the serpent is located there. Some serpents are extremely complex in design, and there may be more than one (cf. Plates 8, 12, 13). A number of rune-stones carry pictures in addition to their inscriptions. A popular motif seems to have been the legend of Sigurðr, the dragon- or serpent-slayer. He is depicted in several carvings thrusting his sword through the zoomorphic band, representing the serpent (Plate 15). Strangely, perhaps, the iconography in these cases bears no obvious relation to the inscriptions, which are of fairly standard memorial type. The Jelling 2 depiction of what is taken to be the figure of Christ (Plate 16) is presumably to be connected with Haraldr's conversion to Christianity and his claim that he 'made the Danes Christian' (p. 73). The portrayal of the Magi and the Epiphany on the Dynna stone (Plate 17) may reflect a desire to commemorate the weaving or embroidery skills modern scholars have attributed to Ásríðr, 'the most dexterous maid in Haðaland' (p. 81).

Scandinavian Viking-Age commemorative rune-stones can also be found outside Denmark, Sweden and Norway – chiefly in the British Isles. The most striking collection is in the Isle of Man. On this small island over thirty

rune-stones or rune-stone fragments have been preserved (Plate 18 shows an example). They are conventionally dated tenth to early eleventh century, and, with the odd exception, form a relatively homogeneous group. They are of fundamentally Norwegian type in terms of language and layout, but have their own peculiar features. Although most of the inscriptions run up a narrow edge of the stone, some are located on a broad face. The stones are either shaped as or carry the depiction of a cross, and their texts tend to begin 'NN raised this cross' rather than 'NN raised this stone'. Many of the personal names recorded are of Celtic origin. The Old Norse grammar of those who composed the wording is occasionally uncertain. Most of the stones are highly decorated with interlacing patterns, and some, like their Scandinavian counterparts, depict scenes from Norse or Germanic mythology and legend. Several of these features reflect the intermixture of Norse with Celtic culture: the raising of crosses (a tradition of the Celtic Church); the frequency of Celtic personal names; the grammatical uncertainty (presumably the result of prolonged language contact resulting in linguistic interference); the interlacing ornament (a feature of the Scandinavian Borre style, which became popular in Ireland). Elsewhere in areas of Scandinavian settlement, the Viking-Age rune-stone occurs only sporadically, and displays no noteworthy features or trends.

Plate 15 *(opposite, above)* Detail of the Ramsundsberg rock, with a depiction of Sigurðr slaying the serpent

Plate 16 *(opposite, below)* Face C of the Jelling 2 stone, northern Jutland, showing what is assumed to be a depiction of Christ

Plate 17 *(right)* The Dynna stone, Oppland, Norway. The runic inscription runs up the narrow edge and the portrayal of the Magi and the Epiphany is placed on the broad face.

Plate 18 The fragmentary Manx rune-stone Braddan 2.
The text runs:]nroskitil:uilti:i:triku:|aiþsoara:siin '[but] Hrossketill
betrayed his sworn friend in a truce [i.e. having plighted his faith]'.

8.4 The rune-stone fashion

Although what appear to be commemorative rune-stones were raised as early
as the older-*fuþark* period, and the practice seems to continue into and through
the early Viking Age, it is only in the tenth, eleventh and early twelfth centuries
we can really speak of a fashion. The fact that the rune-stone raising custom
appears to blossom in Jutland and from there to spread, first across the rest of
Denmark, then into western Sweden, ultimately arriving in eastern Sweden, is
certainly suggestive of fashion. But that observation does not really get us very
far. Rather, it prompts a series of questions. Why did relatively large numbers
of Danes start raising commemorative rune-stones in the tenth century, and
why did very few do so earlier? Why did the trend become hugely popular
in some parts of Scandinavia (e.g. Uppland, Södermanland, Östergötland in
Sweden), while never really catching on in others (e.g. Norway)? What lies

behind the wording of the "raiser formula" (p. 68), with its emphasis on the sponsors of the stone? What caused the fashion to die out – in Denmark early in the eleventh century, in Sweden by about 1130? Why is there a concentration of Scandinavian commemorative rune-stones on the Isle of Man, but an almost total absence in England? These and other questions have been widely debated, but little agreement has been reached on the answers.

An overriding purpose of the rune-stone must have been to commemorate the dead. It is in recognition of this we use the qualifying adjective "commemorative" or "memorial". To begin with the raised rune-inscribed stone was perhaps a development of the earlier *bautasteinn*, an uninscribed stone monument to the dead. In its earliest, or at least simplest, form the commemorative inscription seems to have recorded the name of the deceased (sometimes linking it to a burial spot or monument, as **hnab(u)dashlaiwa** 'Hnaƀuða's grave' or **āiriks:kubl** 'ÆirikR's monument', cf. pp. 30, 67). But even in the older-*fuþark* period the living – presumably (sometimes manifestly) the commissioner(s) of the memorial – may be mentioned too. As we have seen, the prominence given to the commissioner(s) in the late Viking Age, and the apparent emphasis on the precise relationship of the living with the deceased, has been taken to suggest that the rune-stones of that period (at least) were set up to document inheritance rights. But that raises a further set of questions. Why did it become important to document lines of inheritance in Denmark in the tenth century and in Sweden in the eleventh, and not before, and why was it (apparently) never important in Norway? Why did it (seemingly) cease to be important long before roman-alphabet literacy was fully established? And why is there such a striking difference between the few rune-stones that patently document lines of inheritance and the rest? Alternatively (or additionally), as has been argued, many rune-stones may reflect the need to document a family's Christian faith in the absence of effective promotion of the new religion by royal authority. That might explain the wealth of runic monuments, many overtly Christian, in eastern Sweden, where there seem to have been competing centres of secular and religious power, and their paucity in Norway, where the influential missionary kings Óláfr Tryggvason (995–1000) and Óláfr Haraldsson (1015–28, later St Óláfr) were active. But it does not account for the considerable number of runic monuments erected in Denmark apparently after King Haraldr 'made the Danes Christian' (p. 73). The need for documentation – legal, religious or otherwise – in "unsettled societies" has also been mooted. But how settled were any parts of Denmark, Norway or Sweden in the period 900–1100? Various areas of Sweden – even eastern Sweden – have few or no rune-stones. Were these settled and harmonious while neighbouring areas were not? Relative economic strength has also been brought into the debate. The raising of a rune-stone cannot have been cheap, and it has been suggested there could be a correlation between the density of runic monuments and the agricultural and commercial potential of different parts of the Scandinavian world. But the evidence is not persuasive. Even though we cannot be sure about patterns of agriculture in Viking-Age Scandinavia or its colonies, we can be reasonably certain (a) that most of Denmark was as fertile as eastern Sweden, and (b) that the Danelaw (in eastern

England) was in general more fertile than the Isle of Man, yet eastern Sweden and Man have the concentration of inscriptions.

It is probably futile to seek a single explanation for the tenth- and eleventh-century rune-stone custom, because it is unlikely there is one. As noted above, the phenomenon has the appearance first and foremost of a fashion – one that waxed and then waned. But while the rune-stone was in vogue, we may expect that people used it for a variety of purposes: to proclaim religious faith, to assert power and status, to advertise the death of a relative, to document inheritance rights – but above all to commemorate the dead. Once churches and churchyards became widespread, there was no longer the need to set up a monument in a locally frequented spot and the custom lapsed. Even this is not the whole story, however. A few rune-stones were raised by people who could not wait until death to be commemorated. The most prominent of these was one Jarlabanki, an eleventh-century Swedish bigwig, who made, or had made, a series of inscriptions *at sik kvikvan* 'after himself while alive'. It has been claimed the motive was fear his heirs might fail to commemorate him in an attempt to revoke bequests and gifts to the Church. This seems far-fetched, not least when we observe what else Jarlabanki has to say – that he established a local assembly place and "owned" the whole of Täby (Uppland). The passing of a person of such power and influence would hardly have gone unremarked, whether his heirs commemorated him or not. The more likely explanation for his feverish rune-stone raising is a desire to proclaim power, wealth and status – like King Haraldr of Denmark (who on the Jelling 2 stone was ostensibly commemorating his parents; cf. pp. 71–3), but on a more local scale.

Two further matters are finally worth noting. (1) Insofar as any rune-stone is a status symbol of a sort, women feature quite widely, both as commissioners and among the commemorated. It does seem, though, that in some areas women act as commissioners only in the absence of a male relative. (2) The erecting of large numbers of public monuments with texts implies a tolerably widespread ability to read what was written. We have no idea how many Viking-Age Scandinavians were literate in runes, but there must have been a critical mass that made it meaningful to have commemorative inscriptions carved in stone and set up in public places.

8.5 Inscriptions in materials other than stone

The commemorative stone dominates Viking-Age runic writing to such an extent that it is possible to lose sight of the other types of inscription that emanate from the period. A certain number exist, but it is hard to assess their general or particular significance. Two runic sticks and a peg, dated to the ninth or early tenth century, have been excavated in Hedeby (one of the principal Viking-Age trading centres, close to modern Schleswig). These have been seen as containing the same kind of texts as the numerous runic sticks found in medieval Scandinavian towns (pp. 106–7), and from this it has been concluded that runes were used in the Viking Age for everyday communication just as they were later. The rune-forms found on the Hedeby objects are of the simpler younger-*fuþark* type, and that has for some strengthened the view that the simpler runes were developed as a "cursive" form of writing for everyday use (cf. 7.4). Against this line of reasoning it has been argued: (a) that the Hedeby material has not been satisfactorily interpreted and we cannot therefore be sure it represents the same kind of runic literacy we find in the medieval towns; (b) that well-excavated Viking-Age centres such as York and Dublin show nothing comparable – York has revealed no indubitably Scandinavian runic inscriptions, while the twelve or more from Dublin (on wood, bone and antler), many from as late as the mid-eleventh century and most difficult or impossible to interpret, do little to suggest that runes there had any practical or commercial application. The Dublin inscriptions are perhaps rather to be seen as faltering demonstrations of literacy.

Most other runic inscriptions on loose objects from the Viking Age are of such different types and from such different places that any kind of generalisation is difficult. There are small collections from Lund and Schleswig, mostly from the end of the Viking Age, and these do seem to show the beginnings of the kind of runic literacy we find in the medieval towns, although, as with the Dublin material, many individual inscriptions have defied interpretation. From the Ladoga and Novgorod regions of Russia come a wooden stick, a bone fragment and three metal amulets with runes, but apart from the bone, which contains the last eleven characters of the younger *fuþark*, these too have proved hard to get to grips with. Nor is it certain where any of the five inscriptions were made. Also found in Russia are a small number of Islamic coins (from ninth- and tenth-century hoards) with runic (or in some cases possibly runic) graffiti scratched on them. Among the recognisable words is **kuþ/gud** 'gods' 'God', carved with runes of both the younger and the older *fuþark*. Runic graffiti, apparently personal names, are also found in the church of Hagia Sophia, Istanbul, but are of uncertain age. Coins with runic legends make an appearance in the latter half of the eleventh century, in both Denmark and Norway, but these belong in a medieval rather than a Viking-Age context (pp. 105–6).

Of individual loose objects with runic inscriptions from the Viking Age, the following may be mentioned. (1) The eighth-century Ribe cranium (discussed briefly p. 61). (2) Two wooden objects from the Oseberg ship burial (Vestfold, Norway; the burial *c.* 835): a pail on which some have read **asikriʀ** 'Sigríðʀ owns' and a piece of wood with the difficult sequence **litiluism**, sometimes interpreted *lítilvíss maðr* 'man of little wisdom', with the **m** taken – speculatively – as an ideograph (p. 25). The pail inscription might be a precursor of the numerous "name tags" found in the medieval towns, and could thus offer early, if slight, evidence of the practical application of runes, but it is far from certain **asikriʀ** is what it says: some see here little more than a collection of vertical scratches. (3) The Elisenhof comb (southern Jutland; object 850–900, inscription probably contemporary), which sports the word **kãbr** 'comb', and thus belongs in the long tradition of runic inscriptions that identify the object on which they are carved (cf. pp. 46, 114). (4) The Forsa iron door-ring (Hälsingland, Sweden; inscription early or mid-Viking Age), which contains a lengthy inscription of possibly legal import. There has been much disagreement about the dating and the sense of the inscription (pp. 172–3), but if it is indeed a manifestation of legal practice from the earlier part of the Viking Age, it demonstrates a practical use of runic script at this period. (5) The Senja silver neck-ring (Troms, Norway; inscription probably early or mid-eleventh century). Found in the north of Norway, far from the known centres of runic writing, the neck-ring bears an inscription consisting of four lines (a half stanza) of *fornyrðislag* (pp. 81, 83). How the ring got to Senja, and where and by whom the inscription was made, are unknown. The verse form seems to have been common currency throughout Scandinavia, but when we meet it in the Viking Age it is mostly on Swedish or Danish rune-stones (chiefly the former). The half stanza has normally been understood to refer to a raid on the Frisians and the taking of booty, but more recently it has been suggested that it might depict a trading expedition. It is ambiguous enough to support either interpretation: *Fórum drengja Fríslands á vit, ok vígsfǫtum vér skiptum* 'We went to visit the young Frisian warriors/trading partners, and divided up [as booty]/exchanged war-gear'. (6) The Sigtuna copper box (Uppland, Sweden; early eleventh century), which held a pair of scales. The inscription on the box names the owner as Djarfr, and explains that he obtained the scales from a *sæmskr* man (one who probably hailed from the south-eastern corner of the Baltic). It also tells us that a certain Værmundr made the runes, and includes two lines of poetry in *dróttkvætt* metre (p. 83). The runes are perhaps to be seen more as decoration than a statement of ownership; had the latter been the primary intention, 'Djarfr owns these scales' would have sufficed.

Select reading list

Barnes, Michael P., Hagland, Jan Ragnar, and Page, R. I. 1997. *The Runic Inscriptions of Viking Age Dublin*. Dublin: Royal Irish Academy.

Gräslund, Anne-Sofie 2006. 'Dating the Swedish Viking-Age rune stones on stylistic grounds'. In: (Marie Stoklund *et al.*, eds) *Runes and their Secrets: Studies in Runology*. Copenhagen: Museum Tusculanum Press, University of Copenhagen, 117–39.

Jansson, Sven B. F. 1987. *Runes in Sweden*. Stockholm: Gidlunds, 31–161. [In spite of the title, a survey of Swedish runic *inscriptions* of the Viking Age; readable and well illustrated.]

Liestøl, Aslak 1971. 'The literate Vikings'. In: (Peter Foote and Dag Strömbäck, eds) *Proceedings of the Sixth Viking Congress*. Distributed by the Viking Society for Northern Research, London, 69–78. [Argues on the basis of the Hedeby sticks for the existence of widespread runic literacy in the Viking Age.]

Melnikova, Elena A. 1998. 'Runic inscriptions as a source for the relation of northern and eastern Europe in the Middle Ages'. In: (Klaus Düwel, ed.) *Runeninschriften als Quellen interdisziplinärer Forschung: Proceedings of the Fourth International Symposium on Runes and Runic Inscriptions in Göttingen 4–9 August 1995* (Ergänzungsbände zum Reallexikon der Germanischen Altertumskunde 15). Berlin/New York: de Gruyter, 647–59. [Examines Scandinavian rune-stones that document expeditions to the east, and Viking-Age and medieval runic inscriptions found in eastern Europe.]

Moltke, Erik 1985. *Runes and their Origin: Denmark and Elsewhere.* Copenhagen: National Museum of Denmark, 148–69, 184–397. [A detailed and well-illustrated account of the Danish Viking-Age runic material.]

Page, R. I. 1983. 'The Manx rune-stones'. In: (Christine Fell *et al.*, eds) *The Viking Age in the Isle of Man: Select Papers from the Ninth Viking Congress, Isle of Man, 4–14 July 1981.* London: Viking Society for Northern Research, 133–46. [The nearest thing to a modern edition of the Manx rune-stone corpus.]

Page, R. I. 1993. 'Scandinavian society, 800–1100: the contribution of runic studies'. In: (Anthony Faulkes and Richard Perkins, eds) *Viking Revaluations.* London: Viking Society for Northern Research, 145–59. [A critical account of the contribution runic studies have made to understanding of the Viking Age.]

Sawyer, Birgit 2000. *The Viking-Age Rune-Stones: Custom and Commemoration in Early Medieval Scandinavia.* Oxford: Oxford University Press. [A comprehensive study that discusses the purposes for which rune-stones were made and argues that, whatever else, virtually all reflect inheritance claims.]

Spurkland, Terje 2005. *Norwegian Runes and Runic Inscriptions.* Woodbridge: Boydell Press, 86–130. [A general account of the Norwegian Viking-Age runic material, including the Manx corpus.]

Stoklund, Marie 2006. 'Chronology and typology of the Danish runic inscriptions'. In: (Marie Stoklund *et al.*, eds) *Runes and their Secrets: Studies in Runology.* Copenhagen: Museum Tusculanum Press, University of Copenhagen, 355–83. [A detailed reappraisal of the chronology and typology of the Danish runic material.]

9 The late Viking-Age and medieval runes

9.1 The diversification of runic usage

By the end of the tenth century some Scandinavian rune-carvers had clearly seen a need for improvement in their writing system. Starting in Denmark – as far as we can tell – they began to add diacritic dots to ᚾ, ᚲ and ᛁ. As the term "diacritic" suggests, the dots were intended to distinguish the characters so marked from their unmarked counterparts. By and large ᚾ was used for /y/ and /ø/, ᚵ for [g] and [ɣ], ᛁ for /e/ and /æ/ (cf. pp. 6–7). But these dotted characters can have other values – always, though, related to the one suggested by the name of the undotted rune: ᚾ for example sometimes denotes /o/ (like /u/ a rounded vowel, cf. rune name *úr*), and ᛁ [j] (which shares high front, unrounded articulation with [i], cf. rune name *íss*). Occasionally ᚾ, ᚵ, ᛁ can stand for the /u/, /k/, /i/ normally represented by ᚾ, ᚲ, ᛁ respectively. From Denmark – according to our understanding of the sources – the practice of dotting spread into both Norway and Sweden during the first half of the eleventh century.

This innovation has been ascribed by some to awareness of the roman alphabet, coupled with a knowledge of Anglo-Saxon runic writing. As Scandinavian rune-carvers became familiar with roman script, it is argued, they will have begun to observe the shortcomings of their *fuþark*, with its limited inventory of symbols (most notably, perhaps, the lack of equivalents for roman 'e', 'o', 'd', 'g', 'p'). Some will also have been familiar with Anglo-Saxon ᛣ, which stood for /y/ (cf. p. 39). So they borrowed ᛣ, changed its short vertical line into a dot, and went on to apply the dot to two further runes: ᚵ and ᛁ.

There is something to be said for this line of reasoning. As already noted, dotting seems first to appear in Denmark, where it is documented not long after the official introduction of Christianity in the 960s – with which came the roman alphabet. ᚾ is not the same as ᛣ, but the two are similar enough for there to be a connection. The derivation does prompt various questions and doubts, however. ᛣ is not widely attested in Anglo-Saxon runic writing, which in any case seems to have been going out of use towards the end of the 900s (p. 50). How did Danish rune-carvers in England come to select an apparently uncommon character from a seemingly dying script and use it as the basis for a fruitful innovation in their own runic writing? And although there is a credible ᚾ (of uncertain phonetic value) in an inscription archaeologically dated to about 1000 from as far a-field as Dublin, ᚾ appears to be less common than ᚵ and ᛁ, suggesting perhaps that it came a little later than the other two. If the roman alphabet (or the well-stocked Anglo-Saxon *fuþorc* for that matter) provided the impetus, why do we to begin with apparently find just three dotted runes? Why is dotting not used to make good the lack of a character to denote, say, /d/ or /p/? And why does it not correspond with any roman-alphabet practice? A dot may be placed over an 'ı' or 'y' in medieval manuscript writing, but it belongs with the letter concerned; roman script does not differentiate letters by means of a dot (there is no 'ı' versus 'i', for example, according to function).

These uncertainties compel us to acknowledge that the origins of the Scandinavian dotting practice are obscure. There is a faint possibility the innovation began in the British Isles, even if not inspired by English ᚣ: as well as the Dublin ᚤ there are other apparently tenth- or early eleventh-century British examples of dotting, not least in the Isle of Man, and an English manuscript tradition (of uncertain import, cf. p. 155) going back to about 1050, possibly earlier, records ᚤ, ᚵ, ᛔ, alongside other Scandinavian runic characters with a bar (taking the place of the dot, as ᛂ for ᛂ, ᛑ for ᛑ). From Britain the practice could have been exported to Denmark in the second half of the tenth century – a time of lively communication across the North Sea. On the other hand, there is no reason why dotting should not be a purely Scandinavian invention – perhaps, but not necessarily, inspired by comparison with the better-equipped roman alphabet.

At its most basic, the function of dotted runes was "to mark a sound value which the carvers considered it important to mark relative to other sounds which the undotted rune could stand for", as one writer has it. This abstract and conservative formulation is intended to counter the view that dotting heralded the introduction of new runes into the *fuþark*. The regular transliteration of ᚤ, ᚵ, ᛂ as **y**, **g**, **e** has led to the unfortunate misapprehension that the sixteen-character row was expanded through the addition of runes for /y/, /g/ and /e/. But as we have seen, the phonemes and/or sounds denoted by ᚤ, ᚵ, ᛂ can vary. Moreover, these dotted characters do not seem to have been considered part of the *fuþark* by rune-carvers (contrast the English situation, pp. 37–40); rather they are treated as variants of existing runes (see further below). It is also worth noting that neither ᚤ, ᚵ, ᛂ nor other dotted runes are employed consistently: /y/, /ø/ may still be written ᚢ, [g], [ɣ] ᚴ, and so on.

Dotting was not the only device employed to make Scandinavian runic writing a more sophisticated vehicle for the recording of language. Perhaps beginning in Norway, though our earliest examples seem to come from the Isle of Man, some carvers begin to use the fourth rune (mostly in the form ᚬ or ᚭ) to denote a rounded vowel rather than /ã/ (cf. p. 62). The change of value is likely to be connected with a development in the pronunciation of the rune's name (/ansuz/ > /ɔ̃:s:/ > /o:s:/), a development which in Norway led at some point to a shift in the meaning of the name (*áss* 'heathen god' > *óss* /o:s:/ 'river mouth', cf. pp. 161–2). The use of this rune to denote rounded vowels (principally /o/ and /ɔ/) became widespread in Sweden in the eleventh century from where the practice seems ultimately to have spread to Denmark.

In Norway and Norwegian settlements in the west so-called palatal /ʀ/ (p. 6) appears to have coalesced with /r/ somewhen in the tenth century. In these regions the name of ᛦ, the rune that denoted /ʀ/, had by the Viking Age apparently become *ýʀ*, which upon the coalescence changed to *ýr*. Since /r/ was already denoted by ᚱ, ᛦ might well have been judged redundant and jettisoned. However, in accordance with the acrophonic principle, carvers in the Norwegian tradition began to use ᛦ for /y/. The earliest examples are probably from the first half of the eleventh century. Because ᛦ became a regular symbol for /y/ in West Scandinavia, ᚤ was little used there (cf. however below). Ultimately ᛦ for /y/ spread to the whole of Scandinavia.

Another apparently local innovation that became a commonplace of runic writing was the use of ᚼ for [ɣ] (as well as for /h/). This usage seems to have originated in parts of Sweden in the first half of the eleventh century. Its rapid spread is perhaps attributable to the possibility it offered of distinguishing [ɣ] from [g], both of which had previously been written ᚵ, if not ᚴ.

Yet another stratagem adopted to distinguish sounds not hitherto distinguished in younger-*fuþark* writing was to differentiate what had previously been variant forms of certain runes. Thus a distinction began to be made between simpler ᛆ and more complex ᛅ (cf. 7.4): both had originally denoted /a/ and /æ/ (and also /ɔ/), but increasingly ᛆ was used for /a/ and ᛅ for /æ/. The precise development in time and place is difficult to follow, but the differentiation seems to have become more or less consistent throughout Scandinavia by the mid-twelfth century. Hand-in-hand with this innovation went the differentiation of ᚭ/ᚮ and ᚬ/ᚯ: as symbols for rounded vowels all four could stand for /o/, /ɔ/ and /ø/, but many carvers began to limit the variants with single-sided branches to /o/ and /ɔ/, and to use those with crossing branches for /ø/. With three phonemes involved, however, there was less consistency here than in the case of ᛆ /a/, ᛅ /æ/. Sometimes ᚬ/ᚯ is used for /ɔ/ as well as /ø/, occasionally /ɔ/ seems to be distinguished from both /o/ and /ø/ by the shortening of one of the crossing branches (e.g. ᚬ), and in twelfth-century Orkney we find the following correlation: ᚭ /o/, ᚬ /ɔ/, ᚯ /ø/ (cf. pp. 119–20).

Two further runes commonly dotted are ᛐ/ᛏ (usually as ᛑ, ᛑ, standing for /d/) and ᛒ (as ᛔ, standing for /p/). Neither makes a serious appearance in runic epigraphy in dotted form before the twelfth century – and in many areas the dotted variants are not seen much before 1200. Nevertheless, they are recorded earlier in English manuscript tradition (cf. above), and are also found on Danish coins of the period 1065–75, many apparently struck by English moneyers. In the thirteenth century some carvers begin to use ᛕ instead of ᛔ for /p/, the shape perhaps conceived as ᛔ with the highest and lowest branch removed. ᛋ and ᛌ ultimately become differentiated, but practice here is not consistent. Some medieval carvers use ᛌ as the equivalent of roman 'c' or 'z', and ᛋ for 's', but others do the opposite. Further – late and more local – innovations are ᚡ for a sound probably in the region of [v] and ᚧ for [ð]. On the island of Gotland we find ᛛ, seemingly employed to distinguish a particular variety of /l/; and in one Gotlandic inscription ᚴ and ᚿ are used for the consonant combination [ŋg] and a particular variety of /n/ respectively. In Greenland there are several examples of ᚣ for /o/ or /ɔ/, although the more common Greenlandic symbol for these vowels is ᚭ, as normally in western Scandinavian tradition. The ᚣ form has to some suggested Anglo-Saxon influence, but it is hard to see how such influence could have come about. Furthermore, the vowel denoted by Anglo-Saxon ᚣ is /y/.

9.2 The status of the additional characters

The processes whereby ᚢ/ᚭ came to denote /o/ or /ɔ/, and ᚤ /y/, did not result from the diacritic marking or differentiation of existing runes but from sound changes in the language. Neither transition resulted in an expansion of the runic inventory. The dotting of certain runes and the differentiation of others, however, introduced additional characters. ᛂ, for example, was more than a mere variant of ᛁ: in most occurrences it had a different function from the undotted form; ᚿ and ᛂ, which had originally been interchangeable, now each denoted a separate phoneme; and so on.

As we have seen, when the need arose the Anglo-Saxons invented new runes, gave them names, and added them to their *fuþorc*. The Scandinavians followed a different path. The introduction of ᚧ, ᚵ, ᛂ, while extending the range of runic characters, did not increase the number of runes. This may seem a contradiction in terms, but it should be recalled that to begin with none of the three stood for a particular sound, rather the dot served "to mark a sound value which the carvers considered it important to mark relative to other sounds which the undotted rune could stand for". In the light of such lack of specific function it is not surprising that dotted runes were treated by rune-carvers as types of their undotted counterparts rather than as independent characters. The same thinking was apparently applied to traditional variants that became differentiated; thus ᛏ was considered a type of ᚿ, albeit with a specific function, and ᛤ, ᛭ etc. types of ᚿ, with slightly less specific functions. Rune-carvers' perceptions of the additional characters can be deduced from a number of factors. (1) Medieval rune-row inscriptions (of which there are many) rarely consist of more than the sixteen runes of the younger *fuþark*, and such additions as there are seldom comprise more than one or two characters. (2) In the few cases where several additional characters are appended to rune-row inscriptions, they appear in no regular order. (3) The additional characters were not, as far as we can tell, given names. There exist a Norwegian and an Icelandic runic poem (pp. 159–61), the verses of which explain the meaning of the rune names, but these contain only the basic sixteen runes of the Viking Age. Occasional manuscript *fuþarks* (13.1) give names to some of the additional characters, but these have very much the appearance of learned inventions. (4) A common runic cipher based on a division of the *fuþark* into three groups (pp. 149–52) always places five runes in the first and second groups, six in the third; nowhere is there an indication that the system relied on more than sixteen runes.

However rune-carvers may have viewed the additional characters of medieval Scandinavian runic writing, for the modern runologist they have rather uncertain status. They are perhaps best thought of as marked variants, in the same way as, say, the English plural form is marked (e.g. by the addition of /s/), which distinguishes it from the singular, the unmarked and neutral form.

Over time – for some rune-carvers, at least – perceptions of the additional characters probably altered. There exist a few runic "alphabet" inscriptions, i.e. listings of runes where the order is that of the *abc*. Insofar as these can be dated, they would appear to be from no earlier than the late thirteenth century (some considerably more recent), and were probably made by people equally, or more, at home with writing in the roman alphabet. The interesting feature here is that there seems to be an attempt to correlate each rune with a letter of the roman *abc*. That could imply a widely accepted equivalence – that many carvers thought of, say, ᚺ as a 'c'-rune, ᚠ as a 'g'-rune, ᚴ as a 'k'-rune, ᛁ as an 's'-rune, etc., since those are the characters some of their fraternity place in third, seventh, tenth, and eighteenth position in their runic *abc*s (roman 'j' was not differentiated from 'i' at this time) – but it need not. It may instead – or also – reflect simple practicality: the need at any given place or time to settle on one particular rune to represent each roman letter. While there is general agreement, for example, that the runic equivalent of 'e' is ᛁ, 'd' may be ᛁ/ᛏ, ᛏ or ᚦ, and in one runic *abc*-inscription (on a communion wafer baking iron) ᚴ stands for 'g', 'k' and 'q'. This lack of consensus about which rune corresponded to which roman letter certainly indicates that no fixed and unchanging relationship developed between the individual characters of the two systems.

9.3 The medieval runic writing system

By the twelfth century, if not earlier, roman-alphabet writing was well established in Scandinavia. Thereafter, for as long as runes were in common use, the Scandinavian countries were two-script communities (pp. 122, 126). Given the prestige of the roman alphabet as the bearer of European culture, it is not surprising that it exercised some influence on the rune-row and runic writing practices. The surprise is perhaps that this influence penetrated no further than it did.

One noticeable feature is the change, where runes are listed in *fuþark* sequence, from the order **ml** to **lm**. **lm** seems first to be documented late in the eleventh century. It becomes commoner in the 1200s and thereafter, but the original *fuþark* order can still be found throughout the Middle Ages. By the thirteenth century the gemination (doubling) of consonant runes to mark length is a not uncommon feature of runic writing. Whereas, for example, *þetta* 'this [nom./acc. n.]' would traditionally be written **þita** or **þïta**, and *henni* 'her [dat.]' **hini, hinï, hïni,** or **hïnï**, these words sometimes appear in the thirteenth century and later as **þïtta, hïnnï**. The spelling ᚴᚢᚱᚦᛁ **kørthï** 'made' on the Burseryd font from Småland, Sweden (*c.* 1300?), shows the sound [ð] written **th** (as often in roman-alphabet writing) rather than **þ** (as normally in runic; cf. pp. 4–5, 60–61). It has further been suggested that the dramatic increase in the use of bind-runes (p. 20) in the Middle Ages owes something to familiarity with roman ligatures such as 'æ' and 'œ'. And it is also probable that the regular word division characteristic of much medieval runic writing is related to the roman-alphabet practice of inserting spaces between words – though word division in runic inscriptions is almost always indicated by a separator of some kind (pp. 24, 66), very rarely indeed by spacing.

It is finally worth noting that runic orthography tends to be more orthophonic (true to sound) than writing in the roman alphabet. That is presumably because those who mastered roman were trained to write both in Latin and the vernacular, and part of the training will have concerned spelling. There was of course nothing like our modern standardised orthography in the Middle Ages, and most words will be found rendered in a variety of ways in manuscripts. Nevertheless some guidance on putting the spoken word into writing must have been given during a scribe's education, as can be seen not least from the fact that different scriptoria developed different spelling traditions. Runic writing was almost certainly taught in a more informal way. We do not know exactly how, but suggestive evidence comes from: (a) partial or complete *fuþark* inscriptions that appear to be writing exercises; (b) runic syllabaries (repetitions of syllables with regular variations, as, for example, **fu:fo:fi:fy**); (c) texts that have been copied, sometimes imperfectly; (d) nonsense inscriptions, often involving rune-like signs as well as or in place of recognisable runes; (e) inscriptions that specifically mention the process of learning to write with runes (see further pp. 115–16). Most of these sequences are on wood, very often sticks. Taken together they suggest that someone skilled in the art of runic writing would demonstrate the characters of the *fuþark* and how they could be combined into syllables, and then get the learner to practise on a handy object, sometimes the same piece of wood as served for the model. Some learners doubtless practised diligently and became proficient; others clearly struggled. But the individual would probably have been left much more to his or her own devices than the trainee in the scriptorium. Thus rune-carvers would have been freer to make up their own minds about the relationship between sound and spelling than scribes.

The orthophonic nature of runic writing comes out most clearly in inscriptions written in Latin. We find spellings such as **k̇rasia** for *gracia* (< *gratia*) 'grace' (showing the changes [t] > [ts] > [s] before [i]), **inslis** for *in cælis* 'in heaven' (the result, presumably, of [k] > [tʃ] > [s] before [e], the common medieval rendering of *æ*, and the weakening or loss of that [e]), and **uinciþ** 'conquers' ([t] > [ð] in unstressed position). These offer helpful indications about the pronunciation of medieval Latin in Scandinavia (cf. further p. 126). Spellings of Scandinavian words, too, may sometimes reflect everyday pronunciation, though what can appear to be an attempt to reproduce colloquial speech may in fact reflect simple lack of writing skill. Thus **rannr** for the (assumed) name *Ragnarr* may indicate a pronunciation [raɲnr], or even [ranr], **souæk** for *Sólveig* could suggest [so:veɣ]; however, both may instead reveal uncertainty about how to use runes to write words in the native language.

Select reading list

Barnes, Michael P. 2011. 'On the status and transliteration of the additional characters of medieval Scandinavian runic writing'. In: (Guus Kroonen et al., eds) *Thi Timit Lof: Festschrift für Arend Quak zum 65. Geburtstag* (= *Amsterdamer Beiträge zur älteren Germanistik* 67). Amsterdam/New York: Rodopi, 9–21.

Haugen, Einar 1976. 'The dotted runes: from parsimony to plenitude'. In: (Bo Almqvist and David Greene, eds) *Proceedings of the Seventh Viking Congress, Dublin 15–21 August 1973*. Dublin: Royal Irish Academy, 83–92. [A discussion of the origin and function of the dotted runes.]

Knirk, James E. 1994. 'Learning to write with runes in medieval Norway'. In: (Inger Lindell, ed.) *Medeltida skrift- och språkkultur: Nio föreläsningar från ett symposium i Stockholm våren 1992* (Runica et Mediævalia, *Opuscula* 2). Stockholm: Runica et mediævalia – Medeltidsseminariet och Institutionen för nordiska språk vid Stockholms universitet, 169–212. [In addition to the main discussion, this article introduces the reader to the variety of runes in use in medieval Norway.]

Page, R. I., and Hagland, Jan Ragnar 1998. 'Runica manuscripta and runic dating: the expansion of the younger fuþąrk'. In: (Audun Dybdahl and Jan Ragnar Hagland, eds) *Innskrifter og datering/Dating Inscriptions* (Senter for middelalderstudier, Skrifter 8). Trondheim: Tapir, 55–71. [On the basis of Scandinavian *fuþark*s contained in a pair of English manuscripts, this article suggests that the dotting of runes may be earlier than generally believed, and could have arisen among Scandinavian rune-carvers in England.]

Spurkland, Terje 2005. *Norwegian Runes and Runic Inscriptions*. Woodbridge: Boydell Press, 150–53. [A brief account of the expansion of the runic inventory in Norway in the Middle Ages.]

10 Scandinavian inscriptions of the Middle Ages

10.1 Introduction

Medieval runic inscriptions are known from most parts of the Scandinavian-speaking world. Although the majority are of Danish, Norwegian or Swedish provenance, Greenland, Iceland, the Faroes, and the British Isles also contribute a share. The inscriptions come chiefly, but by no means exclusively, from towns and churches. They occur in considerable numbers, and span the period *c.* 1050–1450. Runic writing appears to have been very common in the twelfth and thirteenth centuries, to have declined somewhat in the fourteenth, and to have died out in most parts of the Scandinavian world in the course of the fifteenth. (On runic activity in the post-Reformation era, based largely on printed or written accounts, see chapter 11.) From the island of Gotland there are inscriptions dated as late as the sixteenth and even the beginning of the seventeenth century that seem to represent a continuous tradition, but they are few in number. In Iceland, too, people went on using runes post-1500, but from the eighteenth century on they mostly appear intermixed with roman letters or cryptic symbols of various kinds. In the Swedish province of Dalarna a custom developed – apparently in the 1500s – of carving runic inscriptions into wooden buildings, household objects and message sticks (if the last is not in continuation of medieval practice), and this persisted until the beginning of the twentieth century. As in Iceland, however, the runes became more and more watered down with letters of the roman alphabet. The characters used in Dalarna differ from the generality of late medieval runes, and may be the product of a conscious reform, undertaken perhaps in the sixteenth century (pp. 131–3).

Total numbers of medieval inscriptions are hard to give, since much depends on the precise definition of medieval, but a rough indication might be: Denmark 300 (plus several hundred runic coins from the period 1065–75 – though representing a limited number of designs), Norway 1,300 (again plus a large number of runic coins, representing five basic designs, to be dated between 1067 and roughly 1080), Sweden 800, Greenland 90, Iceland 70, the Faroes fewer than 10, British Isles 60 (some half of which are represented by the Maeshowe collection from Orkney, cf. pp. 119–20).

The medieval runic inscriptions differ greatly in kind. They are found on stone monuments, buildings (principally churches), church furnishings, a wide variety of loose objects, and on boulders and bedrock. The commonest materials are stone, wood, bone, metal, but not a few inscriptions occur in plaster and brick, and other materials are also attested. Texts range from the formal to the highly informal. Such extensive variation makes it difficult to establish a framework within which the inscriptions can be presented and discussed. For purely practical purposes a rudimentary division is made here into five text-types: formal; informal; graffiti; antiquarian; inscriptions in Latin.

This method of classification has its problems: there are, for example, degrees of formality; graffiti are by their nature informal; some inscriptions are partly in Latin, partly in Scandinavian. But a means of organising the material is needed, and this is perhaps as good a way as any to help the reader see the wood for the trees.

10.2 Formal inscriptions

"Formal" is used here of carefully executed pieces of writing intended for public consumption: monuments, declarations and notices. Prominent among the formal runic inscriptions of the Scandinavian Middle Ages are those of memorial type. With the introduction of Christianity and the establishment of churches, the Viking-Age commemorative stone – raised in the countryside, seemingly often in a public spot – eventually went out of use. In its place came the gravestone, located in a church or churchyard. This is often a recumbent slab, commonly of trapezoid or rectangular shape. But more elaborate monuments are also found. Upright stones may be placed at either end of the slab; there are slabs with an arched top (described as *hvalf* 'vault'); and there are sarcophagi (erected on top of the grave, however, and thus not strictly speaking coffins). The rune-inscribed gravestone tends to carry different formulas from the Viking-Age monument. The emphasis is now on the dead. The commissioner or commissioners are sometimes mentioned as in the twelfth- or early thirteenth-century Broddetorp inscription from Västergötland, Sweden, which begins: **bïntikt:romfarari: lïtkïra:hualf:þïnna:ifïr:maknus ...** 'Benedikt Rome-Traveller had this "vault" made over Magnus ...' However, many gravestone inscriptions open with the simple statement *hér liggr* 'here lies' or *hér hvílir/her hvilis* 'here rests' (based on the Latin formulas *hic iacet* 'here lies' and *requiescat* 'may s/he rest'), followed by the name of the deceased. Medieval gravestones often carry a good deal of supplementary text. Occasionally this gives information about the person commemorated; more commonly it requests prayers for them, and/or announces the anniversary of their death (the date on which a mass is to be sung for their soul). A late medieval tombstone from Lye church, Gotland (Plate 19), offers a detailed account of how the deceased met his end:

> *Þinna stain þa lit husfru Ruðvi gjera yfir sinn bonda, Jakop i Mannagardum, sum skutin varð i hel mið en byrsusten af Visborg, þa en kunung Erik var bestallað pa þi fornemnda slot. En þa var liðit af Guðs byrð fjurtan hundrað ar ok ainu ari minna þen femtigi ar. Biðjum þet et Guð naði hans sjal ok allum kristnum sjalum. Amen.*

> 'The wife Ruðvi had this stone made after her husband, Jakop of Mannagardar, who was shot dead by a cannonball from Visborg, when King Erik was under siege in the aforementioned stronghold. And fourteen hundred years and one less than fifty years had then elapsed since the birth of Christ [i.e. it was 1449]. Let us pray that God have mercy on his soul and on all Christian souls. Amen.'

Plate 19 Tombstone from Lye church, Gotland

More run-of-the-mill tombstone inscriptions are the following three: from Bjolderup church, South Jutland, Denmark, perhaps thirteenth-century: *Ketil Urne ligger her* 'Ketill Urn lies here'; from Øye church, Oppland, Norway, probably fourteenth-century: *Hér hvílir Þóra, móðir Eiríks prests. Pater noster* 'Here rests Þóra, mother of Eiríkr the priest. Pater noster [almost certainly an injunction to recite the Lord's Prayer]'; from Årdal church, Rogaland, Norway, partly damaged and of uncertain date: *[Ártíð Ha]llvarðs er einni nótt eftir [allra hel]gra messudag. Brúsi reist* 'Hallvarðr's anniversary day [the date of his death and thus of the anniversary mass for his soul, cf. above] is one night after the Feast of All Saints [i.e. 2 November]. Brúsi carved'.

Medieval inscriptions commemorating the dead are also found incised in wood. On a plank from Hamre church, Hordaland, Norway, apparently salvaged from an earlier church on the same site and reused, we have: *Hér niðri fyrir hvílir jumfrú Margréta. Biðir Pater noster fyrir hennar sál* 'Here beneath rests the maid Margréta. Pray Pater noster for her soul'. In its original setting the plank presumably lay over the burial place in the same way as a tombstone. On runological and linguistic grounds the inscription is thought to be fourteenth-century.

Commemorative texts are not always connected with a burial. A now lost carving from Klepp stave-church, Rogaland, Norway (demolished in the late seventeenth or early eighteenth century) records:

Ártíð er Ingibjargar Káradóttur þrim nóttum eptir Krossmessu um várit. Hverr sá maðr rúnar þessar sér, þá syngi Pater noster fyrir sál hennar. Hjalpi Guð þeim er svá gerir.

'Ingibjǫrg Káradóttir's anniversary day is three nights after spring Cross-mass [*Inventio crucis*]. May every man [who] sees these runes sing Pater noster for her soul. God help him who does so.'

The feast of the finding of the (true) cross was celebrated on 3 May: the date of Ingibjǫrg's death is thus 6 May. The drawing on which the above text is based is not perfect, and needs occasional emendation, but we can be reasonably confident of the sense. The inscription is said to have been carved on a plank in "the north gallery [covered outside walkway] of the church", presumably in a place where it could be seen by large numbers of people. Who might have carved it and in what circumstances are matters for speculation, but this was clearly much more than an idle graffito. Its date cannot be determined with any accuracy, but rune forms suggest the twelfth century.

Formal inscriptions in churches extend beyond those commemorating the dead. Items of church furniture, in particular baptismal fonts and bells, but also censers, door rings and keys may carry runic texts of a deliberate nature. A late thirteenth-century baptismal font from Burseryd church, Småland, Sweden, displays the following carefully executed inscription (Plate 20): *Arinbjorn gørði mik. Vitkunder prester skref mik. Ok hær skal um stund standa* 'Arinbjorn made me. Vitkunder the priest wrote me. And here I shall stand for a while'. Numbers of medieval rune-carvers, like Vitkunder, "sign" their work and many inscriptions identify makers of church objects. A censer from Hesselager

Plate 20 The Burseryd church baptismal font, Småland, Sweden

church, Fyn, Denmark, dated to the first half of the thirteenth century, offers a straightforward example: *Mester Jakop røð af Svineburg gørðe mik. Jesus Krist* 'Master Jakop Red of Svineburg [Svendborg] made me. Jesus Christ'. There are several censers made by the same Jakop still extant, with runic texts in both medieval Danish and Latin.

A totally different kind of inscription appears on a bell from Oslo, almost certainly originating from a lost medieval church, but of uncertain date. The inscription is in two parts, designated A and B, on either side of the lower circumference of the bell. Sequence A contains the complete sixteen-character *fuþark* augmented by ᚯᛅᛍ **øæc**, and B the first seven runes of the sixteen-character *fuþark* framed by ᚱᚴ **rk** at the beginning and ᚠᚢ **fu** at the end. The bell is cast, and the runes are mirror-image (having been cut the right way round on the mould). A adds up to a total of nineteen characters, which corresponds to the cycle of nineteen years at the end of which the new moons start to fall on the same days of the year again (crucial for computing the date of Easter). In that context sequence B would seem to mark the seven days that make up a week. A nineteen-character row and the first seven runes of the younger *fuþark* were used to indicate the nineteen-year cycle and the first seven days of the year (or latterly the days of the week) respectively in so-called runic calendars (pp. 114–15). The inscription as a whole thus seems to symbolise the passing of time, which the bell marks on each occasion it tolls.

Some inscriptions name the donor of a church object, as that on the iron chandelier from Väte church, Gotland, dated around 1300. Its damaged and thus incomplete text proclaims: *Juhan i Grenjum hann gaf þissa krunu fyrst Guði ok vari fru ok þairi helgu kirkju senni sjal til þarfa ok siðan ...* 'Juhan of Grenjar, he first gave this chandelier to God and Our Lady and the holy Church for the benefit of his soul, and then ...'. References are also found to the builders of churches – or those who organised their construction. A striking example comes from the thirteenth-century Tingvoll (stone) church in Møre og Romsdal, Norway. On a marble slab set high in the wall above the altar, we read:

> *Ek bið fyrir Guðrs sakar yðr lærða menn er varðveita stað þenna, ok alla þá er ráða kunnu bœn mína, minnisk sálu minnar í helgum bœnum. En ek hét Gunnarr, ok gerði ek hús þetta. Valete!*

> 'I pray in the name of God you clerics who care for this place, and all those who can read my prayer, remember my soul in holy prayers. And I was called Gunnarr, and I made this house. Farewell!'

From his use of the Latin interjection *Valete* 'Farewell!', as also from his habit of marking consonant length by doubling the relevant rune (as in ᚦᛅᚿᛆ **þæn͡na** 'this [acc. m.]', ᛆᛚᛆ **al͡la** 'all [acc. m. pl.]'; cf. p. 96), it may be deduced that Gunnarr was literate in roman script. That suggests he was not the actual builder of the church, more likely the patron.

Formal inscriptions outside the church context include those few that mark boundaries between properties or seem to document the taking of land. The Huseby stone from Vest-Agder, Norway (perhaps twelfth-century), announces:

Hér skiptir mǫrkunni 'Here the land is divided'. The stone stands on the border between the farms of Huseby and Lunde, which is probably its original position. From Eingjatoftir near Sandavágur, on the Faroese island of Vágar, comes a runic stone with the text: *Þorkell Onondarson austmaðr af Rogalandi bygði þenna stað fyrst* 'Þorkell Onondarson, Eastman [i.e. Norwegian] from Rogaland, settled this place first'. The inscription is dated on linguistic and runological grounds (probably over precisely) to around 1200. Since it is unlikely anyone was taking land in the Faroes as late as that, the probability is the wording records an earlier event. It may well be, though, that descendants of Þorkell set the stone up at least in part to document their entitlement to the property.

Before moving on to more informal types of medieval runic inscription, brief mention should be made of runic coins. These are small, silver pieces with a runic legend, from the period roughly 1065–80 (a specimen is shown in Plate 21). Danish examples (1065–75) tend to give the name of the moneyer (sometimes an English name, suggesting English involvement) and the place where the coin was struck (mostly Lund, in the, now Swedish, province of Skåne). A typical example is: ᚠᚹᚦᚢᚾᛁᚼᛁ:ᛁᚠᚢᚾᚦᛁ **koþuini:ilunti** 'Goðwin in Lund'. Norwegian runic coins (1067 to roughly 1080, which also exhibit onomastic evidence of English involvement), rather than giving the place of production record the name of the moneyer and the fact that he "owned" the

Plate 21 Norwegian runic coin with the right-to-left legend:
kunar:a:motþisa 'Gunnar owns this die'

die from which the coin was struck, e.g. ᚠᚢᚼᛅᚱ:ᛁ:ᛦᛂᛏ ᚦᛁᛏᛂ **kunar:a:mot þita** 'Gunnar owns this die'. Some runic coins show the name of a monarch. The Latin legend *Sven rex danorum* 'Sven, king of the Danes' (with the runes often garbled) appears on one Danish type, while ᛂᛏᛂᚠᚱᚠᚢᚾᚠᚢᚠᚱ **olafrkunukr** 'King Óláfr' occurs on a Norwegian minting. It is fairly certain that *Sven* refers to King Sven Estridsson (1065–75), but whether **olafr** gives the name of Óláfr kyrri 'Óláfr the Quiet' (1066/7–1093), the reigning monarch at the time the coins were struck, or Óláfr the patron saint of Norway, who died at the battle of Stiklastaðir in 1030, is disputed. A question that has been much debated is why runes were used on Scandinavian coins at all, and for such a limited period. Some have attributed their appearance to a rise in national consciousness, but more recently an alternative hypothesis has been proposed. The issuing of new series of coins, it is stressed, was one of the methods by which a ruler could tax his subjects. Only coins issued by the ruler would be legal tender, and he might declare all older types obsolete, thereby compelling the populace to exchange their existing money for the new issue at a rate determined by him. Such a system would require the employment of easily recognisable features on the new coins, and runic characters may have been deemed appropriate to this purpose.

10.3 Informal inscriptions on loose objects

Informal medieval runic inscriptions on loose objects comprise a wide variety of types. Most come from urban contexts – the growing towns of Scandinavia, in particular Bergen, Trondheim, Oslo, Tønsberg in Norway, Sigtuna and Lödöse (by Gothenburg) in Sweden, Lund and Schleswig in (medieval) Denmark. The bulk of these inscriptions are from Norway, Bergen in particular. There, following a fire at Bryggen (the medieval wharf) in 1955, which resulted in the almost complete loss of four building complexes, a veritable treasure of everyday medieval objects (dated roughly between the late twelfth and mid-fifteenth century) came to light in the ground beneath. Among them were some 550 runic inscriptions – a quantity that almost doubled the (then) Norwegian total. Most can be dated to within a specific period according to whether they were found above or below a particular "fire layer", a belt of charcoal and ash marking the periodic fires that ravaged medieval Bergen, and on top of which new buildings were erected.

The discovery of the Bergen runic material, which was followed by similar, smaller finds during excavations in other urban centres, prompted a reassessment of the role of runic writing in medieval Scandinavia. Instead of a gradual decline following the introduction of Christianity and the roman alphabet, there seems to have been something of a renaissance in the use of runes during the thirteenth century. As far as can be seen, however, there was no rivalry between the two scripts, more a division of labour. Roman was used to write lengthy texts with ink on parchment – an expensive and time-consuming business. Runes were employed for the carving of brief, mostly ephemeral, texts; all that was required was a knife or other sharp implement (which most people will have carried as a matter of course) and a piece of suitable material – commonly, but not exclusively, wood. It is possible the upsurge in the writing of everyday messages was (at least in part) inspired by the advent of roman-alphabet literacy. What remains unclear is why runes rather than roman letters were adopted for the carving of such messages. The answer may lie in the way knowledge of the roman alphabet was disseminated. Most people who mastered roman script will have learnt it through studying Latin and only secondarily recognised it as a tool for writing medieval Scandinavian. And the book learning involved will have been slow, laborious and expensive, for the most part the prerogative of the clergy. Runic writing – the rune-row and its uses – was almost certainly taught in a more informal way, though we have only a few pointers to how this was done (pp. 115–16).

The discrepancy between the number of medieval inscriptions found in Bergen and those discovered elsewhere should not be taken to mean that Bergen led the "runic renaissance". It is more likely that the chances of preservation and discovery have skewed the record. Conditions in Bergen were optimal for the survival of wood, and the 1955 fire laid bare what the ground had so helpfully preserved. It is not unreasonable to assume that the levels of runic activity documented at this one site were replicated in other Scandinavian towns.

Prominent among the Bergen and Trondheim inscriptions, because of their sheer number, are owners' tags (Plate 22) – wooden inscriptions consisting of a personal name alone or a name followed by the verb form *á* 'owns', e.g. **þorstæin** 'Þorsteinn', **þorᴋæir:a** 'Þorgeirr owns'. These tags are often shaped in such a way that they can be affixed to a consignment of goods: they may have a hole for tying, or end in a point so they can be thrust into a sack or wrapping. What it was that was owned is seldom stated – for which there are at least two probable reasons: first, it would have been obvious enough when the stick was in use; second, one and the same stick could be used over and over again to mark different wares as required. Just occasionally an owner will state in general or more specific terms what it is s/he owns, as in the Trondheim inscription (late twelfth- or thirteenth-century) **urmrasïk** *Ormr á sekk* 'Ormr owns the sack', or the Bergen example (early thirteenth-century) **rannra:ka͡rn:þætta** *Ragnarr*(?) *á garn þetta* 'Ragnarr(?) owns this yarn'.

There are other inscriptions from the world of commerce. These may be brief, as the note (early thirteenth-century) found on a Bergen stick (which presumably accompanied a consignment of goods): *Þorkell myntari sendir þér pipar* 'Þorkell moneyer sends you pepper'. But they can also be quite extensive, as a letter detailing problems in obtaining merchandise, also unearthed in Bergen and dated to around 1330; this consists of 299 runes in total and covers all four sides of a neatly prepared piece of wood. Sometimes it can be hard to tell whether or not an inscription has a commercial dimension. From Lincoln, England, comes a comb case of antler, to be dated to the late eleventh or perhaps early twelfth century. It bears the runic text: **kamb:koþan:kiari:þorfastr** *Kamb góðan gjarði Þorfastr* 'Þorfastr made a good comb'. This has been described as a "master's signature" and could be

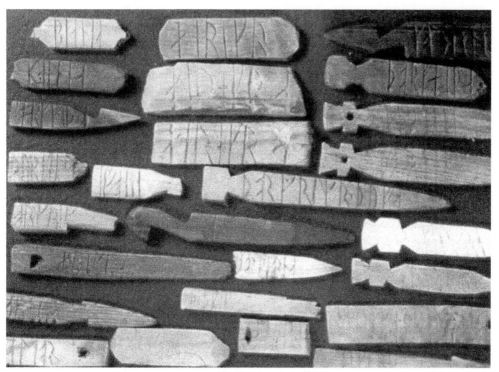

Plate 22 A selection of owners' tags from Bryggen (Bergen), Norway

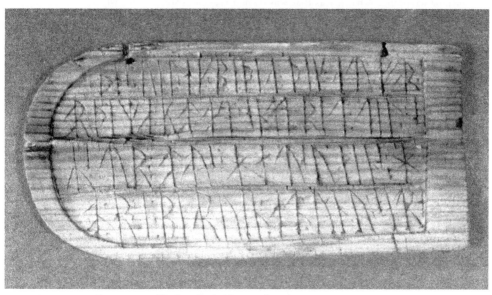

Plate 23 Wax tablet inscribed with runes from Bryggen (Bergen), Norway

seen as a kind of trade-mark. On the other hand, Þorfastr's text may simply express pride in his workmanship. Runic inscriptions on combs vary: some identify owners, some donors; some consist of single names that could belong to owner, donor or maker (and not a few identify the object itself, cf., e.g., p. 89).

Occasionally inscriptions on loose objects have, or seem to have, a political slant. Most notable is a text inscribed into a wax tablet from Bergen (Plate 23). A wax tablet was a piece of wood with a large (slightly) recessed area, surrounded by a rim, into which wax was poured. A message could then be inscribed into the surface of the wax – and could be easily removed by smoothing the surface as and when the need arose. In this particular instance the writer seems to have carved a secret message in the wood and covered it with wax (placing perhaps a more innocuous text on the surface). By no means all of the message can be deciphered, and it is possible it extended beyond the one (two-sided) tablet that survives. What can be read indicates that the recipient was in trouble with an unspecified "earl" – perhaps in hiding from him. The writer offers advice about how to proceed, urging the recipient to take counsel about how s/he might be reconciled with the earl. The inscription is dated to between 1170 and 1198, a period of much civil strife in Norway, and the earl is thus almost certainly to be identified with Erlingr skakki 'Erlingr Crook-Neck', father of King Magnús (1161–84), who died in battle in 1179 (cf. pp. 118–19).

Several loose objects from the medieval period bear runic inscriptions in verse. This can take the form of skaldic poetry – occasional verse, generally by named poets, and notable for its complex diction and metrical structure; of Eddaic poetry – verse in the metre and style of the anonymous mythological and heroic lays that go under the name of the "older" or poetic Edda; and of texts that do not conform to any recognisable verse type but which yet exhibit rhyme and a simple sort of rhythm. To offer here examples of skaldic verse would lead too far, requiring explanation of much that has nothing to do with runes and runic writing. Worth emphasising, though, is the occurrence of this type of poetry in medieval Norway. Although it is in Norway skaldic verse seems to have originated, perhaps in the ninth century, it was in Iceland it was cultivated, ultimately coming to be associated almost exclusively with Icelanders. The medieval Norwegian material, chiefly from Bergen, points to a wider spread of the skaldic form as late as the thirteenth and even into the fourteenth century.

The Eddaic verse found on medieval runic objects can consist of adaptations of lines from known poems, but there are also what appear to be new compositions in Eddaic metres. From approximately 1180/85 comes the following text, inscribed into two adjacent surfaces of a runic stick from Bergen:

> *Heill sé þú*
> *ok í hugum góðum.*
> *Þórr þik þiggi.*
> *Óðinn þik eigi.*

'Be you hale
and in a good frame of mind.
Þórr receive you.
Óðinn own you.'

The first two lines follow almost word for word the opening lines of stanza 11 of the Eddaic poem *Hymiskviða* 'The Lay of Hymir': *Ver þú heill, Hymir, í hugum góðum* 'Be you hale, Hymir, [and] in a good frame of mind'. In the Lay the speaker continues by giving Hymir some news. The second half of the text on the runic stick is in completely different vein, and the intention behind it hard to fathom. It is unlikely that belief in the Norse gods persisted in Norway some 200 years after the introduction of Christianity, so we can probably discount the idea that some unnamed person is being wished safe passage into the heathen after-life. Perhaps the writer intended a curse, along the lines of the well-documented *troll hafi/taki* ... 'the trolls have/take ...'. At the time the inscription was made Þórr and Óðinn might well have been regarded as trolls, masquerading as gods. Alternatively there may be a further literary allusion (though to literature that has not survived), the whole inscription intended to demonstrate the writer's erudition, or simply made for fun.

From twelfth-century Schleswig comes a runic stick with a text in an Eddaic metre:

*Runaʀ jak risti
a rikjanda træ,
sva reð saʀ riki mǫgʀ:
æsiʀ a ardagum,
hullaʀ auk bullaʀ,
mæli þæʀ ars sum magi.*

The sense of this stanza is not clear in every detail, but can be understood as follows:

'Runes I cut
on a ... ing tree,
thus read the mighty son [i.e. he read the message thus]:
gods in days of yore,
hullaʀ and *bullaʀ*,
let them say: for you arse is like belly.'

We have here a mixture of poetic diction with crude insult. The term *áss*, pl. *æsir* 'heathen god(s)' is coupled with *árdagar* 'days of yore' twice in Eddaic poetry, and *mǫgr* is a poetic word for 'son'. The stanza has been described as "mock-pompous": high-flown verse leads up to the punch line, and the balloon is then deflated – the gods are brought in to announce that for 'you', the recipient, the arse is like the belly. Quite what this implies is unclear, but it has been taken as a hint that both are full, that is, 'you' have a reputation as a glutton. The poet seems to have had some trouble composing his stanza: neither *hullaʀ* nor *bullaʀ* is otherwise documented as a Scandinavian word, and both were probably invented on the spot as line fillers (they have something of the

ring of English *helter-skelter*). That may also be true of the present participle
ríkjanda.

An inscription on a twelfth-century weaver's knife from Lödöse (by
Gothenburg), Västergötland, Sweden, exhibits rhyme and simple rhythm, but
the text does not conform to any recognised verse type. It runs: *Mun þu mik!*
Man þik. Unn þu mær! Ann þær 'Think of me! [I] think of you. Love me! [I] love
you'. One can perhaps imagine that the knife was a present from a man to his
loved one. The almost identical text is found on a mid- to late twelfth-century
stick from Bergen, while another early thirteenth-century inscription (also on
a stick) from the same town records: *Unn þú mér! Annk þér. Gunnhildr kyss*
mik! Kann ek þik 'Love me! I love you. Gunnhildr kiss me! I know you'.

A very different piece of rhythmic and alliterative verse from Bergen (late
thirteenth- or early fourteenth-century, yet again on a stick) contains some
kind of incantation designed to upset the cooking:

> *Ími stein heitti,*
> *at arinreykr rjúki,*
> *aldri seyðir soðni!*
> *Út yl!*
> *Inn kyl!*
> *Ími stein heitti.*

'Ími heated the stone,
that the hearth may smoke
and the fire never cook anything!
Out warmth!
In cold!
Ími heated the stone.'

Poetic form apart, this seems a fairly clear-cut case of an attempt to alter the
natural course of events by the invocation of supernatural powers. Sorcery is
not always so easily recognised, however. The extent to which medieval runic
inscriptions are employed in the service of magic is a widely debated question
to which there is no clear answer. Much depends on understandings of magic.
What, for example, is its relationship with religion? Is an object inscribed with
a Christian prayer and worn about the body to be considered an amulet or a
symbol of piety? And was this distinction meaningful at the time the object
was in use? Does an object become magical by virtue of the inscription it
carries or some act with which the inscription is connected? And so on. The
difficulties have been increased by a tendency in runic studies to place any text
that could not be easily understood in the magical category. Many inscriptions,
for example, consist of a partial or complete *fuþark*. Some runologists have
wanted to see these as magical, arguing that the *fuþark*, which contained the
key to writing, embodied and symbolised a certain kind of power. Others have
claimed that the many *fuþark* inscriptions we find reflect writing practice
rather than magic (p. 115). We should be wary of all such blanket assertions.
Each inscription must to begin with be treated individually. In trying to assess
the purpose for which it was made we need to discover as much as we can

about its context. Context may include such things as the find spot, the type of object bearing the inscription, and the totality of the text. Many *fuþark* inscriptions, for example, are accompanied by additional writing, and these may throw light on the purpose of recording a complete or partial rune-row.

A lengthy text whose purpose was clearly to cast out sickness is that found on the so-called healing stick from the town of Ribe, Jutland, dated to around 1300. This is Denmark's second-longest runic inscription and consists of an incantation, partly in Eddaic metre partly in prose, designed to exorcise the "trembler", i.e. malaria. The text invokes earth and heaven, the Virgin Mary and God and ends with *Amen*, followed by its Danish translation **ok:|þæt:sï** 'And so be it'. Although the wider context is Christian, the overall tenor of the words is far removed from prayer. Together with the references to God and Mary comes a hefty dose of sorcery from the world of popular medieval belief (mention is made, *inter alia*, of a stone called Svart, which lies out in the sea and on which lie nine 'needs' – 'need' being the name of ᚾ/ᚿ, for what it is worth).

More difficult to get to grips with are the many medieval inscriptions that (to us, at least) make no sense at all. Some have been interpreted as magic formulas we do not understand (cf. above). Others, it has been suggested, could represent attempts by unskilled novices to create the illusion of magic formulas. Rather like a quack-doctor with his potions, the amateur spell-maker would knock some runes together and sell the result to the illiterate as a charm. As previously emphasised, however, it should not be assumed that that which cannot readily be understood must have magic connotations. Incomprehensible runic inscriptions may simply reflect attempts at writing by people who had learnt the characters of the *fuþark*, but were as yet unpractised in using them to record language. Once again, we must consider the context. A stick or bone with runic gibberish and nothing else offers little to go on. A metal plaque with similar gibberish, on the other hand, is likely to be an amulet or charm (or intended as such). There exist a good many of these objects (most are of lead, though copper and other metals also occur): some are formed as pendants, some rolled or folded together, some are in the shape of a cross, and some simply flat pieces of metal. The evidence suggests that such plaques, whatever their shape, were first and foremost intended to be carried on the person; sometimes to be placed on a corpse before burial. That, together with the content of the interpretable plaque inscriptions, speaks strongly of attempts to harness supernatural powers. We find in particular healing spells, combinations of biblical and incantatory Latin (cf. pp. 123–4), and medieval charm language. An example of the last is the common acronym *agla* (representing the Hebrew *attah gibbor leʾolam adonai* 'Thou art strong to eternity, Lord'). Against this background, it is not unreasonable to assign metal plaques with uninterpretable sequences of runes, or rune-like symbols, to the religious-magical category.

Far removed from the supernatural are the many informal inscriptions – often very informal – that contain statements, jokes, casual comments, and, occasionally, snatches of direct speech or dialogue. These are found chiefly on pieces of wood and bone, and a great many of them stem from the Bergen wharf excavations. What are here categorised as statements can vary widely in sense and purpose. From Greenland comes a small stick, discovered at the bottom of an otherwise empty coffin in the churchyard at Herjólfsnes. It was clearly placed there, in consecrated ground, in the absence of the body, for the inscription (probably from around 1300, and perhaps written by a Norwegian) records: *Þessi kona var lagð fyrir borð í Grœnalandshafi, er Guðveig hét* 'This woman, who was called Guðveig, was put overboard [i.e. her body was consigned to the deep] in the Greenland Sea'. An inscription of a similar date from Lom stave-church, Oppland, Norway, conjures up a lighter, if still serious, context. It is carved into what appears to be the broken-off bottom section of a walking stick. The writer expresses his determination to ask the recipient of the inscription for her hand in marriage – provided she does not wish to be with another. He urges her to consider her position and let him know her decision. A partially successful attempt has been made to erase the personal names from the text, and that, together with the nature of the object on which the message is placed and its find spot – under the floor of the church on the women's side – has led to much speculation about the genesis and fate of this inscription. Where was it made – at home or on the way to church, or even in church? And was it the lady concerned who tried to whittle off the names, before letting the piece of wood drop between the floorboards? Affairs of the heart also concerned the carver of the following inscription, on a stick from Bergen dated to the late twelfth century: *Ann ek svá konu manns at mér þykkir kaldr eldr. En ek em vinr vífs þessa* 'I so love a man's wife that fire seems to me cold. And I am a friend of this woman'. The Bergen runic material contains several heart-felt sighs of a similar kind.

As an example of a joke – in the crudest taste – we may instance a mid-thirteenth century inscription from Bergen carved into an irregular shaped lump of wood (Plate 24). It says: *Jón silkifuð á mik, en Guðormr fuðsleikir reist mik, en Jón fuðkúla rǽðr mik* 'Jón silk-cunt owns me, and Guðormr cunt-licker carved me, and Jón cunt-hump reads me'. *Silki* 'silk', *sleikir* 'licker' and *kúla* 'hump' are all nicknames occurring in medieval

Plate 24 Inscription on a lump of wood from Bryggen (Bergen), Norway

Norway, and one or more persons with the names *Jón silki, Guðormr sleikir* and *Jón kúla* are documented in other sources. Whether a Jón silki, Guðormr sleikir and Jón kúla were actually gathered together in Bergen and there hit upon the hilarious idea of combining their nicknames with a word for the female genitalia cannot be known. Those involved might have borne other names entirely. The inscription need not even be the work of three people: two different hands can be discerned, but whether as many as three contributed is uncertain. While not common, crudities of this kind do appear now and again among the runic inscriptions of the Middle Ages – an indication that medieval man, in this respect at least, did not differ from his modern counterpart.

Yet another inscription from Bergen, this time on bone, and dated to around 1200, comments simply: *Nú er skœra mikil!* 'Now there is great tumult!'. The word *skœra* normally carries the sense 'strife' or 'fight', and possibly some kind of brawl is what is referred to. However, scholars have preferred to set the inscription in the context of a noisy ale-house. A scene is visualised in which a man seizes a handy piece of cattle rib (left over from a meal), furnishes it with a comment on the noise level, and then passes it to his neighbour. Someone has carved another inscription on the same bone – presumably the recipient if we accept the suggested context. The second inscription is incomprehensible, although the runic characters are all clear enough. Perhaps its writer was drunk, or disturbed by the tumult, or both. Whatever lies behind the runic gibberish s/he produced, the context is clearly not one of spells and magic (cf. p. 112). More banal still than this postulated exchange is the comment (probably twelfth-century) on a piece of bone from Lund, Skåne (medieval Denmark): *Ben es þetta, ben es þetta* 'This is a bone, this is a bone'. Possibly we have here a bit of writing practice – the final word is garbled – but the inscription belongs to a common enough medieval type in which a writer painstakingly identifies an object everyone would have recognised at first glance.

An ale-house has also been suggested as a likely venue for the genesis of another pair of inscriptions from Bergen, carved on a stick and dated to around 1200 or the early thirteenth century. First we have *Gyða segir at þú gakk heim!* 'Gyða says: go home!', then a clumsily written and incomprehensible sequence that has been taken as an attempt to reply. The supposedly initial message exhibits a grammatically mixed construction: 'Gyða says that' leads us to expect a subordinate clause, but the writer abruptly switches to direct speech: 'you go home!'. It has been surmised that Gyða (a female) instructed someone to fetch her husband, or other male relative or friend, and the messenger, for whatever reason, wrote the summons down. The recipient tried to frame an answer, but through incompetence or incapacity succeeded only in producing nonsense.

It is a leap from such very informal communication to the appearance of runes in calendars. Indeed, it could be argued that calendars present a formal context. The way runes are deployed in that context, however, is as labels or rubrics. We are far removed here from the monument or public notice. It was the practice in medieval calendars to mark (a) the Sundays in a particular year with a number or letter denoting whichever of the first seven days of a year the initial Sunday fell upon (so-called dominical numbers or letters), (b) – also with a number or letter – the nineteen years of the lunar cycle (p. 104). In Scandinavia runes were sometimes used for this purpose: the first seven characters of the younger *fuþark* for the first seven days of the year (and in later calendars for the seven days of the week), and for the lunar cycle the sixteen runes of the complete younger *fuþark* augmented by three additional symbols, seemingly created for calendar use. The earliest extant runic calendars appear to be from the second half of the thirteenth century, but there is no reason why the phenomenon should not be somewhat older. Formats vary greatly. Many of the calendars are written or painted on parchment or paper (and occasionally on permanent fixtures), some are carved into wood, bone or antler – so-called "calendar sticks". The practice of carving such sticks (some with runes for the relevant numbers or letters) persisted for many centuries. Indeed, after the Reformation it positively blossomed.

Finally among the informal inscriptions on loose objects we turn to those that indicate, or are at least suggestive of, the teaching of runes and runic writing. No account exists of how people learnt to write in runes, so we have to form our own picture from the various bits of evidence that survive. The medieval Norwegian evidence has been categorised as follows: (1) inscriptions containing complete or partial rune-rows; (2) runic syllabaries – inscriptions consisting of or including sequences of syllables, often a particular consonant symbol followed by different vowel runes (e.g. **fufafïfifoþoþaþiþu, funẗ:punẗ:runẗ: k̈unẗ:lunẗ:** – and yet more in a similar vein – on a late thirteenth- or early fourteenth-century stick from Bergen); (3) meaningless inscriptions, particularly those consisting of or including repeated runes or rune-like symbols (e.g. on a stick from Trondheim, late twelfth- or thirteenth-century: **iiii iii ii i kkkkk:kkkk kkk:kk:k**); (4) inscriptions indicative of model and copy (e.g. **æinar:sikr:amïk** *Einarr sikr á mik* 'Einarr Whitefish owns me' and, by another hand, the imperfect copy **ainarsikr:ïmak,** on a mid-fourteenth century stick from Bergen); (5) inscriptions that mention the learning of runes.

Complete or partial rune-rows abound, but they cannot automatically be interpreted as writing exercises. As has been emphasised previously, the context must be taken into account. To be reasonably sure a runic novice is at work, we need something suggestive of teaching or learning, as for example rune-rows in different hands, one or more with errors. Sequences of syllables also occur relatively often, but these may not all be syllabaries. Where they appear on unadorned pieces of wood they are commonly assumed to be writing exercises, for it is not easy to see what other purpose they could have had, but where a spindle-whorl, for example, or a stone column in a cathedral bears such an inscription, we ought at least to consider other explanations. In some people's view these latter are more likely to be protective formulas. Repeated runes or rune-like symbols are not uncommon, and may well have to do with the teaching and learning of runes, but, once again, context must as far as possible be taken into account. There are not many inscriptions in which texts appear to have been copied by a second hand, but of those that exist, most are best interpreted as writing practice. Of particular interest are inscriptions that mention the learning of runes. Again, these are not plentiful. There is, however,

Plate 25 Runic stick from Tønsberg, Vestfold, Norway

a striking example on a runic stick (Plate 25) dated 1250–1325 from the town of Tønsberg, Vestfold, Norway. The text begins: **mit:stæin:k̃rimr:hafum: mælt:mart:okk̃arimilli:firir:þasok:atïk:uil:nïma:afþi:runãr:** *Mit Steingrímr hafum mælt mart okkar í milli fyrir þá sǫk at ek vil nema af því rúnar* 'Steingrímr and I have talked much between ourselves for the reason that I want to learn runes from so doing'. There follows a demonstration of various kinds of runic versatility in two or more hands. There is no sign anywhere in the writing of uncertainty; rather, the people involved seem concerned to demonstrate the depth and breadth of their knowledge. We have here, perhaps, the fruits of the conversation with Steingrímr – a record of a runic master class?

10.4 Graffiti

Medieval runic graffiti are found principally in churches, wooden or stone, and in places where people congregated, sought shelter or rested up, and there was a suitable surface for carving (almost always stone).

Church graffiti cover a wide range of topics, from the religious to the profane, and even banal. A good many are in Latin (pp. 123, 125). Some, in the manner of the medieval memorial text, call for divine help or prayers, for the carver himself, for others, or for both. On a wall plank in Hopperstad stave-church, Sogn og Fjordane, Norway, is the following inscription, perhaps from the second half of the twelfth century: *Nú er palmsunnuaftann. Dróttinn hjalpi þeim manni er þessar rúnar reist, svá þeim er þær ræðr* 'Now it is the eve of Palm Sunday. The Lord help the man who carved these runes, as also the one who reads them'. Inscriptions of this type are by no means always anonymous: commonly the writer adds his name and the fact that he 'carved runes', rendering the message part prayer part a record of the visit (a medieval equivalent of "Kilroy was here", cf. below). A plank in the gallery round the outside of Borgund stave-church, Sogn og Fjordane, Norway, provides an example (of uncertain date, but on the basis of the rune forms perhaps late twelfth-century): *Klemetr reist rúnar þessar sunnudag þann er næstr er eptir jól. Guð gæti hans ok in helga María* 'Klemetr carved these runes on the Sunday immediately after Christmas. God and the Blessed [Virgin] Mary preserve him'. A prayer for two unnamed people (almost certainly twelfth-century) occurs elsewhere on a plank in the Borgund gallery: *Guð fagni sál þeirra beggja* 'God receive the soul of them both' (the initial word is damaged but can be reconstructed on the basis of what remains and the context). In many medieval Scandinavian churches the single name *María* can be found carved in runes – a pious reference to the Virgin Mary. Yet other types of inscription declare that God or a relevant saint 'owns' the church, or record an event of religious significance, as the runes on a stone from Niðaróss (Trondheim) cathedral, which, though damaged, seem to say: *Jón ok Ívarr vaktu Ólafsvakunótt hér*

'Jón and Ívarr held a vigil here on the night of the feast of St Óláfr [28–9 July]'. These were perhaps pilgrims who had come to the cathedral simply to pray, or who hoped to be cured of an illness or handicap through the intercession of Óláfr. At what date they were there is impossible to say, but it cannot have been much before 1200 from what is known of the history of the cathedral's construction. Also a possible pilgrim is the person who carved the following into yet another plank in the gallery round Borgund church: *Guð styði hvern er mik styðr til útferðar* 'God support each person who offers me support for my journey abroad'. The inscription appears to be an appeal for financial and material aid, most probably towards a pilgrimage given the church context. A date in the second half of the twelfth century or perhaps a little later has been suggested on linguistic grounds, but the recent dendrochronological dating of Borgund to 1180–81 narrows the period somewhat.

Some church inscriptions are not of a religious nature at all. On a stone in the western wall of the south transept of Carlisle cathedral is carved **tolfinuraitþisarunraþisastain**, which gives the rather odd piece of medieval Scandinavian: *Dólfinn wreit þessa rúnr á þessa stein* 'Dólfinn wrote these runes on this stone'. The inscription, perhaps from somewhen in the twelfth century, has *þessa stein* for expected acc. m. sg. *þenna stein* 'this stone', *rúnr* for *rúnar* 'runes', and what appears to be the English word *wrat* 'wrote' (Scandinavianised as **urait**) in place of usual *reist* 'carved'. This suggests a demotic form of Scandinavian, appropriate to such an apparently casual piece of writing. Cut into a limestone door-jamb in Allerslev church, Zealand, Denmark, is the inscription (of uncertain date but perhaps thirteenth-century): *Jordan risti runu. Raði þæn ær kann* 'Jordan carved runes. Let him who is able to, read/interpret'. The verb *ráða*, cognate with English *read*, often seems to mean something like 'make out', and thus 'read' or 'interpret', depending on the context. Where inscriptions contain an injunction to *ráða* the runes, it is commonly the precursor to some kind of puzzle, or obfuscation of the text, making 'interpret' a reasonable rendering. In this case there is no puzzle; the inscription is of the common "Kilroy was here" type, with the injunction to read/interpret added for fun or possibly because the carver felt he was one of an elite group who had mastered the art of runic writing.

A good number of church inscriptions are made in the plaster covering the walls – incised either while the plaster was still wet (identifiable from a small ridge on either side of the furrows of which the characters are made up), or after it had dried out. These do not differ in kind from other church graffiti: appeals to Jesus, the Virgin Mary, or a saint; prayers, commonly in Latin; rune-rows; names, with or without the phrase 'carved runes' (some made by workmen); banal comments and jokes. In Lye church on the island of Gotland, some forty such inscriptions can be found covering almost the whole range; most of them, if not all, appear to date from the late fourteenth or the fifteenth century.

Workmen, stonemasons in particular, have left runic records of their activity in many Scandinavian churches. Running across several sandstone blocks that form a corner of the tower of Vallentuna church, Uppland, Sweden, is the inscription: *Andorr telgdi þenna fagra sten ...* 'Andorr dressed this beautiful stone ...'. Construction of the church began towards the end of the twelfth century, and the tower belongs to the earliest phase. Bricks were used in the building of some churches, and these occasionally carry runic inscriptions – usually traced into the wet clay before it was fired. The texts are almost always brief: the odd religious sentiment apart, they consist of personal names (most probably those of the brick makers) with or without additions, partial rune-rows, banal comments, and what appears to be gibberish. As an example of the banal we may take **tihlstïn** 'brick', decorating one of the bricks in Nørre Løgum church, Jutland, built in the first half of the thirteenth century or a little earlier. Another brick inscription from Søborg church, Zealand, **þæn:fürstæ** 'the first', seems to have a practical purpose. This was perhaps the first brick (of a particular batch?) to be made; alternatively the inscription may indicate the first one destined to be laid in a particular spot, or have served as some other kind of marker. Runes were certainly used by workmen to mark both wood and stone. Timbers have been found in the roofs of Danish churches with individual runes on them, clearly used like numbers to distinguish one timber from another. Stones in church buildings may also exhibit single characters probably intended as runes. These are generally interpreted as masons' marks – symbols that identify the work of a particular stonemason, the character possibly representing the initial letter in his name.

Two runic inscriptions carved into the outer edge of portal planks flanking the south door of the stave-church that once stood in Vinje, Telemark, Norway (demolished 1796), have – uncommonly – a political context. The church seems at one point (or just possibly on separate occasions) to have served as a hideout for two prominent fugitives, and the church timbers must have afforded a handy surface on which they could record their plight. One of them inscribed a message in prose (Plate 26) outlining the circumstances in which he came to be at the church, the other composed a quite complex stanza of skaldic verse, breathing contempt for his enemy and striking a note of defiance. The prose text runs:

> *Sigurðr Jarlsson reist rúnar þessar laugardaginn eftir Bótolfsmessu, er hann flýði hingat ok vildi eigi ganga til sættar við Sverri, fǫðurbana sinn ok brœðra.*

'Sigurðr, the Earl's son, carved these runes on the Saturday after the feast of St Bótolfr [17 June], when he fled hither and would not be reconciled with Sverrir, the slayer of his father and his brothers.'

Sigurðr was one of the sons of Earl Erlingr, slain in battle against the pretender to the Norwegian throne, Sverrir, in 1179. Sigurðr's half-brother, King Magnús

Plate 26 The opening of the Vinje 1 (prose) inscription, Telemark, Norway

of Norway, died fighting Sverrir in 1184, and his full brother, Finnr, seems to have met the same fate a year later. Not surprisingly, Sigurðr became a central figure in various revolts against Sverrir, who in the late twelfth century managed to seize the crown of Norway by force of arms. Comparison with other historical sources makes it possible to narrow down the year in which Sigurðr's inscription was carved to 1194 (or possibly 1197). The verse inscription, carved by a man styling himself Hallvarðr grenski (i.e. from Grenland, Telemark), was most probably made on the same occasion, though we cannot be wholly certain of this.

Medieval runic graffiti outside the church context come from various sites. Most notable are: Storhedder, a place in the mountains of Aust-Agder, southern Norway, where hunters and travellers seem to have rested up and where a huge overhanging soapstone rock provides shelter and a suitable surface for carving; Hennøy, Sogn og Fjordane, Norway, a good haven in a storm or windless conditions, with a number of sizeable stones along the shoreline on which runes can be, and have been, inscribed; Maeshowe, a large prehistoric chambered cairn on the Orkney Mainland; Holy Island off the east coast of Arran in the inner Hebrides, like Hennøy a good place to anchor up, and with a handy rock face close to the shore. In the main the inscriptions in these and similar places record the names of passers-by (often accompanied by the superfluous statement that they 'carved runes'), comment on women and sex, and speculate about hidden treasure.

Maeshowe offers the most extensive and interesting collection. Two of its inscriptions state that 'Jerusalem farers' or 'Jerusalem men' broke into the cairn. This is almost certainly a reference to the band of (largely Norwegian) crusaders organised by the Orkney earl, Rǫgnvaldr, who spent the winter of 1150–51 in Orkney on their way to the Holy Land. With little to occupy them during the long Orcadian winter, it would be no surprise that they forced their way into Maeshowe, a place that must have seemed to them likely to conceal objects of value. Whether all thirty-three runic inscriptions and the sundry other medieval carvings in the cairn were made immediately or soon after the break-in cannot be determined, but rune forms and language both point clearly to the middle decades of the twelfth century. About half the texts are of the "Kilroy was here" type. A couple laud a woman's appearance, as: *Ingigerðr er kvennanna in vænsta* 'Ingigerðr is the most beautiful of women'. One inscription gets straight down to the essentials: *Þorný sarð, Helgi reist* 'Þorný fucked, Helgi carved'. Yet others speculate about the treasure the cairn-breakers clearly failed to find. A series of carvings across two huge stones in the south-east wall record an exchange of views on the matter (Plate 27). *Útnorðr er fé folgit mikit* 'In the north-west great treasure is hidden' proclaims one writer. *Hǫkon einn bar fé ýr haugi þessum* 'Hǫkon alone carried treasure from this mound' counters another. *Sæll er sá er finna má þann auð hinn mikla* 'Happy is he who can find the great wealth' sighs a third. *Þat var lǫngu er hér var fé folgit mikit* 'It was long ago that great treasure was hidden here' opines a fourth. Women also contributed to the Maeshowe graffiti. It was Líf, the earl's housekeeper, who informed the world that 'Jerusalem-farers' broke into the cairn. Whoever the writers were, they knew their runes; none of the

Plate 27 A series of carvings from Maeshowe, Orkney. These deal, among other things, with the possibility of hidden treasure and the breaking open of the cairn. Some of the inscriptions run across both stones.

inscriptions betrays uncertain command of the script and several demonstrate considerable versatility.

The Holy Island corpus, found on a rock overhang close to the shore, is less interesting runologically and textually. Most of its inscriptions consist of names, with or without the addition 'carved' or 'carved runes'. These texts do, however, have a certain historical importance. There is reason to connect most or all of them with the campaign launched by the Norwegian king, Hákon Hákonarson, to reassert his authority over the Hebrides and the Isle of Man. Hákon set sail for Scotland in the summer of 1263, but met defeat later in the year at the battle of Largs.

10.5 Antiquarian text-types

There is evidence, of various sorts, of an antiquarian interest in runes and runic inscriptions as early as the Middle Ages.

In the porch of Norra Åsum church, Skåne, (medieval) Denmark, stands a remarkable rune-stone. Its text is laid out in the manner of a Viking-Age commemorative inscription, but cannot have been made earlier than the last quarter of the twelfth century. It records: *Krist Mariu sun hjalpi þem ær kirkju þessa gerðu, Absalon ærkibiskup ok Æsbjorn Muli* 'Christ, son of Mary, help those who made this church, Archbishop Absalon and Æsbjorn Muzzle'. Absalon became archbishop of Lund in 1178 and died in 1201. It seems likely he commissioned the stone himself, and it has been surmised that its traditional format reflects the archbishop's interest in the past.

Viking-Age in layout, wording, rune forms and orthography is the Oddum stone from Jutland. Set between neat, quasi-zoomorphic bands, the text proclaims: **þurulfs:sati:stain:uftiʀ:tuka:tuka:sun|hin:usta:kuþ:hialbi|hans:** 'Þorolf placed the stone after Toki, Toki's son, the ?foremost [in rank]. God help his ...'. The meaning of **usta** is uncertain: some believe it represents the superlative of *ung* 'young', and thus means 'youngest' rather than 'foremost'; and a word for 'soul' is missing at the end of the inscription because there was no room for it. Of more immediate significance, however, is the fact that the carver employs only the sixteen runes of the younger *fuþark* (in their "long-branch" forms). There is no sign here of any of the developments associated with medieval runic writing (pp. 92–4). That accords with the early and mid-Viking Age spelling **stain**, suggestive of diphthongal pronunciation ([stæin] rather than later [ste:n]), and the distinction made between ᚱ **r** and ᛆ **R** (a feature of Viking-Age and early medieval runic orthography in Denmark). Yet against these indications of a relatively early date must be set the serifs that form the ends of many verticals: this is a practice the carver has copied from roman capitals. Other features smack of pastiche, notably the shapes of the word separators (which vary between a short vertical stroke and a single dot) and the style of the bands between which the runes are placed. There can be little doubt the inscription was made well into the Middle Ages. What is unclear is why someone decided to commemorate Toki by setting up a rune-stone of Viking-Age type 200 years or more after the fashion had died out. Admiration for, or at least interest in, the past seems not unlikely.

From Bergen, Norway, comes a runic stick bearing a damaged, but almost complete staveless rune-row (p. 64), deposited in the ground in the last decades of the twelfth century. Insofar as staveless runes are otherwise documented only in Sweden, and seem to belong to the late Viking Age, the find is unexpected. As well as the staveless row, the stick exhibits a sequence of complex, rune-like characters and a group of medieval consonant runes (for which latter an intricate but plausible interpretation has been suggested). The choice of lettering here suggests that the inspiration for the carvings may have been an interest in runic writing, past and (perhaps) present.

Although runes are almost exclusively an epigraphic script, there do exist two runic manuscripts. They seem to have been written in Skåne, (medieval) Denmark, and are dated to around 1300. One contains a version of the provincial law of Skåne, along with various shorter texts, the other part of a 'Lament of Mary', in which the mother of Jesus pours out her grief at the persecution and crucifixion of her son. A traditional explanation for the sudden appearance of runic manuscripts at this late date is that they represent an attempt to promote the native script as a rival to roman-alphabet writing. It is perhaps more likely that an antiquarian interest developed in one or more scriptoria, and that some scribes became curious to find out how well suited runes were to extensive pieces of writing.

10.6 Inscriptions in Latin

Just as the roman alphabet was adopted for the writing of medieval Scandinavian, so runes could be employed to write Latin. Choice of script seems to have depended more on situation and material than language. Runes were used to record brief messages, statements, quotations, etc. in materials that required the characters to be carved or scratched. Roman letters belonged first and foremost in the scriptorium: there, lengthy texts addressing themselves to an extended audience and demanding a degree of permanence were written with ink on parchment – laws, religious treatises, works of scholarship, sagas, letters patent. The distinction is by no means absolute, however. The two runic manuscripts mentioned above are exceptional, but roman-alphabet inscriptions are not uncommon in Scandinavia, especially on gravestones. Some of these carry inscriptions in both runes and roman. In such cases it can be difficult to discern what motivated the choice of script. A few gravestones exhibit a clear division according to language – runes for the vernacular, roman for Latin – but others deploy the two writing systems differently: roman *and* runes for Latin, runes for the vernacular; both roman and runes in an almost wholly vernacular text; and so on. Sometimes Latin texts carved in roman letters occupy pride of place on a memorial, suggesting that the universal language and script were accorded a higher status than the native equivalents. But in other cases practical considerations seem to have played a part, not least the recognition that runes by and large occupied less space than roman letters. The age of an inscription can also be a determining factor. On gravestones of the eleventh and twelfth centuries carvers opt mainly for runes and Scandinavian; thereafter roman and Latin are increasingly used, becoming dominant in many areas in the fourteenth century.

The Latin found in runic inscriptions is of different kinds. Scandinavian names may be latinised, as in **ïrikus amik** 'Ericus [Scand. Erikr] owns me', carved on a wooden measuring gauge from Lödöse, Västergötland, Sweden, dated around 1300 (the gap between name and what follows copied from roman-alphabet writing), or a Latin word or phrase inserted into a vernacular text, as the **uaĺïtï** 'Farewell!', with which the Tingvoll church carver concluded his message (p. 104). Strictly speaking, these examples do not belong in the corpus of Latin runic inscriptions. A carver writing in Scandinavian is demonstrating knowledge of the language of the Church and European learning, much as someone writing in English today might use a foreign word or inflection for particular effect.

The quality of "runic Latin" varies considerably, from good to indifferent or downright poor. A number of inscriptions are in what is termed "pseudo-Latin", sequences that suggest Latin words and inflections, but which make no obvious sense. Some of these may have been written out of ignorance, others by people – with or without proper knowledge of the language – trying to harness magic powers. Much depends on context. A small stick from Oslo, dated around 1200, carries the following runes: **kalïs:falïs:akla|hakla**. Here the Christian charm-acronym *agla* (p. 112) is combined with what look like (but are almost certainly not) Latin verb forms. The **h** that precedes the second

akla (on the other side of the stick from the main inscription) has been taken as a "Christ monogram" (based on the perceived similarity between runic ᛯ and greek χ, the initial letter in the Greek form of the name *Christ*). The general context suggests perhaps the stick was fashioned as an amulet. The rhyming words **kalïs:falïs** may derive from a meaningful piece of Latin, as *hocus pocus* from *hoc est corpus* [*meum*] 'this is [my] body', said during Holy Communion, but they could simply have been invented; probably not on the spot, though: a series of three very similar rhyming words, **alïs:talïsarfalïs** (conjecturally construed by some as 'you shall nourish such farmers' – a puzzling statement) occurs on the broken-off handle of a wooden measuring tool from Lödöse (also dated to around 1200).

The Latin runic inscriptions come from more or less the same environments as their vernacular counterparts, chiefly churches and towns. That may be because those were places where large numbers of people congregated, and because Latin was the language of the Roman Church. But modern activity – church restoration and the excavation of urban sites – may have distorted the pattern of distribution somewhat. The Latin inscriptions also tend to be carved into the same materials as their vernacular counterparts, and into the same types of fixture or object. The chief materials are thus stone, wood, bone, metal, plaster and brick. The fixtures or objects that bear the Latin texts are church buildings and furnishings; gravestones; wooden crosses; wood and bone implements and utensils; sticks; unworked pieces of bone; metal plaques; metal crosses; rings; the occasional coin. An unusual find is the leather upper of a shoe into which a Latin text in runes has been embroidered (see below).

Content, as well as language, marks the Latin inscriptions out as a distinct group. Unlike the vernacular texts, which often arise from the need for spontaneous communication between individuals, those in Latin tend to reflect Christian and European culture. Many of the Latin inscriptions are renderings – accurate or garbled – of well-known prayers. Others quote, or attempt to quote, fragments of classical or medieval Latin literature. The latter do not presuppose familiarity with the works concerned; almost certainly, well-known quotations were reproduced from medieval florilegia (compilations of excerpts).

The prayers that occur most regularly (complete or incomplete) are *Pater noster*, the Lord's Prayer, and *Ave Maria* 'Hail Mary!', but many others are attested. Various quotations from the mass are found, for example, *Gloria in excelsis deo* 'Glory to God in the highest', carved on a stick from around the 1180s found in Bergen. The names *Maria*, *Jesus* and *Christus* are cited (the latter two often as a pair), as also those of the evangelists and other apostles and saints – sometimes with additional text, sometimes without. Many of these names are of course of Hebrew or Greek origin, but they have become part of "Church Latin", just as the Hebrew charm acronym *agla* (p. 112) or the Greek prayer *Kyrie eleison, Christe eleison* 'Lord have mercy, Christ have mercy', which in the form **kirialæisun:kristalæison** occurs on a Bergen stick from the period *c*. 1250–1335.

Some Latin inscriptions hover uncertainly between Christian prayer and sorcery. That is especially true of those on lead plaques (p. 112). Like their vernacular counterparts, the purpose of many of these plaque inscriptions seems to be either to offer general protection or drive out illness. Some are in pseudo-Latin, some combine runes with rune-like signs or other symbols. But there are also those with fully or largely comprehensible texts, as for example that on the lead plaque from Odense, Fyn, Denmark (of uncertain date but clearly medieval; Plate 28). This lengthy inscription begins with what seems to be an incantation, consisting of some seven words among which it is possible to see garbled references to anointing and "prime-signing" (*prima signatio*, the preliminary to baptism). Then comes a prayer: *Christus vincit, Christus regnat, Christus imperat, Christus ab omni malo me Asam liberet, crux Christi sit super me Asam, hic et ubique* 'Christ conquers, Christ reigns, Christ commands, Christ deliver me, Asa, from all evil, the cross of Christ be over me, Asa, here and everywhere'. More incantatory words follow, then the charm acronym *agla*, and finally: *Sanguis Christi signet me* 'the blood of Christ bless me'. The plaque, folded so its inscription could not be seen, was found in a churchyard lying among a number of skeletons. Given the find spot and the fact that several lead plaques have been recovered from coffins, it is assumed that the Odense example too was originally placed in a grave, the purpose perhaps being to transfer to the deceased some sickness that afflicted Asa.

Notable among the profane Latin texts are quotations from Virgil and from ribald Latin verse of the twelfth and thirteenth centuries (so-called "Goliardic" poetry). Embroidered on the leather upper of a left shoe found in Bergen is the sequence: **imulilamoᷓru|iciþomniaoþ**. Following the uninterpreted **imulil**, with which the text opens, we discern *amor vincit omnia* (and perhaps also a mis-spelt *et*), a garbled and incomplete version of the famous Virgilian sentence *omnia vincit amor et nos cedamus amori* 'love conquers all, and let

Plate 28 The Odense lead plaque, Fyn, Denmark

us too yield to love'. The shoe was discovered above the 1198 fire-layer and thus probably belongs to the early thirteenth century. In all likelihood the right shoe continued the quotation. Certainly the complete sentence will have been well known to many in Bergen, for it was used in teaching the writing of Latin in the Middle Ages. On a four-sided rune stick from the town, dated about a quarter of a century later, Virgil's words accompany a skaldic (p. 109) love strophe. Interestingly enough, someone has tried to copy the Latin on an unused side of the same object, but with only limited success. On another (mid-thirteenth century) stick from Bergen are fragments of love songs, somewhat mixed up, from the famous medieval collection *Carmina Burana*.

By no means all the profane Latin inscriptions consist of quotations. A thirteenth-century bell from Bollebygd church, Västergötland, Sweden, carries what seems to be a freshly composed text in poetical Latin celebrating its chimes: *Dat Katerina sonum fideli populo bonum. Hic sonus auditur, hic mens turbata blanditur* 'Katerina gives a fine sound to a faithful congregation. Here the sound is heard, here a troubled mind is calmed'. In Björkeberg church, Östergötland, Sweden, someone proficient in Latin (probably a member of the clergy) has written in the plaster of the chancel arch: **hik:lo͡kus:illo͡rum:kui:ka͡nta͡nt:no͡n:alio͡rum** 'Here is the place of those who sing, not of others' (Plate 29). The inscription is late medieval and (in serious or jocular fashion) signals the boundary between clergy and people. A small lead plaque from Lödöse, Västergötland, Sweden, bears the runes **unmarka**, presumably an imperfect version of Latin *una marca* 'one mark', giving perhaps the weight of the original sheet, of which the plaque may have comprised about a quarter. If that is the true interpretation, the inscription, dated on the basis of the context in which it was found to *c.* 1250–1300, represents a rare

Plate 29 The Björkeberg church plaster inscription, Östergötland, Sweden

commercial use of Latin. Some Latin inscriptions, like many in the vernacular, are simply banal. A brick from Lösen church, Blekinge, (medieval) Denmark, informs the reader: *ego sum lapis* 'I am a stone'.

The Scandinavians who used runes to write Latin were from different backgrounds. This can affect the way they approach the task. The varied renderings of 'c' in the common word *gracia* (< *gratia*) 'grace' provide an illustration. The learned follow medieval Latin orthography and write **k̇racia**; those used to hearing Latin but unused to reading it tend to spell the word **k̇rasia** in accordance with medieval pronunciation; those aware of Latin orthography but more familiar (or content) with runic spelling conventions ignore pronunciation and write **k̇rakia**, presumably reasoning that **k**, which denotes /k/, is a common runic equivalent of roman 'c'. The fact that many who write Latin in runes follow pronunciation rather than traditional orthography offers us insights into the way the language was pronounced in medieval Scandinavia (cf. p. 97). The person who (probably in the thirteenth century) scratched **patïrnostïrkiïs|inslis**, i.e. *Pater noster qui es in cælis* 'Our father which art in heaven' into the wall of Gol stave-church, Buskerud, Norway, was presumably trying to reproduce what s/he heard, or thought to hear: [ki] rather than [kwi] for *qui* 'which', [slis], or perhaps [səlis], rather than [tʃelis] for *cælis* 'heaven'. A revealing orthographic feature is the regular substitution of **þ**, denoting [ð], for unstressed Latin /t/, as **uinciþ** for *vincit* 'conquers', **æþ** for *et* 'and'. The latter spelling also suggests a lowering of the vowel from [e] to [æ].

10.7 The two-script community

As this chapter has demonstrated, the introduction of the roman alphabet into Scandinavia did not spell the end of runic writing. On the contrary, the advent of Latin literacy seems to have led to an upsurge in literacy in general, leading people to make much wider use of runes than they had done earlier. But, as has also been emphasised, roman and runic literacy occupied different positions in the community. Roman writing was the province of the learned, of schools and scriptoria. It was the medium for lengthy texts, written with ink on parchment, which addressed themselves to a general audience. The ability to write in runes appears to have been spread more broadly across society, and those who had the skill used it chiefly for spontaneous communication directed at individuals or small groups. Because they are concerned with matters of the moment and spring from a largely oral culture, runic texts give us a more intimate picture of everyday life and linguistic usage in the Middle Ages than the more formal, literary texts we find in manuscripts. Those texts record the law, set out the beliefs of the Church, chronicle historical events, tell stories, document legal transactions. Runic inscriptions, memorial and certain other formal texts aside, comprise prayers, quotations, spells, statements, comments, exclamations, pleas, musings, declarations of love, and lavatory humour. As a genre, they reinforce the conviction that medieval man had much in common with his modern counterpart.

Select reading list

Barnes, Michael P. 1994. *The Runic Inscriptions of Maeshowe, Orkney* (Runrön 8). Uppsala: Institutionen för nordiska språk, Uppsala universitet. [A complete edition of the Maeshowe corpus.]

Barnes, Michael P., and Page, R. I. 2006. *The Scandinavian Runic Inscriptions of Britain* (Runrön 19). Uppsala: Institutionen för nordiska språk, Uppsala universitet, 251–78. [Provides an edition of the Holy Island, Arran, corpus.]

Gustavson, Helmer 1994. 'Latin and runes in Scandinavian runic inscriptions'. In: (Klaus Düwel, ed.) *Runische Schriftkultur in kontinental-skandinavischer und -angelsächsischer Wechselbeziehung* (Ergänzungsbände zum Reallexikon der Germanischen Altertumskunde 10). Berlin/New York: de Gruyter, 313–27. [A discussion of the interaction between Latin, roman-alphabet writing, and runes.]

Hagland, Jan Ragnar 1998. 'Runes as sources for the Middle Ages'. In: (Klaus Düwel, ed.) *Runeninschriften als Quellen interdisziplinärer Forschung: Proceedings of the Fourth International Symposium on Runes and Runic Inscriptions in Göttingen 4–9 August 1995* (Ergänzungsbände zum Reallexikon der Germanischen Altertumskunde 15). Berlin/New York: de Gruyter, 619–28. [A general discussion of the contribution runic *inscriptions* can make to our understanding of medieval Scandinavian society.]

Jansson, Sven B. F. 1987. *Runes in Sweden*. Stockholm: Gidlunds, 162–73. [An outline account of medieval runic inscriptions from Sweden.]

Knirk, James E. 1994. 'Learning to write with runes in medieval Norway'. In: (Inger Lindell, ed.) *Medeltida skrift- och språkkultur: Nio föreläsningar från ett symposium i Stockholm våren 1992* (Runica et Mediævalia, Opuscula 2). Stockholm: Runica et mediævalia/Medeltidsseminariet och Institutionen för nordiska språk vid Stockholms universitet, 169–212. [Discusses different types of inscription from medieval Norway that offer insights into how people learnt to write with runes.]

Knirk, James E. 1998. 'Runic inscriptions containing Latin in Norway'. In: (Klaus Düwel, ed.) *Runeninschriften als Quellen interdisziplinärer Forschung: Proceedings of the Fourth International Symposium on Runes and Runic Inscriptions in Göttingen 4–9 August 1995* (Ergänzungsbände zum Reallexikon der Germanischen Altertumskunde 15). Berlin/New York: de Gruyter, 476–507. [A detailed survey of the material.]

Knirk, James E., Stoklund, Marie, and Svärdström, Elisabeth 1993. 'Runes and runic inscriptions'. In: (Phillip Pulsiano and Kirsten Wolf, eds) *Medieval Scandinavia: An Encyclopedia*. New York/London: Garland Publishing, 545–55. [A general introduction to runes and runic writing is followed by more detailed treatment of medieval inscriptions.]

Moltke, Erik 1985. *Runes and their Origin: Denmark and Elsewhere*. Copenhagen: National Museum of Denmark, 398–500. [A detailed and well-illustrated account of the Danish medieval runic material.]

Spurkland, Terje 2004. 'Literacy and "runacy" in medieval Scandinavia'. In: (Jonathan Adams and Katherine Holman, eds) *Scandinavia and Europe 800–1350: Contact, Conflict and Coexistence*. Turnhout: Brepols, 333–44. [A discussion of the interaction between Latin and the vernacular, and between roman and runic script, exemplified by Norwegian inscriptions.]

Spurkland, Terje 2005. *Norwegian Runes and Runic Inscriptions*. Woodbridge: Boydell Press, 131–202. [A general account of the Norwegian medieval runic material, including the Maeshowe corpus; deals briefly, in addition, with the development of runic writing in Norway in the Middle Ages.]

Steen Jensen, Jørgen 2006. 'The introduction and use of runic letters on Danish coins around the year 1065'. In: (Marie Stoklund *et al.*, eds) *Runes and their Secrets: Studies in Runology*. Copenhagen: Museum Tusculanum Press, 159–68. [Argues that the purpose of the runic legends found briefly on Danish coins was to distinguish a new issue from earlier types.]

Stoklund, Marie 1993. 'Greenland runes: isolation or cultural contact?' In: (Colleen E. Batey, Judith Jesch and Christopher D. Morris, eds) *The Viking Age in Caithness, Orkney and the North Atlantic* (Select Papers from the Proceedings of the Eleventh Viking Congress, Thurso and Kirkwall, 22 August – 1 September 1989). Edinburgh: Edinburgh University Press, 528–43. [A summary presentation and discussion of the Greenlandic runic corpus.]

Stoklund, Marie 2005. 'Faroese runic inscriptions'. In: (Andras Mortensen and Símun V. Arge, eds) *Viking and Norse in the North Atlantic* (Select Papers from the Proceedings of the Fourteenth Viking Congress, Tórshavn, 19–30 July 2001). Tórshavn: Faroese Academy of Sciences, 109–24. [A presentation and discussion of the small Faroese runic corpus.]

11 Runic writing in the post-Reformation era

11.1 Introduction

As is made clear in chapter 10, runic writing had died out in most parts of the Scandinavian-speaking world well before 1500. Only on the Baltic island of Gotland, in Iceland, and in the Swedish province of Dalarna (though see below) did it openly survive as a continuous tradition into the post-Reformation era. There are occasional hints from other areas that runes continued to be known by some. In the early sixteenth century a German craftsman employed to supervise the restoration of Lund cathedral made two inscriptions in the building using both roman letters and runes. One of them begins k̇ot:hïlḃ 'God help': the language here is Low German, but the script is runic. The craftsman, Adam van Düren, is unlikely to have learnt runes in North Germany, so it is plausible there were one or more persons in Lund at the beginning of the sixteenth century in a position to teach him. Where and how they might have gained knowledge of runic writing at that period is unclear: outside Gotland, Iceland, and Dalarna virtually no sixteenth-century inscriptions are known that indubitably (or in the case of Dalarna probably) reflect an inherited tradition. Unclear, too, is why people stopped writing in runes. As the Middle Ages progressed, outside influences on Scandinavia increased, not least in the shape of the North-German Hanseatic traders, who came to form a sizeable proportion of the population in the growing Scandinavian towns. Closer and more regular exposure to European culture may have led people to abandon old traditions and embrace what they perceived as modernity. That cannot be the complete explanation, however. Some maintain that feudalism and the Church hierarchy contributed, each in its own way, to the demise of the vernacular script. And while it might be argued that Iceland retained runic writing because it was relatively isolated, the same cannot be said of Gotland or Dalarna, the latter a point of contact between Sweden and Norway, the former an important trading centre with the town of Visby at its heart. All three areas, though, nourished small, culture-conscious communities that preserved much from the past, not least highly distinctive forms of speech. It may be that linguistic conservatism, common to Gotland, Iceland, and Dalarna, extended to the written form and thus helped perpetuate the use of runes in these places.

11.2 The survival of traditional runic writing after 1500

On Gotland the sixteenth century saw a sharp decline in runic writing, but the script seems to have survived into the early decades of the 1600s. That we are dealing here with a living tradition and not a new creation can be deduced from two factors. First, the rune forms employed do not differ in any significant way from those favoured by Gotlandic rune-writers of the late Middle Ages.

Second, the inscriptions are of traditional type, from traditional contexts. Virtually all are found in churches. Many are carved into plaster; there is also a rune-inscribed gravestone, and a crucifix base or stand. The texts range from the pious to the banal, and some consist solely of an individual's name. Fairly representative is the collection from Bunge church in the north of the island. It consists of five inscriptions, all cut into plaster. One gives the name of a sexton, another the name of a man who seems to have been pastor of the church for much of the second half of the sixteenth century. The third says *Sanctæ Lafrans* 'Saint Lawrence', the fourth *þaun helga kirkja* 'the Holy Church', and the fifth *Guð hann jær goðær. Þæt jær sant* 'God, he is good. That is true'. The latest datable inscriptions ascribable to a living Gotlandic tradition come from Atlingbo church in the middle of the island. Unfortunately they are known only from an 1852 report. This observes that on each of two columns supporting the entrance to the choir could be seen the name *Jakop Isem* written with red crayon. On one column it appeared as ᛁᚴᚱᛆᛒ:ᛁᛋᛁᛘ together with the date 1568, on the other as ᛁᚴᚱᛆᛒ:ᛁᛋᛁᛘ, or perhaps ᛁᛋᛁᛘ, with the date 1621, both years in arabic numerals. The name *Isem* (more properly *Isums*) seems to belong to a local farming family. Possibly we have here father and son or grandfather and grandson, with the years of their birth or, perhaps more likely, death.

Iceland does not appear to have had an ancient runic tradition (pp. 190–94). Settlement of the island began in the last decades of the ninth century, but virtually no runic inscriptions have been found there dated earlier than the thirteenth (in 1993 a rune-inscribed stick was discovered on the island of Viðey, just north of Reykjavík, dated from the archaeological context to before 1200, but how long before is unclear, as is the provenance of the stick). Many have considered runic writing in Iceland to be a late import, connected perhaps with the upsurge in the use of runes that took place in Norway in the late 1100s and 1200s (pp. 106–7). Not all have agreed. The existence of a runic tradition in Greenland from the time of settlement there (*c.* 1000), together with the Icelandic origin of many of the settlers, has been deployed as a counter-argument. In reality, direct evidence for runic activity in Greenland before the thirteenth century is rather sparse, although the dating of the Greenlandic inscriptions is by no means straightforward. Whatever the truth of the matter, Icelandic tradition as we have it effectively begins in the thirteenth century, and extends into the seventeenth, quite possibly even the eighteenth.

The reason we cannot say for certain when runes ceased to be a traditional script in Iceland is that it is harder there than elsewhere to discern the difference between inherited usage and learned re-creation. Rune forms change a little over the centuries, but not radically. The starting point appears to be the medieval system as found in Norway, augmented to ensure there was a runic equivalent for every letter of the roman alphabet (as ultimately tended to happen elsewhere). Icelandic preferences include the substitution of rings for dots (as ᚯ for ᛁ **ë**, ᚯ or ᚯ for ᛁ **ï**), the extension of **s** to full height (ᛚ or ᛚ for ᛚ), a distinctive form of **y** (ᛁ), the introduction of various shapes for **q** (e.g. ᛉ, ᛉ), and the complete abandonment of ᛒ **b** in favour of ᚴ **p**. The custom of inscribing memorial inscriptions on gravestones (mostly beginning *Hér hvílir ...* 'Here rests ...') lasts into the seventeenth century, to be superseded by an interest in

Plate 30 The Bergþórshvoll runic stick, Rangárvallasýsla, Iceland

decorating household objects with runic texts. In the same century a learned interest in runes becomes apparent. Icelanders start to treat them as an antiquarian script, and runic material from printed books (pp. 133–5) finds its way to the country. From then on it can often be difficult to decide whether an inscription represents unbroken tradition or is based on something found in a book or manuscript. As an example we may take a rune-inscribed stick said to have been unearthed in 1925 at the farm Bergþórshvoll in the south of Iceland (Plate 30). This has on one side a list of runes in roman-alphabet order from **a** to **u**, and on the other a formula widely quoted in medieval Europe (though originating in an earlier period): **sator:arïpo:tïnït:opïra:rotas**. The runes are a mixture of common medieval types (ᛏ, ᛆ rather than ᚦ, ᚬ) and distinctive Icelandic ones (ᚦ, and ᚴ **p** throughout). The formula, an extended palindrome of disputed meaning (if meaningful at all), appears several times in medieval Scandinavia written with runes (and may be laid out as a square, each "word" occupying one line, so the characters can be read forwards, backwards, and up and down). It is generally taken to have protective function, and in that context magical significance has also been ascribed to the listing of the runic characters. The Bergþórshvoll stick comes from what is described as a 'rather recent [archaeological] layer', and having regard to that, a date in the seventeenth or eighteenth century has been suggested. Another dating, based on the stick's runic alphabet, is in the sixteenth or seventeenth century. Lists of runes in roman-alphabet order are known from as early as the 1300s (pp. 95–6), but the combination of medieval ᛏ and ᛆ (the latter extremely rare in Iceland) with ᚦ and ᚴ on a stick from a 'recent layer' is perhaps suggestive of learned reconstruction. However, whether the inscription was made in the sixteenth, seventeenth or eighteenth century is impossible to decide with the limited evidence at our disposal. And indeed there can be no absolute certainty it *is* post-medieval.

How far back runic writing extends in the Swedish province of Dalarna is unclear. One Viking-Age inscription is known (of uncertain significance), and there are a few from the Middle Ages. This may indicate that the script was a rather late arrival, but the tradition could of course be older than the somewhat meagre sources imply. Even though the material is sparse, there is enough to suggest that by the fifteenth century runes were in decline in Dalarna, as elsewhere. In the 1500s, however, the province experienced something of a runic renaissance. In the old parish of Mora in upper Dalarna inscriptions begin to appear in what looks like a reformed, or at least substantially reorganised, writing system. Several inscriptions from the period 1575–95 contain an inventory of runes that matches the roman alphabet character for character (Fig. 19 depicts a model alphabet of the type). Some of the shapes are new. While Ð for roman 'd' is late medieval, ᚷ for 'g', or ᛘ for 'p', for example, are innovations, as are runes for 'å', 'ä', 'ö'. Clearly, the roman alphabet is the model (as it increasingly came to be for many late *medieval* rune-writers).

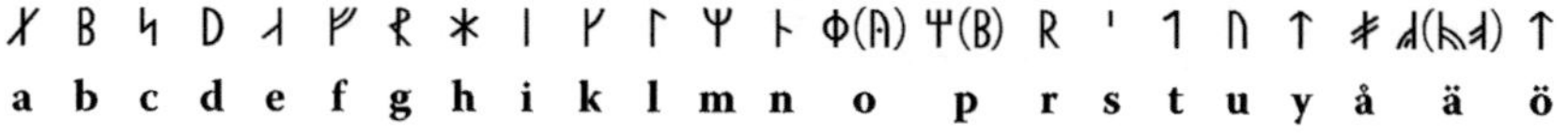

ᚴ B ᚼ D ᛆ ᚠ ᚱ ᛉ I ᚼ ᚠ Ψ ᚽ Φ(ᚨ) ᛉ(B) R ' ᛏ ᚿ ᛏ ᚵ ᛆ(ᚼᛆ) ᛏ
a b c d e f g h i k l m n o p r s t u y å ä ö

Fig. 19 Runes in use in Dalarna in the late sixteenth century
(those in brackets are less common variants)

What lay behind the reorganisation is uncertain. It has been suggested the aim may have been to enable more people to read. The Reformation emphasised the importance of bringing the word of God to the people, but most had to content themselves with hearing the Holy Scriptures in church. Possibly, it is reasoned, someone in Mora concluded simple texts like the catechism might be more easily taught if they could be written out and read. Paper or parchment would have been expensive and difficult to come by, but wood was plentiful. For writing in wood runes represented the traditional medium, carved with a knife or other sharp implement. What was needed was thus a runic alphabet that mirrored the roman. The difficulty with this explanation is that none of the extant post-Reformation inscriptions from Dalarna contain religious texts of quite the kind envisaged. They do suggest an ambition to use the developing standard language as found in the sixteenth-century Swedish translation of the Bible, and a number quote from Scripture or repeat well-known prayers, but none of them look like aids to teaching. By and large the inscriptions concerned are found on calendar sticks, wooden buildings, tools and utensils, and reflect everyday life in the village community. Many record notable events: these may be of importance to individuals, e.g. numbers of fish or birds caught in a particular place, or of collective interest, e.g. a lament about a particularly hard year. Some inscriptions carry summonses to attend village meetings, e.g. 'Tonight there is a public meeting at the usual place'. Yet others are makers' inscriptions, which can vary from the simple **ulåfä:afä:kart** 'Olof has made' on a loom-block from the early seventeenth century, to **andersolsun:hafer:giort:sklä:utaf:grån:at:hån:skal:giera:sina:tinest**   1608 'Anders Olsson has made the bowl from spruce that it may perform its function 1608' (Fig. 20; transliteration here and below follows existing practice for the different types of post-Reformation runic writing).

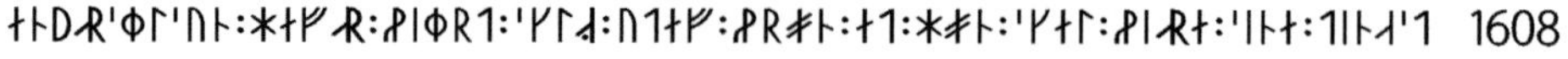

ᚼᚽDᚱ'Φᚠ'ᚿᚽ:✳ᛏ�473ᚱ:ᛈIΦRᛏ:'ᛏᚱᛆ:ᚿᛏᛏᛉ:ᛈRᚵᚽ:ᛏᛏ:✳ᚵᚽ:'ᛉᛏᚠ:ᛈIᚱᚽ:'Iᚽᛏ:ᛏIᚽᛆ'ᛏ   1608

Fig. 20 Schematic representation of 1608 bowl inscription from Dalarna

Whatever the precise origin of the Dalarna runes, they represent a popular, and in part at least continuous, tradition. Although someone (or some group of people) seems to have reorganised the system in the sixteenth century, the resulting set of characters was based on existing medieval usage rather than printed material. Once introduced, the new system was adopted by a whole community, which employed it to write relatively uniform types of text. Moreover, the system did not stand still, but continued to develop. In the course of the seventeenth and eighteenth centuries the runic character of the script was gradually watered down by the introduction of more and more roman letters. In many inscriptions from the late 1700s and 1800s, only a few runes survive in texts that are otherwise written in roman, as BODKAfLA 'summons stick' on a piece of wood specially fashioned for the purpose and dated 1832, where only **f** is runic. Some inscriptions of comparable or later date exhibit a higher proportion of runes. On a piece of wood dated 1893, we read: KaS **gä**T 'K[arl] A[nders]s[on] tended [the flock]'. But such inscriptions represent the dying embers of the last surviving popular runic tradition. By the 1900s the only runes in Dalarna, as everywhere else, were those based on material taken from written or printed sources.

Post-Reformation runic writing on Gotland, in Iceland, and in Dalarna existed in the shadow of the roman alphabet. However traditional and close-knit, these three communities – no less than the rest of Scandinavian society – had become fully reliant on roman letters for written communication. Runes found a small niche, but were not really needed, as witness the fact that they ultimately went out of use.

11.3 Learned interest in runes in the sixteenth and seventeenth centuries

Antiquarian interest in runes seems to go back as far as the Middle Ages (pp. 120–21). It continued into the post-Reformation era and grew. In the sixteenth and seventeenth centuries lists of runes and a fair number of runic inscriptions were presented in printed works (see further chapter 17). A runic alphabet (i.e. a row arranged in *abc*-order) entitled "Alphabetum gothicum" 'Gothic alphabet' appeared in two histories of the North, published in Rome in 1554 and 1555 respectively, but compiled by the Swedish brothers Johannes and Olaus Magnus (Fig. 21). In 1599 the Swedish scholar Johannes Bureus began writing and publishing on matters runic. One of his works was *Rvna ABC boken* 'The Runic ABC Book' from 1611 (Fig. 22), an unsuccessful attempt to reintroduce runes for the writing of Swedish. In 1603 the Norwegian-Danish historian Arild Huitfeldt included a runic alphabet in his history of Denmark. This is called "Alphabeticum gothicum" and seems to be taken from the Magnus brothers' illustration, with whose rune forms it agrees almost entirely. Another Danish history published in 1622 presents a few inscriptions. Serious study of runes in Denmark began with the works of Ole Worm: most notably a book about runes, their origin, development and use, published first in 1636 and again in 1651, and an edition of all the then known Danish, Norwegian and Gotlandic inscriptions (Norway and Gotland being at the time under Danish

Fig. 21 The "Alphabetum gothicum" of the Magnus brothers

Fig. 22 Title page of Johannes Bureus's *Rvna ABC boken*

sovereignty), published in 1643. Of these various works, it is likely the Danish histories reached the greatest number of people. They were in Danish, while the Magnus brothers and Worm wrote in Latin. Bureus used Swedish as well as Latin, but with the exception of the rather impractical runic ABC, he was writing for the specialist.

It is clear, once lists of runes with roman equivalents became available in printed books, that anyone with a mind to adopt the script had a ready-made source. There is seldom much difficulty, however, in distinguishing between genuine tradition and runic writing based on printed material. The rune forms themselves usually betray their origin. Thus writers who use ↓ for 'c' and Þ for 'd' are likely to have taken their runes from "Alphabet(ic)um gothicum" – more than likely if they also have ᛩ for 'q', ᛘ for 's' or ᚠ for 'y' (see Fig. 21). Further, occurrences of post-Reformation runic writing that do not come from a genuine tradition tend to occur sporadically: they are not associated with a particular community, and often do not serve a purpose for which runes were commonly employed (the commemorative stone, the gravestone, the owner's tag, the expression of piety in a church context, etc.). Their authors may also reveal themselves through use of modern language or incorrect use of earlier forms of language, unusual ways of organising their texts, or anachronisms of various kinds.

11.4 Runes and runic inscriptions as re-creations

People have used knowledge of runes gained from manuscripts and books (and in recent times from electronic sources) for a multiplicity of purposes. Simplifying, we can perhaps identify five main areas of activity: (1) the recreation of runes out of antiquarian interest or simply for fun; (2) the employment of the script to conceal what is being written; (3) the perpetration of forgeries; (4) the application of runes to commercial purposes; (5) the promotion of superstition (on the use of the script for literary and political purposes, see chapter 16). The dividing lines between these five areas are not always sharp. Kirkwall airport in Orkney has a sign above the entrance announcing its name in runes: ᚠᚱᛁᛣᛋᛁᛏᛁᚱ **krimsitir** – the local place-name Grimsetter. This exemplifies the commercial use of runes in a modern setting, but it springs from an antiquarian interest in the script that is particularly strong in Orkney (cf. p. 142). Forgeries can sometimes be hard to distinguish from runic texts made out of interest or for fun. A piece of writing can only be labelled a forgery if there is reasonable evidence it was made with the intent to deceive, but such intent can often be difficult to establish. These uncertainties should be borne in mind when examples of post-Reformation runic activity are considered.

The majority of runic texts from the first four centuries or so of the post-Reformation era were undoubtedly made out of antiquarian interest or for fun. In sixteenth-century Denmark members of the upper classes would sometimes employ runes (commonly handwritten or printed) as symbols of the past. The purpose seems to have been to emphasise age and tradition, rather as "Ye Olde Tea Shoppe" in an English country-town context. Thus, when in 1528 a certain Petrus Jacobi Skjold writes his name, he uses roman letters for *Petrus Jacobi* but runes for *Skjold*, presumably in oblique reference to King Skjold, a legendary ruler of Denmark. Most runic *inscriptions* of the modern period that reflect an antiquarian interest in the script are found on utensils or tools of one kind or another, though not a few appear on stones, rock faces and buildings. The writers are usually individuals, occasionally a small group, but never more widely spread.

Of uncertain origin, but discovered in Skåne (now south-western Sweden), and probably to be dated to the seventeenth century, is a drinking horn with a long piece of courtly verse inscribed in runes. As a set the runes cannot be traced back to any published source, but certain forms are indicative of a post-Reformation origin, e.g. ⅄ for /r/, a correlation apparently based on too superficial a reading of the works of Bureus or Worm. The language of the inscription is a kind of early modern Danish. From Oppdal, Sør-Trøndelag, Norway, come several inscriptions – on wooden objects (mostly sticks) and a stone. They consist of a runic alphabet, a personal name, initials, and dates. The runes almost certainly go back to the "Alphabet(ic)um gothicum". The dates come in the form of roman numerals where each roman letter has been transliterated into its runic equivalent. Not all of them are entirely straightforward renderings, however. One (Fig. 23) begins **anno** 'in the year', continues ᛘᚦ↓↓ **mdcc** '1700', and ends Φᛁ, presumably **xi** '11'. Three characters that come in between, roughly ᚳΛΛ, have been taken as attempts to carve **l** with an extended branch, adding perhaps 50 and thus giving the date 1761, but why there should be three **l**s, two of them identical, is unclear. An alternative reading is **uuu** (for roman 'vvv'), which, added together, give 15 and so the date 1726, but that would normally be written mdccxxvi. The exact intention of the writer cannot be established, but unambiguous runic roman-numeral dates from Oppdal (e.g. ᛘᚦ↓↓↓Φᛁᛁ **mdcccxii** '1812' on the flyleaf of a book, with the same rune-forms as the stick), confirm the general interpretation. Use of runes in numerals as replacements for roman letters extends well beyond eighteenth-century Oppdal. The practice is found in other parts of Norway and elsewhere in Scandinavia.

Fig. 23 Runic roman-numeral date on a stick from Oppdal, Sør-Trøndelag, Norway

Inscriptions made closer to our own time than those just discussed employ a greater variety of rune forms. By the 1870s the main lines of development in runic writing were well understood and much had been written and published on the subject. More modern rune-writers were thus able to avail themselves of the older *fuþark*, the Anglo-Saxon *fuþorc*, the younger *fuþark* (with or without the medieval expansions), cryptic runes (pp. 148–52), and homemade runic inventories derived from any or all of these. A stone inscription from the suburbs of Stockholm records in the older runes, but colloquial modern Swedish, **beŋt:okk:ulla|telta:her** 'Bengt and Ulla camped here'. In Bracadale on the Isle of Skye is a cairn erected in 1887 to celebrate the Golden Jubilee of Queen Victoria. One of the stones in the cairn carries the inscription (the second **i** of which is hard to make out) ᚠᛁᛆᚱᚴᛁ ᛃᚢᚾᛏᚴ **kiorki younk**, i.e. 'George Young' written with runes that appear to be derived from Norwegian late Viking-Age or early medieval usage. These two carvings are the products of private initiative. Some modern inscriptions have official sanction. In 1997 a newly carved rune-stone was unveiled on Plymouth Hoe, "a gift from the five Nordic countries" according to contemporary reports. The design, with the text placed on a relief band that curves round the surface, owes something to the typical eastern Swedish stone of the eleventh century (p. 68). The runes are of Viking-Age type and the text is in Old Norse alliterative verse, part made up, part based on the wording of the late Viking-Age Hällestad 1 commemorative inscription (Skåne, Denmark). The Plymouth stone was put up to commemorate the thousandth anniversary of a Viking raid on south-west England, and runs in translation: 'Vikings we were, now we are friends. The stone stands as a token, made firm with runes'.

Various other modern inscriptions take their texts from an ancient source, manuscript or runic. Round the base of the statue *Bältespännarna* 'The belt fighters' in Stockholm is a quotation from verse 5 of the Eddaic poem *Hamðismál* written in late Viking-Age runes, and exactly the same inscription (bar one minor detail) occurs on a large limestone slab found on a property in Örebro, Närke, Sweden. It seems likely the Örebro inscription is a copy of the one in Stockholm. A teacher at Lindhult school, Västergötland, Sweden, copied part of the wording of the eleventh-century Ågersta rune-stone (Uppland, Sweden; Plate 8). Preceding the Viking-Age text is: **runa:risti:r:m:**1926 'R[udolf] M[agnusson] carved runes 1926'. In the wall of a chapel in Skien, Telemark, Norway, someone has tried to copy the older runes of a famous inscription on a gold horn found at Gallehus, southern Jutland (**ekhlewagastiz:holtijaz:horna:tawido:** 'I Hlewaȝastiz, son of [?someone the first element of whose name was] Holta made the horn'; cf. pp. 194–5), but with only partial success. Shortly after the excavation of the Orkney Maeshowe cairn (pp. 119–20), one of its inscriptions scaled off the wall and broke in pieces. An almost exact copy of part of the inscription came to light in the Yorkshire Dales in the late 1930s. It is perhaps significant that the chief excavator of Maeshowe, James Farrer, lived only a few miles distant from where the copy was discovered.

As a secret script, or code, runes do not seem to have been employed very often. At least, there are few clear examples of the practice. Olaus Magnus (p. 133) mentions that it was still common in his day for runes to be used in a military context, but does not make clear how they were used. In all probability he is referring to the need to keep things secret, for which runic script might well have been deemed a handy and adequate device. Two notable instances of the use of runes for concealment come from the sixteenth and seventeenth centuries. One concerns Bent Bille, a Danish court official and navy captain. He made a number of lists and log-book notes in runes, and several from the period 1543–51 have survived. Of particular interest are the runic log-book notes. These occur side-by-side with entries in ordinary roman-alphabet handwriting, but there is a noticeable tendency to employ runes to record sensitive material, be it to do with naval affairs or Bille's sexual adventures. Where and how this sixteenth-century Danish official achieved his runic literacy is unclear. He was writing before the appearance of the Magnus brothers' historical works, and the majority of the rune forms he uses – though not all – can be found in late medieval inscriptions. However, Bille's runic jottings are hardly indicative of a continuing runic tradition. Had runes still been in relatively common use in his day, he could hardly have employed them as a secret script. From 1628 come a couple of letters concerning Swedish military affairs in Livonia (an area corresponding roughly to present-day southern Estonia and northern Latvia). Again, sensitive information is written in runes. These seem to owe something to the works of Bureus, but not all the forms, nor all the sound-symbol correspondences, can be traced back to known sources.

There is nineteenth-century evidence from Karmsund (Rogaland, Norway) of runes' being used for concealment of a rather different nature. A newspaper article from the 1970s, which furnishes a brief account of runic writing in the Karmsund district a century or so earlier, draws attention to a letter dated 1872 from a local tailor to one Hans Knud Sørensen: the tailor refers to a bill but issues a warning in runes against letting anyone else see the bill since the price asked was lower than normal. The same article mentions a marginal note in runes contained in an 1874 letter from a Karmsund emigrant in the USA to Sørensen: the note urges him not to let Mangela (a dialect form of the name Magnhild) 'hear anything about this'. Unfortunately, neither of these letters appears any longer to be extant. Other runic material from Karmsund of a similar date reveals a set of runes different from any of those to be found in printed literature. Opinion favours the belief that they stem from one individual, but whether he obtained his runes from a single source or constructed them on the basis of several is unclear.

Demonstrable runic forgeries are uncommon. One reason for this is the difficulty in showing intent to deceive. On two prehistoric stone monuments in Orkney the name *Ingibjǫrg* appears, written ᛁᚿᚵᛁᛒᛁᚭᚱᚼ **ink̈ibiorh**. Rune forms and spelling bear a marked resemblance to the beginning of one of the Maeshowe inscriptions (pp. 119–20), prominently illustrated on a postcard on sale in Orkney. The two occurrences were not observed until recently and are clearly modern creations. What cannot be known is whether they were made just for fun or with the aim of deceiving simple-minded runologists. But we can hardly declare them certain fakes. Indeed, given the wide availability of the postcard and the fame of the Maeshowe inscriptions they could not have deceived anyone for long.

An apparent forgery from the 1600s is the inscription on a knife discovered on the Danish island of Fyn. The object makes its appearance in 1699, but has since been lost and is now known only from a drawing. The runes run along one side of the blade and seem to say, in a failed attempt to write medieval Scandinavian, '[to] sacrifice for Þórr'. As if that were not enough, we have Λ for apparent /y/, a usage that can be traced back to Johannes and Olaus Magnus, and ᛦ for /r/, which probably stems from a misunderstanding of Bureus or

Worm (pp. 133–5). The inscription contrives to suggest the knife was used in sacrifices to Þórr and is thus of pre-Christian origin – a complete impossibility. From the nineteenth century come two British forgeries, the Barnspike and Hazel Gill rock inscriptions. Found by shepherds near Bewcastle, Cumberland (now Cumbria), in 1864 and 1872 respectively, they were taken seriously by scholars of the time, edited, published and discussed. The runes are of late Viking-Age or early medieval Scandinavian type, but with various oddities. The texts seem to hark back to the Viking-Age commemorative stone, even incorporating the uncommon phrase *í tryggu* 'in a truce', found on the Manx runic cross Braddan 2 (Plate 18), and the designation *hemþegi* 'retainer', known from a number of Danish stones. It is possible these two rock inscriptions were originally carved as a joke. If so, however, they became forgeries through the force of events, for at no point did anyone step forward to advise the scholarly community of their modern genesis.

An early twentieth-century forgery that gained a certain notoriety is the Maria Saaler Berg inscription from Carinthia, Austria. Six runes of older-*fuþark* type were identified on a bone awl found during excavations in 1924 and dated to the second century BC. Read right-to-left and expanded these were declared to say 'Nefo sowed me [with runes]'. Considerable importance was attached to the inscription because it appeared to offer geographical and chronological support for the belief that the runes were derived from north italic scripts (pp. 10–13). In 1930, however, a member of the work force involved in the excavations admitted to having forged the inscription. In this case the motivation seems to have been a desire to fool the scholarly world. That the perpetrator succeeded was in part the fault of contemporary runologists. The reading of the symbols was uncertain, the expansion unwarranted, and the suggested text, which in medieval fashion has the object speaking in the first person, fanciful.

Reminiscent of the Barnspike and Hazel Gill efforts are the four or so stone inscriptions from Vörå, Österbotten (Vaasa), Finland. Written in what are largely late Viking-Age runes, these are worded not unlike a typical tenth or eleventh-century commemorative stone (although the layout is different from anything found in that period). As with Barnspike and Hazel Gill, some of the phrasing seems to have been lifted from published inscriptions: ᚠᛁᛅᚱᚱᛁ:ᛅᚢᛌᛏᛅᚱᛚᛅ:ᛑᚭ **fiarri:austarla:ẗo** 'died far away in the east' carries distinct echoes of the Gripsholm text (pp. 77–8; Plate 12), although the doubling of ᚱ and the use of ᛑ for /d/ is anachronistic (pp. 94, 96). It is possible the Vörå inscriptions were made in an attempt to document Viking-Age Scandinavian settlement in Österbotten, and thus have a political dimension. They appear to be of comparatively recent origin.

A considerable number of runic finds have been reported from the United States, but so far the runological and wider scholarly community has refused to accept any of them as genuine. Best known is the Kensington stone from Minnesota (Plate 31). Reportedly found between the roots of a tree in 1898, it carries a lengthy inscription, telling of an expedition from Vinland and of the demise of ten of the participants, who were found 'red with blood and dead'. The inscription is dated 1362 by the carver himself, using pentadic numerals

Plate 31 The broad face of the Kensington stone, Minnesota, USA

(a system with signs for 1, 5, 10, 15, the numbers in between being marked by the addition of side-strokes; Fig. 24). Much effort has been expended to show that the Kensington inscription is what it purports to be: an account written in 1362 by a member of a Scandinavian expedition to the heart of North America. Apart from the circumstances of the find – and there has been much argument about these – the inscription itself is an oddity. The rune forms are highly unusual (unparalleled until a recent discovery, cf. below). The language is a strange mixture of older and more modern Scandinavian (with a hint of interference from English); in addition it seems to derive from different parts of Scandinavia. The layout of the inscription is most unusual with the runes running horizontally across the stone. The content is unique: no other inscription presents a narrative in the manner of Kensington (the closest approximation might be the Hønen stone, Buskerud, Norway, but that exists only as a copy of a drawing, and its interpretation is suspect). Finally, pentadic numerals, although known in the Middle Ages, seem to be used by the Kensington carver as a substitute for arabic equivalents. Thus he writes the number 14 (which also occurs in the inscription), not as the sign for '10' with four side-strokes in the medieval way, but as ⌈F, the sign for '1' followed by the sign for '4'. ⌈FⱣ⌈ for the year 1362 also seems to be a pentadic rendering of a date conceived in arabic numerals.

| 1 | 2 | 3 | 4 | 5 | | 6 | 7 | 8 | 9 | 10 | | 11 | | 15 etc. |

Fig. 24 The pentadic numeral system

The concentration of so many unusual features in a single inscription has convinced most dispassionate observers that Kensington is a modern creation, and many consider it an out-and-out forgery. American geological expertise has argued that the incisions on the stone must be at least 200 years old (and thus from a time before nineteenth-century Scandinavian immigration into Minnesota), but this view has been challenged. Some have also wondered why, if the intention really was to deceive, the forger did not do a better job. Unfortunately we have no way of knowing who made the Kensington inscription or for what purpose, but it looks to be more than the result of a bit of fun. Apart from anything else, it must have taken a good deal of time and trouble to carve. Recently a runic alphabet almost identical to that used by the Kensington carver has come to light in Sweden, copied independently by two brothers together with various other alphabets, runic and non-runic. The relevant documents are dated 1883 and 1885 respectively – in pentadic numerals, used in the same way as on the Kensington stone. The copyist of the 1885 document was a travelling tailor and musician, and may in principle have come across these unusual runes anywhere in Sweden. His family was from the province of Dalarna, but although there are certain similarities between the 1883/1885 alphabet and the post-Reformation runes of Mora (pp. 132–3), no direct connection can be established. Given the totality of the evidence, it seems likely that whoever made the Kensington inscription had access to an alphabet and numerals of the kind recorded in 1883/1885, coupled with some grasp of medieval Scandinavian idioms. The person concerned, however, does not seem to have been familiar with genuine medieval runic writing. There is little reason to believe the Kensington stone is an artefact from the fourteenth century.

The commercial application of runes certainly goes back as far as the late nineteenth century. At that time a foundry in Fredericia, Jutland, was manufacturing a number of items with runic inscriptions on them. In the early decades of the twentieth century an enterprising Icelander began to make runic artefacts on a small scale for sale to tourists. One of these, a beautifully ornamented and rune-inscribed ox horn, turned up in Waukegan, Illinois (north of Chicago), in 1952. It was subsequently claimed to be a genuine medieval artefact, further proof of the presence of Norse settlers in North America in early times. But the sketches for the horn had remained with the family of the craftsman in Iceland, demonstrating beyond any doubt that the carving is modern.

The more extensive exploitation of runes for commercial gain belongs to the modern era. Rune-inscribed jewellery in particular has become popular. Some of the pieces on sale are copies of early, Viking-Age or medieval artefacts, but many are new creations, the runes often an inelegant jumble of characters from different rows and the "text" more or less meaningless. In Orkney, runic cardigans and pullovers are manufactured (a common type repeats the name *Orkney* over and over again), as well as rune-inscribed wooden objects and sundry bric-à-brac. There are even "Historic Orkney" chocolate bar wrappers adorned with a sequence of runes that gives no sense. It is doubtless in part the heightened awareness of the script brought about by this industry that leads tourists to deface public monuments in Orkney with their attempts at imitation (cf. p. 138).

The promotion of runic superstition – what might be termed "modern rune-lore" – is also at heart commercial. However, it differs from the straightforward commercial exploitation just described (a) by coming chiefly in printed or electronic form, (b) by implying that runes are imbued with magical powers of one sort or another. A few representative book titles from the early 1990s give something of the flavour: *Discover Runes: Understanding and Using the Power of the Runes*; *Esoteric Rune Magic: the Elder Futhark in Magic, Astral Projection and Spiritual Development*; *Lady of the Northern Light: A Feminist Guide to the Runes*; *The Mysteries of the Runes*; *Rune Divination for Today's Woman*; *Rune Power: Runic Power Course, 18 Lessons*; *Rune Sex Gymnastics: Body Work for Sportsmen and Magickians* [sic]. Anyone keen to gain a wider view of the field need do no more than type "runes" into an Internet search engine (cf. pp. 195–6). Characteristic of such works is their reliance on assertion in preference to evidence. This stems in part from ignorance. The author who knows little of a subject is not in a position to argue a reasoned case. But ignorance (or the deliberate suppression of knowledge) is also a prerequisite for the launching of wild claims and unsubstantiated ideas. No one with real insight into runes and their use could with good conscience recommend them as tools for "astral projection", "divination" or the attainment of "power".

The depth of ignorance or obfuscation on display is well illustrated by *The Book of Runes: A Handbook for the Use of an Ancient Oracle: The Viking Runes* (1982). Its author continually describes as "Viking runes" what are in all essentials the characters of the older *fuþark*. Yet the older *fuþark*, as has been amply demonstrated, went out of use before the Viking Age began.

Modern rune-lore is unfortunately little more than mumbo-jumbo – *esoterica*, as one journal puts it. It exemplifies what a distinguished runologist has called "the flight from reason", which he finds "such a sad feature of the modern world". Runes are an alphabetical form of writing, no more, no less. To associate them with the supernatural is to pervert the evidence. There is no more justification for considering runes magic symbols than the characters of the roman, greek, or cyrillic alphabets.

Select reading list

Åhlén, Marit 1986. 'On the younger and the youngest runic inscriptions in Sweden', *Saga-Book* 22:1, 73–9. [A brief account of late medieval and post-Reformation runic inscriptions from Sweden.]

Barnes, Michael P., and Page, R. I. 2006. *The Scandinavian Runic Inscriptions of Britain* (Runrön 19). Uppsala: Institutionen för nordiska språk, Uppsala universitet, 19–43, 338–41. [The sections cited contain discussion of a number of inscriptions that are probably or clearly modern.]

Hagland, Jan Ragnar 2006. 'Runic writing and Latin literacy at the end of the Middle Ages: a case study'. In: (Marie Stoklund *et al.*, eds) *Runes and their Secrets: Studies in Runology*. Copenhagen: Museum Tusculanum Press, University of Copenhagen, 141–57. [On Bent Bille, the sixteenth-century Danish writer known for his use of both roman and runic script.]

Haugen, Einar 1981. 'The youngest runes: from Oppdal to Waukegan', *Michigan Germanic Studies* 7:1, 148–75. [On a local runic tradition from eighteenth-century Oppdal, Norway, and the Waukegan horn.]

Moltke, Erik 1985. *Runes and their Origin: Denmark and Elsewhere*. Copenhagen: National Museum of Denmark, 500–04. [A summary account of post-Reformation runic inscriptions from Denmark.]

Nielsen, Karl Martin 1987. 'The numerals in the Kensington inscription'. In: *Runor och runinskrifter: Föredrag vid Riksantikvarieämbetets och Vitterhetsakademiens symposium 8–11 september 1985* (Kungl. Vitterhets Historie och Antikvitets Akademien: Konferenser 15). Stockholm: Almqvist & Wiksell International, 175–83. [On the use of pentadic numerals within the arabic system and the implications such usage has for the age of the Kensington inscription.]

12 Cryptic inscriptions and cryptic runes

12.1 Introduction

Rune-carvers do not always write plain messages or use plain runes. Sometimes they employ devices that disguise the text to a greater or lesser extent. Their reasons for doing so are not always easy to understand. In some cases the intention may be to restrict readership to a small circle of initiates, but since most of the puzzles can be solved without too much difficulty, other factors must be involved. On occasion it looks as though disguisement serves to highlight parts of a text, or simply to draw attention to the versatility of the carver.

The term most often used to describe runic inscriptions disguised in one way or another is "cryptic". Runes altered so as to conceal their normal shape are known as "cryptic runes". The association of the adjective "cryptic" with "mysterious", "esoteric" and the like has led to an occasional blurring of the distinction between "hidden" and "magic". It should be emphasised at the outset that cryptic inscriptions and cryptic runes are *encoded*. They are in themselves no more magical than the Enigma or Morse codes, or encrypted e-mails. Naturally a cryptic runic inscription can be used for magical purposes, but so in principle can any kind of written text.

12.2 Cryptic and pseudo-cryptic

The extent to which a runic inscription and/or its runes may be disguised varies considerably, raising the question of what can sensibly be termed cryptic. A few rune-writers of the late Viking Age and early medieval period deploy the occasional staveless rune among the more common characters of the younger *fuþark* (pp. 61–4), as on the Sigtuna copper amulet (Uppland, Sweden, from perhaps the end of the eleventh century) and a number of (probably eleventh-century) commemorative rune-stones from the Swedish province of Medelpad. This usage has at times been described as cryptic, but can hardly count as such. Staveless runes are simply reduced versions of the sixteen characters of the younger *fuþark*, and seem to have been quite widely known, at least in parts of Sweden. Their sporadic appearance together with more traditional rune-types is not likely to have disrupted the reading of an inscription. There could be several reasons for their use: to save space, for example, or to impress. For some carvers staveless runes were doubtless simply part of the stock of characters on which they might draw, just as the more complex and simpler Viking-Age types were often employed side by side (pp. 62–3). That was almost certainly the case in Medelpad, which lies immediately north of Hälsingland, a province that boasts several commemorative stone inscriptions written entirely in staveless characters.

A few rune-writers of the late Viking Age place the branches of their runes on a central line – a kind of extended vertical (Plate 32). The resulting characters are known in English as "same-stave runes" (a literal translation

Plate 32 "Same-stave" or "bound" runes on the Sønder Kirkeby stone from Falster, Denmark. The main part of the inscription is of common commemorative type, but the "bound" (upside-down) runes say: *Þorr vigi runaʀ* 'Þorr hallow the runes'.

of Scandinavian *samstavsruner*/-*runor*) or "bound runes". They can make an inscription laborious to read, but are hardly cryptic. Very occasionally the branches of such runes are attached to the arms of a design resembling a St Andrew's cross. There are two sixth-century southern German manifestations (on a sword from Schretzheim and a fibula from Soest), and a late Viking-Age example from Ludgo, Södermanland, Sweden (Fig. 25; see also Fig. 27: iv), while from the Norwegian town of Tønsberg, Vestfold, comes a bone inscription

Fig. 25 "Same-stave" or "bound" runes attached to a St Andrew's cross design on the late Viking-Age Korpbron stone from Ludgo, Södermanland, Sweden. The runes have been read **siþiþur** and interpreted as *Siði Þorr* '?May Þorr safeguard'.

dated to the thirteenth century in which the branches of the runes are attached to a cross within a circle. The first two instances are hard to interpret, but the difficulty resides not in identifying the runes, but understanding what they say. That can often be the case with inscriptions of this early date written in plain runes.

Some rune-writers make use of abbreviation. The tenth-century Bække 2 commemorative stone from Jutland offers an illustrative example. It says: **hribnã:ktubi:kriukubþsi|aft:uibrukmþusin**. The name or names with which the text begins are uncertain, but it seems plausible most of the remainder is to be expanded: **k[i]ri[þ]ukub[l]þ[u]si|aft:uibrukm[u]þu[r]sin[a]**, i.e., *gærðu kumbl þøsi aft Viborg moður sina* 'made this monument after Viborg his/their mother'. Abbreviation seems to be limited to words easily recoverable from the context. Anyone familiar with the commemorative formula of Viking-Age stones would have had little trouble filling in the gaps as has been done here. Personal names will have needed more careful handling. Accordingly, *Viborg* has either been written out in full (with transposition of **ur**) or abbreviated in a way that would ensure it was still recognisable (**uibruk** for **uib[u]ruk**, with epenthetic vowel between /r/ and /k/ denoted). The opening **hribnã:ktubi**, too, may well have been clear enough to the contemporary reader, but the passing of some 1,000 years has rendered it obscure. Most modern readers have thought to see here the female name *Hrefna* and male *Tobbi*, connected by an abbreviated **[au]k** 'and', but some have argued for an abbreviation of the compound name *(H)rafnunga-tofi*, not least because a person so called features on two nearby rune-stones. The evidence of the inscription speaks against *(H)rafnungatofi*. If that is indeed what the writer intended he has done a poor job. Rather than abbreviating the name he has mangled it, and his verb form **kriu**, if that is indeed what it is, ends in *-u*, the 3rd person plural marker, suggesting a grammatical clash with the subject. In addition, we have to assume that **b** is twice used for [β] (rather than just once), an uncommon correlation in the Viking Age. All in all, the chances are that *Hrefna* and *Tobbi* are what was intended, and the carver thus only abbreviates where it will cause the reader little difficulty. That seems to be the general pattern of runic abbreviations, which makes it hard to regard the feature as a cryptic device (indeed the primary purpose, one would think, was to save space or effort). It is a different matter when scholars wrestling with troublesome sequences of runes conjure up abbreviations as a solution to their problems. Interpretations of this nature tend to assume a high level of ingenuity in writer and reader. But such desperate attempts to create sense where none seems to exist should be recognised for what they are. It is enough to refer to the **mknfsz** of the Maria Saaler Berg forgery, expanded into the fanciful text: *Mik Nefo sezo* 'Nefo sowed me [with runes]' (p. 139).

A more radical form of abbreviation is exemplified by an inscription (thirteenth-century or later) in Gol stave-church (Buskerud, Norway; now preserved in the Norwegian Folk Museum, Bygdøy, Oslo). Its sequence **ætþffssantætþffssant** appears at first glance incomprehensible, but closer consideration reveals that each of the runes stands for the initial character in the names of the Old Norwegian numerals 1–20: *æinn, tvæir, þrír, fjórir, fimm,* *seks, sjau, átta, níu, tíu,* and so on. Again, the procedure can scarcely qualify as cryptic. It is not hard to work out how the runes are to be understood, even for modern man. And such a stale recital scarcely calls for concealment – whatever the precise intent behind the carving. Use of single runes as abbreviations for words beginning with the sound they denote does not seem to be a particularly common practice in runic writing. However, as with less drastic abbreviation of the type discussed above, a good few interpretations have been offered that assume rune-writers regularly shortened words in this way. Stray **rs** are particularly exposed: given a helpful context, a lone **r** is readily assumed to stand for the appropriate form of 'runes', while two in succession in a Viking-Age or medieval inscription easily become *reist/risti rúnar* 'carved runes' in the minds of some runologists.

12.3 Cryptic inscriptions written with plain runes

Cryptic inscriptions may be written with ordinary runic characters. Encryption in such cases involves either transposition of the runes or a code in which one or more characters are substituted for the intended rune. A simple case of transposition (according to common opinion) is **lua** for presumed **alu** (pp. 30, 32) on two fourth-century arrow shafts from Nydam, Jutland. A more striking example comes from the tenth-century Rimsø stone, Jutland. Following what seems to be a standard formula commemorating a mother (parts of the inscription are lost), we have: **ikam:tsrau:mas:iþua***[, a sequence that does not look Scandinavian at all (certainly, no word can begin /tsr-/). However, if read backwards, the first part of this section metamorphoses into: **sam:uarst:maki** 'the worst for a son' Subjected to the same treatment, the remaining **iþua** becomes **auþi**, which has generally been expanded to **[t]auþi** 'death'. Further runes are missing after **iþua**, allowing broader scope for the imagination. One suggestion is that the lacuna contained the words *moður es,* giving a short piece of verse – or perhaps rhythmic prose: *Moður es dauði sæm værst megi* 'A mother's death is the worst [thing] for a son', with alliteration between *moður* and *megi* (pp. 81, 83).

The clearest and most famous examples of a runic substitution code occur on the ninth-century Rök stone from Östergötland, Sweden. In certain parts of the lengthy inscription that covers all five faces of this stone the intended rune is replaced by the one immediately preceding it in the *fuþark.* Knowledge of the procedure enables the reader to transform an unpromising sequence like **airfbfrbnhn**, for example, into **sakumukmini** (Fig. 26), a recurring phrase in the inscription, to be understood, perhaps, as *sagum ok minni* 'I/we also tell the ancient tale', or *sagum ungmænni* 'I/we tell the young men' (or yet something other). This type of substitution (well documented in roman-alphabet writing) can in theory follow any pattern. It may proceed in either direction, and by as many places in the *fuþark* as desired. If, for instance, single backward replacement as in the Rök example is chosen, intended **s** will be written **a**; with backward replacement by two or three places it will be written **i** or **n** respectively; and so on. Backward and forward replacement by one is attested in runic epigraphy; various interpretations involving forward and backward replacement by two or more places have been suggested, but few if any have won approval.

$$
\begin{array}{ccccccccccccccc}
f & u & þ & ã & r & k & h & n & i & a & s & t & b & m & l & ʀ \\
| & | & | & | & | & | & | & | & | & | & | & | & | & | & | & | \\
u & þ & ã & r & k & h & n & i & a & s & t & b & m & l & ʀ & f
\end{array}
$$

Fig. 26 A runic substitution code of a kind used on the early ninth-century Rök stone from Östergötland, Sweden. In the upper line are the runes to be written, in the lower the key to how they are to be read.

On an early or perhaps mid-thirteenth century runic stick from Bergen, Norway, we meet a different kind of substitution code. The inscription reads: **f:ff:fffo:oo:oooh:hh:hhha:aa:aaab:bb:bbb**. This is clearly an encrypted *fuþark* in which the first rune stands for itself, the second is represented by the first rune doubled, the third by the same rune trebled, the fourth by itself, the fifth by the fourth rune doubled, and so on, giving: **fuþorkhniastbml** (the final rune is lacking). The context of this particular inscription is perhaps teaching or learning (pp. 115–16), not of runes as such but of a relatively simple runic cipher.

12.4 Cryptic inscriptions written with cryptic (graphically deviant) runes

Writers sometimes disguise runes by changing their appearance. They accomplish this in different ways. In one passage on the Rök stone, for instance, the carver uses older-*fuþark* runes (some with aberrant forms) as replacements for equivalent characters of the younger *fuþark*. That we are dealing here with code and not a piece of older-*fuþark* writing is clear from the way the runes are deployed. For example, in the older system, Ⴖ stood for /u/ and ᛟ for /o/, ᚷ for /g/ and ᚲ for /k/; on Rök ᛟ is used in place of Ⴖ for both /o/ and /u/, ᚷ in place of ᚠ for both /g/ and /k/.

The author of one of the Maeshowe carvings (pp. 119–20) adopted a different strategy. His inscription consists in the main of otherwise unknown characters with something of the appearance of runes (Plate 33). ᚼ and ᛉ (characters 4–5) can be clearly recognised, both cut with double lines, and also ᚻ (character 18), but the other symbols require decipherment. The distribution of the last fifteen suggests **ræistrunarþïsar** *reist rúnar þessar* 'carved these runes', especially since the phrase (or variations on it) occurs so often in Maeshowe. The name of the person who carved the runes is then presumably to be found in the first five symbols. The second character, on the evidence of the rest of the inscription, might well stand for r, which, with plain **hr** as characters 4–5, gives the sequence *r*hr. Some have taken this as a way of writing *Tryggr* (though **h** for [g:] is scarcely otherwise documented). But there is of course no guarantee the double-lined **h** and **r** are plain runes: they may also be cryptic, especially in view of the suggestion that **r** has been given an encoded form in all other instances.

The intention behind the use of cryptic runes can be hard to discern. It

Plate 33 Inscription with a unique series of cryptic runes from Maeshowe, Orkney

doubtless varies from inscription to inscription. On the Rök stone it may be connected in some way with the content, but precisely how is unclear. In the case of the Maeshowe carving the intention was almost certainly to demonstrate runic versatility. There are other cryptic runes in the cairn (see below), as well as several unusual and embellished forms, and the standard of runic writing is generally high.

The most common of runic ciphers is based on a division of the *fuþark* into three groups. Such a division seems to go back as far as the older *fuþark*. The rune-row on the Vadstena bracteate, for example, is set out in three groups of eight (p. 17). However, no cryptic inscriptions are known based on an 8:8:8 division, although Continental manuscripts of the ninth to eleventh century (pp. 154–5) assume their existence. In Viking-Age and medieval Scandinavian tradition, where the *fuþark* consists of sixteen runes, there is normally one group of six followed by two of five, i.e. **fuþärk:hnias:tbmlʀ**, later **fuþork:hnias:tbmly** (pp. 93–4). The system works by substituting for plain runes characters in which the number of the group and the number of the rune within the group can be identified. Such characters are most commonly "twig-runes", composed by arranging twigs or branches on either side of a vertical, the total on one side denoting the group, that on the other position within the group. In Scandinavian epigraphic tradition group designation regularly precedes indication of position within it, and the groups seem always to be numbered in reverse order, **tbmlʀ/y** counting as the first, **fuþä/ork** as the third. Thus ᛏ, reading from left to right, gives group 1, position 2, and stands for **b**; ᛦ gives group 2, position 4, **a**; and ᛦ group 3, position 3 **þ**. Several ingenious alternatives to twig-runes are found, for example fishes with fins, men with beards, and, somewhat further removed, the writing of a particular rune once, twice or thrice to indicate group, followed by a different rune, or the same rune in slightly different form, one to six times to indicate position within the group.

Plate 34 Inscription with twig-runes from Maeshowe, Orkney

Plate 35 Bone from Schleswig, Germany, displaying a complete younger *fuþark* and a key to the 6:5:5 cipher

One of the Maeshowe carvers writes the phrase þisarrunar *þessar rúnar* 'these runes' using two varieties of twig-rune (Plate 34). On the Rök stone the cipher appears in four different guises (Fig. 27). Fishes' fins, men's beards and yet other realisations appear on runic sticks from Bergen (Figs 28–9). A key to the 6:5:5 cipher is found on a twelfth-century bone from Schleswig, northern Germany (Plate 35). This bears a complete sixteen-character *fuþark*, each of whose runes is preceded by a series of dots. By the top of **f** there are three dots in horizontal line following the direction of writing, by the top of **h** two, and by the top of **t** a single dot. Before each rune one or more dots are set vertically: one before **f**, two before **u**, and so on, rising to six before **k**; then one before **h**, rising to five before **s**; and finally one before **t**, rising to five before **R**. Clearly, the dots by the top of **f**, **h** and **t** indicate the number of the group they head, while those placed vertically before each rune denote its position within the group. While the Schleswig bone shows how the 6:5:5 cipher works, its exact purpose is unclear. It might have been carved as a memory aid, or perhaps as a tool for teaching the 6:5:5 cipher.

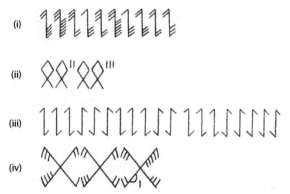

Fig. 27 Schematic representation of four different manifestations of the 6:5:5 cipher found on the early ninth-century Rök stone from Östergötland, Sweden. (i) reads:]2/4 3/6 3/2 1/3 3/2 3/6 1/3 2/3 2/2 2/3 (a few twigs lost through damage have been supplied) – transliterated:]akumukmini, undoubtedly **sakumukmini** (cf. p. 147; the initial rune has scaled off). (ii) reads 2/2 2/3, i.e. **ni**; this sequence is followed by a rune whose reading is uncertain, and it is unclear how the three characters are to be interpreted. (iii) reads 3/3 3/2 3/5 **þur**, by most taken as an invocation of the god Þorr. (iv) is most probably to be read clockwise, starting at the top left of each cross, giving: 3/2 1/4 2/2 2/3 3/5 3/2 **þR**, to be transliterated **ulniruþR**, interpreted by many as *ol nirøðR* 'begot as a nonagenarian'.

Fig. 28 The remains of a runic stick from Bryggen (Bergen), Norway, with the hairs of men's beards indicating the intended runes according to the 6:5:5 cipher. The runes read 2/5 2/3 1/3 1/4 2/3 1/2 2/3 2/5 2/3 2/2 3/2 – **simlibisinu**, *sem lífi sínu* 'as his/her life'.

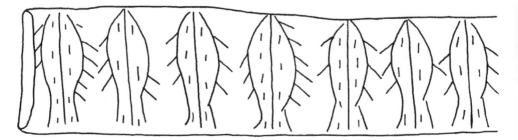

Fig. 29 Part of a runic stick from Bryggen (Bergen), Norway, with fishes' fins indicating the intended runes according to the 6:5:5 cipher. The runes read: 3/6 3/2 3/3 3/6 2/3 3/1 2/3 – **kuþkifi**, *Guð gefi* 'May God give ...' and the inscription continues, with different manifestations of the 6:5:5 cipher intermixed with the occasional plain rune: '... us a good wind and Mary [give us] good fortune'.

12.5 Final thoughts

There were without doubt more ways of encrypting runic inscriptions than those presented here. The problem is to distinguish the cryptic from doodling, failed demonstrations of literacy, decoration, and so on. Where we are faced with a sequence of runes that do not appear to record language, or a sequence of symbols that are only "rune-like", we have no way of knowing for sure what they represent unless and until we can interpret them. Recognisable patterns of distribution (as with the otherwise unknown characters in the Maeshowe inscription discussed above) lead one to suspect something meaningful; a confused jumble suggests no sense was intended; but we cannot be certain. Context is also important, as so often in runology.

Select reading list

MacLeod, Mindy 2002. *Bind-Runes: An Investigation of Ligatures in Runic Epigraphy* (Runrön 15). Uppsala: Institutionen för nordiska språk, Uppsala universitet, 265–89. [On complex runic shapes as encoding devices.]

McKinnell, John, and Simek, Rudolf (with Klaus Düwel) 2004. *Runes, Magic and Religion: A Sourcebook* (Studia Medievalia Septentrionalia 10). Vienna: Fassbaender, 26–30. [An outline account of cryptic inscriptions and cryptic runes.]

Moltke, Erik 1985. *Runes and their Origin: Denmark and Elsewhere*. Copenhagen: National Museum of Denmark, 132–4. [A brief survey of cryptic inscriptions and cryptic runes, but with total emphasis on the Scandinavian tradition.]

Page, R. I. 1999. *An Introduction to English Runes* (2nd ed.). Woodbridge: Boydell Press, 80–88. [A general account of cryptic inscriptions and cryptic runes with emphasis on the Anglo-Saxon tradition.]

13 *Runica manuscripta* and rune names

13.1 Introduction

The term *runica manuscripta* in its broadest sense refers to manuscripts that contain runes. Manuscript runes are by most runologists set apart from their epigraphic counterparts. That is because runic writing is in essence epigraphic and the presence of runes in manuscripts often reflects scholarly interest. Indeed, some argue that manuscript runes should be distinguished entirely from those in inscriptions and treated as a separate tradition. There are, however, points of contact between the two. (A minimal epigraphic example occurs in Corpus Christi College, Cambridge, MS 57, dating from the late tenth or early eleventh century. At the outer margin of one of its pages are two lines of runes cut in dry point, giving, *inter alia*,]auarþ, almost certainly the Norse personal name Hávarð(r).)

The rune names are almost exclusively preserved in manuscripts; hence their place in this chapter. In inscriptions they occur very sparingly (chiefly on Gotland where in late medieval times the perpetual calendar is occasionally used to specify particular years or dates and rune names can be used in place of the relevant characters; cf. pp. 114–15). There are nevertheless clear indications that rune-carvers knew the names and used them as a mnemonic tool – and sometimes for other purposes.

13.2 Runes in manuscripts

Manuscript runes appear in many guises. In Anglo-Saxon England, probably in the eighth century, þ and ƿ were incorporated into the version of the roman alphabet used for writing English in the cursive forms 'þ' and 'ƿ' (the latter sometimes open at the top, resembling 'y'). The purpose of the scribe or scribes who came up with this idea was probably to make the writing more precise, or at least more elegant. 'þ' furnishes a symbol for the dental spirants [θ] and [ð] (previously written either 'th' or 'd'), sounds which did not occur in Latin, and 'ƿ' for the rounded semi-vowel [w], which the Romans did not distinguish from [u]. These two cursive runes persisted in English writing well into the Middle English period, and were exported to Scandinavia. Both are found in the earliest (mid-twelfth century) Norwegian and Icelandic manuscripts ('ƿ' only sporadically in the latter), and 'þ' appears in a few early Swedish codices (dated shortly before or around 1300). 'þ' continued to be used in Norway until the late Middle Ages, and is still part of Icelandic orthography today; 'ƿ' disappeared from both Icelandic and Norwegian writing around 1300. The adoption of þ and ƿ to augment the roman alphabet suggests that some English scribes were familiar with runes as a practical, everyday script.

A few runes are used in manuscripts as abbreviations, where they represent the word that supplies their name. Abbreviation was a common scribal practice in the Middle Ages: it saved time and especially parchment, which was scarce and expensive. In English writing ᛗ may stand for the word or syllable *dæg*(-) 'day', ᛗ for *monn*(-) 'man'. The practice is particularly common in compounds, as *sunnan*ᛗ 'Sunday'. Such abbreviation can even occur where no English word or syllable is intended, as *Salo*ᛗ 'Solomon'. English scribes also use ᛟ *œþel* or *eþel* 'ancestral possession' 'land' and ᚹ *wynn* 'joy' to shorten the writing, though much less often than ᛗ or ᛗ. The Scandinavians wrote ᛦ for *maðr* 'man' (and very occasionally ᚠ for *fé* 'wealth'). ᛦ is found in Norwegian, Icelandic and Swedish manuscripts, and while the practice is almost certainly copied from the English, the rune form itself is Scandinavian. In Anglo-Saxon, Scandinavian and Continental manuscripts runes are sometimes used as reference marks, in place of roman letters or other signs.

Certain, mainly ninth-century, Continental manuscripts contain scribal signatures in runes sometimes accompanied by further text in the same script, often expressions of satisfaction or joy that the labour of copying has been completed. How close any of these scribes were to epigraphic runic tradition is unclear. Text additional to the signature tends to be written in Latin, and greek or other letters may be employed as well as runes. The likelihood is the runic symbols are taken from manuscript sources and that their function is purely ornamental. As an example we may cite the Latin text (from a south German manuscript, Munich Clm. 6250): **cundpato me parte scripsit in primis** 'Cundpato wrote me in part at the beginning'. The runes, which show some peculiarities, are probably derived from an Anglo-Saxon model; **e** is inexplicably replaced by roman 'e' in **me** (the scribe was clearly familiar with the relevant rune since he uses it in **parte**).

There exist a great many manuscripts in which runes are presented in one form or another. These go back as far as the eighth century, and continue into the nineteenth. The content is varied. We find lists of runes set out either in *fuþark* or roman-alphabet order, often with roman equivalents indicating their sound value. The rune names may also be included. Cryptic runes (cf. chapter 12) are sometimes discussed and exemplified. Rune forms and names may be garbled, which suggests writers at some remove from epigraphic tradition. The early manifestations of this rune-lore are found in Anglo-Saxon and Continental manuscripts, where the runes are mostly of Anglo-Saxon type. The appearance of Anglo-Saxon runes on the Continent has to do with English missionary activity and the loss of Continental traditions of runic writing in the seventh century (pp. 33–4). The earliest manuscript manifestations of the Scandinavian younger *fuþark* also come from Anglo-Saxon and Continental sources, the oldest of which is ninth-century. In Scandinavia itself manuscript writing was a late arrival. As elsewhere, it followed in the wake of Christianity, which in the course of the late tenth and eleventh century brought the roman alphabet, the Latin language, and European culture to the North. There are references to a runic tract from early twelfth-century Iceland, but many scholars have doubted whether such a work ever existed (see below). Be that as it may, the Icelanders exhibit a lively and abiding interest in runes. From the high Middle Ages and until long after the Reformation writers subject the script to a variety of treatments, some sober, some fanciful. They discuss the shapes, sound values, names, and uses of runes. A particular favourite is runic cryptography.

Much of the discussion of cryptography in Icelandic manuscripts, as in their Continental forerunners, concerns the runic cipher based on a division of the *fuþark* (*fuþorc/fuþork*) into groups (cf. 12.4). Interestingly, while the Icelandic material (operating with a *fuþork* of sixteen runes) largely agrees with known epigraphic practice in counting the groups backwards, with **fuþork** group 3, Anglo-Saxon and Continental tradition (operating with a *fuþorc* of twenty-eight runes or more) counts forwards, making **fuþorcgw** group 1.

It is hard to know what to make of this diverse collection of material. Clearly some writers and scribes considered runes a mere curiosity – one among a number of esoteric scripts. Their knowledge of runic writing may have been minimal or all but non-existent. Such collectors and transmitters of uncommon scripts could have developed traditions of their own, making it unwise for us to draw conclusions about runes and runic writing from sources of this kind. Yet there are points of contact between manuscript and epigraphic tradition. To take a pertinent example: an English manuscript of the early twelfth century (St John's College, Oxford, 17) contains a Scandinavian *fuþork* of twenty-three characters (surrounded by various exotic alphabets and rune-rows). There are indications this *fuþork* goes back to the eleventh century. It contains several dotted or barred runes, including **ẗ** and **b̈** (cf. p. 93), and it differentiates **a** and **æ**. These are developments that hardly appear in runic inscriptions (apart from **ẗ** and **b̈** on coins) until the twelfth century. It is difficult to believe that manuscript and epigraphic tradition here are unconnected. The uncertainty is how. We can probably dismiss the notion that the relevant characters were made up by a scribe and from there migrated into inscriptions. That does not chime with what we otherwise know of developments in runic writing. The far more plausible alternative is that a scribe was aware of the epigraphic use of such characters (whether in England or Scandinavia, or both), and incorporated them into his *fuþork*. If that is accepted, it has some bearing on the generally accepted chronology of the younger-*fuþark* expansions. Whichever view one takes, there are indications here of contact between manuscript and epigraphic tradition.

Rather different from the manuscript material so far presented is the discussion of the expanded younger *fuþark* as a representation of speech found in the thirteenth-century Icelandic work known as the *Third Grammatical Treatise*. This is one of four treatises on orthography, grammar and style appended to a fourteenth-century manuscript of the Icelandic historian Snorri Sturluson's treatise on poetics known as the *Prose Edda* (part of the *Third Grammatical Treatise* also exists in a copy dated to around 1300). According to a prologue that precedes the four grammatical treatises, a certain Þóroddr rúnameistari 'Þóroddr rune-master', together with the renowned early twelfth-century Icelandic scholar Ari the learned, instituted an expansion of the sixteen-character younger *fuþark*, or at least systematised and improved on existing expansions (the sense is not wholly clear). The obvious implication is that the thinking behind the additional characters (such as **t**, **k**, **↑**) presented and discussed in the *Third Grammatical Treatise* goes back to a tract compiled by Þóroddr and Ari. Though there are certain novelties in the *Treatise*, the relevant characters and their values cannot (in general, at least) be ascribed to Icelandic scholars of the early twelfth century since in most cases they reflect developments known from inscriptions that pre-date or are contemporary with the supposed runic reform. This suggests that Þóroddr and Ari's names were included in the prologue simply to lend weight to the runic section of the *Third Grammatical Treatise*. Whatever else, the author of the *Treatise*, by general agreement one Óláfr Þórðarson, had kept abreast of developments in runic writing, and clearly viewed the script as a practical Norse equivalent to the roman alphabet. Only in one case does he seem to misinterpret, or perhaps resort to invention. This concerns the form ⸕, which he claims denotes the diphthong *ey* or *æy*. In runic epigraphy ⸕ is almost always a variant of ᛁ **ï**, and it is possible Óláfr has been misled here by the use of ⸕ᛁ to denote the sequence [eyj-], in which the second element of the diphthong and the glide [j] are apparently marked by the single rune ᛁ. Yet there are two examples of the name Eyjólfr written ⸕ᛁᚤᚱ: one from the Maeshowe collection (mid-twelfth century, cf. pp. 119–20) and one on a runic stick from Bergen (late thirteenth-century). This may indicate that Óláfr was aware of a quite rare nuance of runic orthography, implying, in this instance at least, a relatively close connection between epigraphical and manuscript runes. Or it may simply reflect independent speculation, leading in Iceland to Óláfr's analysis, elsewhere to the sporadic occurrence of diphthongal ⸕ in inscriptions.

Manuscript runes occur in yet other contexts. Reference was made in 10.5 to two Old Danish manuscripts written entirely in runes. Nothing comparable is known from Anglo-Saxon England, but runes were sometimes used by English scribes to give prominence to individual letters. In the didactic poem *Solomon and Saturn I*, Solomon (one of the characters of the poem) portrays each letter of the Latin text of the Lord's Prayer, *Pater noster*, as a warrior fighting the enemy of mankind. Thus, 'P' '... keeps on beating the fell fiend', 'A' '... knocks him down too', and so on. In one of the two manuscripts of the poem (Corpus Christi, Cambridge, 422) the letters of the Prayer are given in runes as well as roman. In the *Exeter Book* (a manuscript of Old English Poetry), sequences of runes or individual runic characters are used to give cryptic clues to the meanings of a series of riddles. And the eighth-century poet Cyn(e)wulf uses runes to insert the letters of his name into certain verses, as a signature. Each rune stands for its name, and the words that supply the names form part of the text of the poem at the relevant points. In one case **cynwulf** appears as an anagram: distributed among the words of nine lines of verse are ᚠ ᚹ ᚢ ᛚ ᚲ ᛣ ᚾ **f w u l c y n**, the runes immediately preceded and followed by a point to set them off from the surrounding text.

A runic riddle is also found in the Icelandic *Bósa saga*, one of the mythical-heroic "sagas of ancient times". A troll-woman, concerned to save the lives of two captured heroes, recites a riddle to their captor, King Hringr. The king is either to solve the riddle or release the captives. Dire consequences are threatened in the event he fails to do either. The riddle consists of the runes ᚱ ᛆ ᚦ ᚴ ᛘ ᚢ **r a þ k m u** followed six **i**s, six **s**s, six **t**s, six more **i**s and six **l**s. The troll-woman asks for the names of six men, hidden in the runes. The king is unable to solve the riddle and agrees to let the captives go. The solution that evaded him seems to be to add **istil** to each of the first six runes, giving **ristil, aistil, þistil**, etc. The clue is in the numbers – six initial runes and six of each of the others. There is epigraphic evidence for the existence of this riddle stretching back well into the Viking Age. On the late ninth- or early tenth-century Gørlev stone from Zealand, Denmark, and the eleventh-century Ledberg stone from Östergötland, Sweden (Plate 36), we find the following sequence: **þmkiiissstttiiilll**. Borgund stave-church, Sogn og Fjordane, Norway, offers a solution in the form of the following inscription (end of twelfth century or later) carved into a plank in the gallery that runs round the outside of the church: **tistilmistil ok*nþiriþiþistil** '?, mistletoe, and the third: thistle'. No word *tistil* is known in Old Norwegian, and with the evidence for **þmk** from the two rune-stones and (in different order) from the riddle in *Bósa saga*, we may perhaps assume that some confusion in the tradition led to the replacement of *kistill* by *tistill*. That gives *þistill, mistill, kistill* 'thistle', 'mistletoe', 'little box' as the common elements of the formula, which some scholars have sought to connect with ancient burial rites. The grounds are largely contextual – the occurrence of the formula in memorial inscriptions and on the outside of a church in an area possibly used for the burial of aborted foetuses. This is all rather speculative, however, and the role the plants and the 'little box' might have played in the rites is obscure. What the occurrence of the formula does demonstrate is a further connection between epigraphic and manuscript runes.

13.3 Rune names

As outlined in 3.4, runes had names (or more precisely, perhaps, designations). Whatever their significance otherwise, these must have served to indicate the sound-value of each rune, not least because, with few exceptions, the initial sound of the name appears to have coincided with the value (in the case of the multifunctional runes of the sixteen-character younger *fuþark* with the original value). ᚠ, for example, was called *feoh* in Old English, *fé* in Old Norse, and denoted /f/, ᚢ was called *ur/úr* and denoted /u/ (in the younger *fuþark* other rounded vowels as well), and so on. This is known as the acrophonic principle. The way of dealing with sounds that never occurred in initial position seems to have been to incorporate them into the middle or end of the name.

The evidence for the rune names and their meanings is not as clear and straightforward as some accounts imply. Most of it comes from manuscripts rather than inscriptions. These hardly go back further than the ninth century, and appear in the majority of cases to have been compiled by scribes without practical experience of runic writing. A consequence of the relatively late transmission is that we have no record of the names of the older-*fuþark* runes. These have to be reconstructed on the basis of Anglo-Saxon and medieval Scandinavian tradition. In the case of the eight runes that were lost from the *fuþark* in Scandinavia, we have only the Anglo-Saxon attestations to guide us.

The most useful sources for the Anglo-Saxon rune names include three ninth-century manuscripts, two of *c.* 900 and 1000 respectively, and the early twelfth-century St John's College, Oxford, 17 referred to on p. 155 above.

Plate 36 The Ledberg stone, Östergötland, Sweden,
showing the sequence **þmkiiissstttiiilll**

These set out the Anglo-Saxon runes in *fuþark* order (more or less) together with their names, and sometimes their values (expressed by giving the roman equivalent, e.g. ᚾ u). The number of runes (and variant forms) included in the rows can vary, and the manuscripts do not always agree about the names of particular runes (or variants), but comparison between the texts can facilitate the identification of scribal error and confusion. An important further source is the so-called Anglo-Saxon *Rune Poem*, which in twenty-nine stanzas of (riddling) alliterative verse defines the Anglo-Saxon rune names. Each stanza begins with a rune and its name, and the immediately following lines expound the meaning of the name, as (in modern English translation):

> '*ᚠ feoh* [wealth] is a comfort to all men. Yet every man must give it away readily if he wants to gain glory before the Lord.'

The *Poem* survives only in printed form, in George Hickes's *Thesaurus* (1705). The text is based on a transcription made in the early 1700s from a manuscript of *c.* 1000, the relevant part of which was destroyed by fire in 1731. Some of the printed text (which contains extraneous material) seems to stem from more than one source, and deserves to be treated with caution, but scholars have found no reason to doubt the Anglo-Saxon pedigree of the *Rune Poem*.

The names of the sixteen Scandinavian runes are first attested in a handful of manuscript sources dated between the late ninth and early twelfth century (some preserved only in more recent transcripts). Here, too, the runes are listed together with their names, and sometimes their values. Once again, the number of runes can vary, and there can be disagreement about the names of certain characters, in particular their precise form. However, if all these sources are compared, a reasonably unified picture of the sixteen Scandinavian rune names emerges. There also exist an Icelandic and a Norwegian *Rune Poem*, which like their Anglo-Saxon counterpart expound the sense of the names in riddling verses (there is even a comparable Swedish "poem", recorded in a letter from the end of the sixteenth century, but it adds little to our understanding of the rune names and their development). The oldest version of the Icelandic *Poem* is from the fifteenth century and does not include the names themselves. The Norwegian *Poem* survives in three seventeenth-century versions: two transcripts, and one printed text derived from a lost manuscript (all three versions in fact probably derive from the same medieval original). The transcripts do not include the rune names; the printed text has them, but they may well owe their inclusion in this edition to the compiler. In spite of the late date at which the Icelandic and Norwegian *Rune Poem*s are preserved, there is reason to believe they go back to a much earlier period – or at least that the material in them does (see below). They differ in form from the Old English *Poem*, and from each other, as the two following examples illustrate. First is the Icelandic then the Norwegian *Poem*'s treatment of **f** (in English translation).

> '*ᚠ* [wealth] is family strife and men's delight and grave-fish's path.'

> '*ᚠ* [wealth] causes strife among kinsmen; a wolf is reared in the forest.'

The Icelandic *Poem* presents the meaning of the name in the form of three "kennings" (poetic circumlocutions – the last, 'grave-fish's path', is somewhat obscure, at least to the modern reader). The Norwegian *Poem* offers a kenning-like clue to the sense of the name, followed by a second line that alliterates and rhymes with the first (*fé veldr frænda rógi / fœðist ulfr í skógi*), but has no obvious semantic connection with it. Each *Poem* follows the pattern established in verse 1 throughout (although the Icelandic variant has a few two-kenning stanzas).

At this point it must be stressed that the texts of the Icelandic and Norwegian *Rune Poem* normally presented to readers are the products of heavy editorial intervention (which may include normalisation of the spelling, as above). The manuscript versions (which here includes the seventeenth-century printed text of the Norwegian *Poem*) differ somewhat or considerably among themselves. The discrepancies between the three versions of the Norwegian *Poem* are mainly orthographical (one reason for thinking they derive from a common original) – though not entirely. The Icelandic *Poem* exhibits wide differences of wording. The second kenning of the **f**-stanza, for example, can appear as *flæðar viti* 'flood-tide's beacon' (fire glinting in the water is an image of gold), and in an eighteenth-century version as *Fáfnis bani* 'death of Fáfnir' (with oblique reference to Germanic myth concerning the Nibelungen treasure, in pursuit of which Fáfnir was slain). There are also differences in the order of the kennings in individual stanzas of the Icelandic *Poem*, and the order in which the runes are listed can vary in both (though affecting only **ml/lm** in the Norwegian versions; cf. p. 96).

These disparities may be due to copyists, who have over time altered a medieval original. But it is also possible – perhaps likely – that there never was a single original text of either *Poem*. From Bø church, Telemark, Norway, comes a runic inscription (to be dated perhaps *c.* 1200), which begins **suæfnbanarmïr** *Svefn bannar mér* 'prevents me sleeping'. There follow six kennings, identical in import to six of those in the Icelandic *Rune Poem* but with slightly or completely different wording. The third, by way of example, is *fjalls íbúi* 'mountain dweller', which can be compared with the *kletta íbúi* 'cliff dweller' on which the Icelandic versions of the *Poem* mostly agree. Both *fjalls íbúi* and *kletta íbúi* are kennings for 'giant', Old Norse *þurs*, the name of **þ**. Taken in order and interpreted in this way, the six kennings spell **kuþrun**, the female name *Guðrún*. The inscription ends with the words *Þat skulu ráða* '[people] will have to interpret it'. What the carver is thus saying is that (the thought of) Guðrún prevents him sleeping, but to find the message the reader will have to work out the puzzle. This important inscription indicates that medieval rune-carvers were familiar with a tradition by which rune names could be described in riddling ways. Comparison of its text with those of the *Rune Poems* also suggests that the form of the riddles could vary. The different versions of the Icelandic and Norwegian *Poems* may thus reflect diverse oral traditions rather than gradual alteration by copyists. This could apply equally to differences between the Scandinavian *Poems* and the English. One can envisage a world in which a large and varied stock of rune-lore circulated orally among rune-carvers, regularly subject to change and innovation. Much of what has come down to us in manuscripts and early printed books could then be viewed as a random sample. A further important feature of the Bø inscription is the additional link it establishes between epigraphic and manuscript runes.

There is some epigraphic evidence for rune names, direct and indirect. On one or two loose objects from medieval Norway personal names are written with the relevant rune names taking the place of the runes themselves, as *ár sól maðr úr nauð Týr reið* for *Ásmundr* on a stick from Bergen (undated, since the find information is lost). In 7.2 (see especially pp. 57–8) arguments were advanced in favour of a close connection between a rune's name and its sound value. Here we may take as an example the original twelfth rune, which denoted /j/, but in Scandinavia came to denote /a/ instead. The English and Scandinavian evidence is unanimous that the name of this rune was 'year'. That suggests a form **jāra* for the earliest Scandinavian, which with the loss of initial /j-/ in the North will have changed to *ár(a)* – a development that corresponds well with the change in the rune's sound value. Further epigraphic evidence for rune names comes from their occasional use as ideographs. Now and again, it seems, carvers would let runes stand for their name instead of the sound they normally represented. The Stentoften inscription (p. 25) supplies a convincing example, with ᚼ denoting not /j/ or /a/ but **(j)āra* '(good) year' 'good harvest', and there are perhaps one or two other fairly clear-cut cases of such usage, but many of the claims made for the occurrence of ideographs appear speculative. As we have seen, however (pp. 153–4), manuscript usage offers supporting evidence, with Anglo-Saxon ᛗ, ᛉ, ᛟ, ᚹ representing *monn*, *dæg*, *æþel/eþel*, *wynn* respectively, and Scandinavian ᛦ, ᚡ standing in for *maðr, fé*.

This is, in outline, the testimony on which our knowledge of the rune names is based (on the "gothic letter names", see p. 21). One important point to emerge is that there are eight instances of etymological and (basic) semantic correspondence between the Anglo-Saxon and Scandinavian rune names:

OE	ON	
feoh	fé	'wealth'
rad	reið	'riding' 'ride'
hægl	hagall	'hail'
nyd	nauðr	'need' 'affliction'
is	íss	'ice'
ger	ár	'(good) year'
mann/monn	maðr	'man' 'human'
lagu	lǫgr	'water' 'liquid'

The agreement here points to a common origin and thus to the antiquity of the rune names (unless we are to assume the one tradition was heavily influenced by the other – for which there is no evidence).

The other eight runes found in both the Anglo-Saxon and Scandinavian rune-rows have names that do not correspond quite so neatly. In four cases there is complete or partial correspondence of form but not of meaning:

OE		ON		
ur	'aurochs'	úr	'drizzle' (Icel.)	'slag' (Nw.)
os	'mouth'	óss	'god' (Icel.)	'river mouth' (Nw.)
tir	'guiding star'	Týr	'the god Týr'	
beorc	'?poplar'	bjarkan	'birch-twig'	

To enter into detailed discussion about the relationship of these names would lead too far in the present context. Suffice to say: of **u**, that **ūruz* 'aurochs' is the preferred candidate for the earliest name on the grounds that the extinction of this animal from northern Europe led to the adoption of replacement names (further: that Norwegian *úr* may originally have meant 'sparks' – the "drizzle" from hot iron); of **o**, that 'god' is presumed to have been the sense of the earliest name because Icelandic *óss* comes from older *ǫ́ss/ǻss*, which in turn come from early Scandinavian **ansuz* 'god', a suitable name for a rune that originally denoted /a/; of **t**, that the Germanic rune name is almost universally taken to be that of the god Týr, but on differing and sometimes rather uncertain grounds; of **b**, that some form of a name for 'birch', or part of that tree, is likely to underlie the extant attestations – notwithstanding the difficulty that one of the Anglo-Saxon *Rune Poem*'s definitions of the name ('without seeds it produces shoots') cannot apply to a birch.

s seems to have had a name meaning 'sun' in Germanic, but the English and Scandinavian traditions disagree about the form of the name – OE *sigel*, ON *sól*; attempts have been made, not entirely successful, to trace both words back to a common ancestor.

Although younger-*fuþark* ᛦ **R** is clearly derived from the fifteenth rune of the older *fuþark* (ᛉ **z**), the name given to it in Norse sources, *ýr* 'yew' 'bow', may be cognate with the name of the thirteenth character (ᛇ) of the Anglo-Saxon *fuþorc*, *eoh/ih* 'yew' (< **īwaz*??) – one of the runes lost in Scandinavia. In a few Scandinavian inscriptions, however, ᛦ denotes [e] or [æ], which has led some to propose the name **elgʀ* or **ælgʀ* (as an alternative to **eʀ/*æʀ*, the suggested eastern Scandinavian cognates of *ýr*), derived from **algiz* 'elk', cognate with OE *eolh*, which may have been an earlier name of the fifteenth rune in the Anglo-Saxon *fuþorc* (rather than the attested *eolhx*, *iolx*, etc., the *x* of which seems to have been added when ᛉ was adopted as the runic equivalent of roman 'x').

þ is called *þurs* 'giant' in Old Norse, but *ðorn/þorn* 'thorn' in Old English. Some scholars have argued that OE 'thorn' is a replacement for 'giant', the latter having too many pagan associations for the christianised English. It is true that giants play a part in Norse heathen mythology, and perhaps that was also the case in the mythology of the pre-Christian Anglo-Saxons, but it is still hard to see why a word meaning 'giant' should be considered so irredeemably pagan it had to be replaced by the innocuous 'thorn'. On the other hand, the Anglo-Saxon *Rune Poem*'s definition of *ðorn/þorn* is relatively unspecific and could, with slightly different wording, be applied to 'giant' – which might imply that this was the original designation.

k is named *cen* in Old English, a word not otherwise found in the language, but interpretable as 'torch' from its *Runic Poem* definition, and from the apparent Old High German cognate *chien, ken* 'pine-torch'. In Old Norse **k** has the name *kaun* 'boil' 'sore'. It is impossible to determine which of these names, if either, is derived from a putative Germanic original.

Given the extent of the disagreement between the Old English and Norse sources, the reconstruction from English evidence alone of the Germanic names of the eight runes lost from the Scandinavian row is a hazardous undertaking (cf. above on the apparent mix-up between the names of the thirteenth and fifteenth rune). There is perhaps a modicum of indirect evidence from Scandinavia if we believe that sound changes affecting certain rune names curtailed the usefulness of the runes to which the names belonged and ultimately led to their demise (cf. pp. 57–8). The Old English name for ᛗ **e**, for example, was *eh*, suggesting an earlier form *ehwaz*, which in Scandinavian would have developed to *jóʀ*, perhaps leading to a situation where ᛗ could no longer be used by Scandinavian carvers to denote /e/. But there is a good deal of hypothesis here, and the danger of circular reasoning (ᛗ was probably lost because its name changed from *ehwaz* to *jóʀ*; because ᛗ was lost its name is likely to have suffered drastic sound change). It seems relatively uncontroversial to reconstruct Germanic *dagaz* on the basis of OE *dæg* 'day', given the existence of rune names like 'year' and 'sun'. At the other end of the spectrum is OE *peorð*. The word is otherwise unattested in Old English and the verse defining its meaning (partially defective) too vague to be of much help. OE *gyfu, wynn, Ing, eþel/œþel* – together with cognates in other Germanic languages – suggest the respective Germanic etymons *gebō, *wunjō, *ingwaz, *ōþila*, but whether all four names really do go back to Germanic, and whether they were the only names applied to the relevant runes, we cannot know for sure.

Using the supposed original names of the runes (pp. 21–2), some imaginative scholars have tried to reconstruct a primitive Germanic cosmology or belief system. Their more conservative colleagues, on the other hand, tend merely to suggest the names represent areas of life important to the early Germanic peoples: natural phenomena, objects of veneration, aspects of human existence. Given our uncertainty about the earliest names and the period and manner of their creation, it is unlikely any attempt to "interpret" them will have the power to convince.

Select reading list

Barnes, Michael P. 1994. *The Runic Inscriptions of Maeshowe, Orkney* (Runrön 8). Uppsala: Institutionen för nordiska språk, Uppsala universitet, 48–53. [On ᚦ and its possible values in Maeshowe inscription no. 2.]

Derolez, R. 1954. *Runica Manuscripta: The English Tradition* (Rijksuniversiteit te Gent: Werken uitgegeven door de Faculteit van de Wijsbegeerte en Letteren 118). Brugge: "De Tempel".

Page, R. I., and Hagland, Jan Ragnar 1998. 'Runica manuscripta and runic dating: the expansion of the younger fuþąrk'. In: (Audun Dybdahl and Jan Ragnar Hagland, eds) *Innskrifter og datering/Dating Inscriptions* (Senter for middelalderstudier, Skrifter 8). Trondheim: Tapir, 55–71.

Page, R. I. 1999. *An Introduction to English Runes* (2nd ed.). Woodbridge: Boydell Press, 60–79, 186–99. [On the rune names, the Anglo-Saxon runic poem, and the occurrence of runes in Anglo-Saxon manuscripts.]

Page, R. I. 1999. *The Icelandic Rune-Poem.* London: Viking Society for Northern Research (earlier published in *Nottingham Medieval Studies* 42, 1998, 1–37).

Page, R. I. 2003. 'On the Norwegian Rune-poem'. In: (Wilhelm Heizmann and Astrid van Nahl, eds) *Runica – Germanica – Mediaevalia* (Ergänzungsbände zum Reallexikon der Germanischen Altertumskunde 37). Berlin/New York: de Gruyter, 553–66.

Raschellà, Fabrizio D. 1993. 'Grammatical treatises'. In: (Phillip Pulsiano and Kirsten Wolf, eds) *Medieval Scandinavia: An Encyclopedia.* New York/London: Garland Publishing, 235–7. [A brief introduction to the four Icelandic grammatical treatises.]

Thompson, Claiborne W. 1978. 'The runes in *Bósa saga ok Herrauðs*', *Scandinavian Studies* 50, 50–56.

14 The making of runic inscriptions

14.1 Introduction

As is clear from many of the preceding chapters, runes are found carved into a variety of materials – chiefly, however, stone, wood, bone, and metal. There exist no accounts of the tools or carving techniques used in the making of runic inscriptions, so our conception of the processes involved is based largely on evidence derived from the inscriptions themselves (with a little help from preserved tools, medieval drawings and modern experimentation). "Carve" as used here and widely throughout the book is to be understood as a generic term covering different methods of incising lines and points into materials of varying hardness. It does not necessarily imply the use of a knife.

14.2 Inscriptions in stone

Most studied have been runic carvings in stone – the Viking-Age rune-stone in particular, and also the early medieval grave-slab. The general consensus seems to be that the tools employed were primarily hammer and/or mallet and different types of chisel. Certainly, chisel marks have frequently been identified in the grooves of runes. One runologist has argued strongly for the use of the pick hammer, an implement with one or two pointed ends used for cutting directly into the surface of a stone. However, this claim has been rejected on practical grounds. While the pick hammer might well have been suitable for hewing out large surfaces (as, for example, in relief carving), it would have been difficult to use it to incise thin, even lines. Apart from hammer, mallet and chisels, punches seem sometimes to have been employed. It is at least hard to think that neatly rounded dots of the kind found, for example, in the separators and some branch ends of the Inchmarnock cross inscription (Strathclyde, Scotland, perhaps early eleventh-century; Plate 37) can have been made by a chisel. Many stone inscriptions are so weathered that all traces of the tools used to carve them have been obliterated.

How the production of a Viking-Age rune-stone proceeded from conception to finished product has been much discussed. A possible scenario is the following. A relative of the deceased commissioned the monument from a craftsman, suggesting roughly or precisely what he wanted the text on it to say. The commissioner (or in some cases perhaps the craftsman) sought out a suitable stone. The stone was transported either to a workshop or a location specified by the commissioner and laid on the ground, whereupon the craftsman sketched in the design using a substance such as charcoal that could subsequently be washed off. He then lightly incised the lines he wanted to carve before setting to work in earnest. Finally, the completed monument was transported to its ultimate destination (if not already there), raised up and embedded in the ground. This may be an accurate account of how things were sometimes done, but it leaves out much, and the emphasis is firmly on *sometimes*.

Plate 37 The Inchmarnock cross fragment, Strathclyde, Scotland

The availability of stonemasons and their ability to carve runic texts must have varied greatly. In parts of late Viking-Age Sweden there is good evidence for the existence of workshops – of groups of craftsmen acting together, with several often involved in the production of an individual runic monument. Not only, for example, might ornament and runic inscription be made by different people, the inscription itself seems sometimes to have been the work of more than one carver. The fact that a rune-stone is "signed" (pp. 68, 81) does not therefore necessarily mean it was made from start to finish by a single person, any more than, say, Rembrandt was necessarily the sole painter of a "Rembrandt", or Ford cars were made by Henry Ford himself. What the signature may instead imply is that the inscription was produced by a workshop that the individual named as the carver ran. In areas with few preserved Viking-Age rune-stones, such as Norway, it is hard to envisage groups of craftsmen devoted solely or chiefly to the production of runic monuments. More likely, stonemasons engaged on other work turned their hand to the carving of monuments as the need arose. That may well sometimes have been the case in the rune-stone rich areas of Sweden and Denmark too. There is evidence that certain Swedish workshops produced both grave-slabs and rune-stones (which may thus to some extent have been contemporary; cf. however p. 100), and that these workshops developed in connection with ecclesiastical centres, where stonemasons would have been in demand, literacy common, and liturgical knowledge (for the formulation of prayers, cf. p. 71) readily available.

Decisions about the final wording of rune-stone texts must to some extent have depended upon who had the ability to read and write. Where the commissioner of a runic monument was literate, he or she may well have written down the precise text they wanted ready for the stonemason to copy. Where that was not the case, the mason would presumably either have had the necessary competence or have been able to seek help from his fellow workers or elsewhere. There are apparent exceptions, however. Some rune-stones carry texts that do not seem to be cryptic and are yet uninterpretable, or partly so. The eleventh-century Hjälsta inscription, Uppland, Sweden, provides an example. It runs: **fast…ʀ:þuliak:oaʀtþiol:atiurai:fasatiʀ:þaloi:oaʀfsai**, a sequence that hardly contains a recognisable Scandinavian word. Attempts have been made to find a hidden message here, not least because the inscription is otherwise competently executed, but none has proved successful. In this and similar cases we are likely to be dealing with a carver who knew runes but had little or no understanding of how to use them to write language (and was unable to seek help, or disinclined to do so). Such "nonsense" inscriptions also seem to presuppose a commissioner who was illiterate and thus unable to check the wording. Even comprehensible commemorative texts can exhibit great variation in orthography, and there has been considerable discussion about the strategies their carvers adopted in moving from speech to writing. Some have assumed the existence of an orthographical norm of sorts, but it is hard to see how such a norm would have been imposed, and the variation attested hardly lends credence to the idea. Others have urged, in stark contrast, that composers of runic commemorative texts simply followed their own pronunciation. This assumes an ability to undertake rudimentary phonetic analyses that many may not have possessed, but perhaps some of the more unlikely spellings encountered (e.g. **istn, itin, stnia, stun** for /stæin/ or /ste:n/) are simply evidence of a lack of phonetic awareness. A further hypothesis is that rune-stone writers – and others who wrote in runes – copied existing spellings of at least the more common words, and from the understanding they thus gained of the relationship between speech and writing, went on to tackle the less common items.

Sometimes, it seems, stone raiser and carver were one and the same. That, at least, is the most obvious interpretation of a text such as: *Suni retti stæin ok gjærði bro æftiʀ Sigbjarn ok Þjagn. Suni risti* 'Suni raised the stone and made a bridge after Sigbjarn and Þjagn. Suni carved' (Lunda kyrka, Uppland, Sweden, eleventh century). Introductory formulas of the type 'NN carved runes after

Plate 38   The Högby stone, Östergötland, Sweden. The runes tend to become more cramped as the inscription proceeds, and the final **naʀ** of the word **runaʀ** 'runes' is placed outside the main design.

MM' have been thought to imply that the raiser did the carving him- or herself too, but that is perhaps less assured. It is true that many rune-stone texts state specifically 'NN *had* the stone raised', but absence of the phrase 'had raised' 'caused to be raised' need not perhaps automatically be taken to mean that raiser and carver were the same person. People today may say: "I cut my hair" or "I built a house", without meaning literally they performed the tasks themselves, and similar modes of expression doubtless existed in times past. A few Viking-Age runic monuments proclaim the runes to have been carved by a named individual who was in the service of the deceased. This is probably to be taken at face value, especially if the erection of the monument is separately attributed to close relations of the person commemorated, as on the Glavendrup stone from Fyn, Denmark (pp. 75–7; Plate 11), part of which runs: *Alla syniʀ gærðu kumbl þausi aft faður sinn, auk hans kona aft ver sinn. En Soti ræist runaʀ þassi aft drottin sinn* 'Alli's sons made this monument after their father, and his wife after her husband. But Soti carved these runes after his lord'. Soti may of course have been an accomplished stoneworker as well as one of Alli's retainers: the Glavendrup runes certainly suggest a practised hand.

As noted above, it is assumed rune-stones were normally laid flat on the ground to be carved. This is far easier than working on a raised stone – and an approach from different directions may in part explain the not uncommon confusion of ᛏ and ᛐ. Nevertheless, not all monumental stone inscriptions were carved into flat surfaces or transportable pieces of stone. Some are found on huge boulders, others on bedrock or cliff-faces, and these must have been carved at whatever angle the face presented to the rune-writer.

Evidence for the sketching in of inscription and ornament lies to some extent in the finished products themselves. Without a preliminary drawing, it is hard to see how carvers could have achieved the evenness and symmetry exhibited by many runic monuments. Yet not all appear to have been planned, or not very thoroughly at least. Runes may, for example, be well spaced out at the beginning of an inscription, but become more and more cramped towards the end (Plate 38). And/or the carver may simply run out of space and have to place the final runes outside the main design (Plate 38). Occasionally he may misspell a word and correct it (Plate 39), or forget a word completely and add it later (Plate 12). Neither of these latter phenomena, though, need imply the inscription was made without a preliminary sketch, since the mistake can go back to the drawing. There is some direct evidence that incisions might first be made lightly and subsequently opened out. A runic cross from Thurso, Highland, Scotland (probably eleventh-century), exhibits what appear to be the remains of layout lines, and there are a few rune-stone inscriptions from Scandinavia suggestive of the same. A different – yet similar – case is the Ingla boulder (Uppland, Sweden), whose inscription appears never to have been finished: runes and ornament are very shallow or only faintly outlined. (On the colouring of runic monuments, see p. 81.)

By no means all runic inscriptions in stone are monumental. A fair number of the many medieval runic graffiti are carved into rocks or stone buildings (see 10.4). The making of such inscriptions must often have involved different

Plate 39 Part of the Iona cross slab, Argyll, Scotland, with **brþu** apparently corrected to **bruþ** in the word **bruþur** 'brother'

techniques from the production of formal monuments. For one thing, people killing time while resting, waiting, or sheltering from a storm, would not necessarily have had ready access to hammers, mallets and chisels. They would have used any sharp implement they had to hand (with little regard for the type of stone that confronted them). The Maeshowe inscriptions from Orkney (pp. 119–20) bear witness to a variety of both implements and carving techniques, though without the use of specialist technology it is hard to say with assurance how any one of them was made. Most appear to have been scratched with a sharp implement, probably the blade and point of a knife (the stone is for the most part quite soft). Some incisions were almost certainly opened out by running the implement over the initial furrow several times. Cutting appears mostly to have been top-to-base, but there is some evidence of base-to-top direction (particularly where lines are opened out). One inscription consists of a sequence of verticals and very little else, suggesting perhaps that carvers sometimes incised their verticals first, with distinguishing features to be added afterwards. Maeshowe inscription no. 20 claims it was carved 'with the axe, which Gaukr Trandilsson [an Icelandic saga figure] owned', and many scholars have taken this statement at face value, one even attributing the straightness, evenness and regularity of the lines of the runes to the use of an axe with a long handle. However, simple experimentation indicates that the closer one can get to the surface of a stone, the easier it is by and large to achieve the shapes one wants; a long handle is no advantage. The claim that the inscription was made with a famous axe is probably no more than an empty boast; or it may simply reflect the same jocular spirit as much of the Maeshowe corpus.

14.3 Inscriptions in wood and bone

Most runic inscriptions in wood and bone come from the Middle Ages. Whether this reflects changes in writing practices or the vagaries of preservation is uncertain. The tool used for carving runes in these materials – at whatever period – is commonly described as a "sharp implement", which is a cautious way of saying "knife", since knives were the principal "sharp implements" in common use. Knives could of course vary widely in size and shape, affecting the appearance of any carving made with them.

The technique of cutting runes with a knife has been the subject of some experimentation, but there has been little published discussion. As part of an account of two ninth- or early tenth-century runic sticks, and a runic peg of similar age, excavated from Hedeby (Schleswig, medieval Denmark, now northern Germany), a carving technique is described capable of replicating the lines and points found in the inscriptions. Assuming a right-handed carver, part of the handle and most of the blade of the knife is gripped by the four fingers of the right hand, the sharp edge of the blade turned towards the thumb. The stick is held by the thumb, index, middle and ring finger of the left hand and rests on the thumb of the right. The point of the knife and the front of the blade protrudes from between the thumb and index finger of the right hand, from which position both parts can be used for carving, the blade producing a thin cut, the point and thicker top edge a broader one (Plate 40).

Plate 40 Cutting runes into a stick with a knife

Lines, straight or curved, require relatively even pressure, whereas points are made by pushing the knife deep into the wood. This is of course merely a suggested technique, and we have no way of demonstrating that that is how the Hedeby objects, or any runic artefacts of wood or bone, were in fact carved. The likelihood is that techniques varied from person to person and from situation to situation. Some runic inscriptions are found on quite thick lumps of wood, and many are cut into wooden walls. Bones rarely have the flatness and evenness of a runic stick, and their curves and ridges clearly often caused rune-carvers difficulty.

14.4 Inscriptions in metal

Runic inscriptions occur in a variety of metals, and range from the carefully engraved to the crudely scratched. Other techniques are also found (see below).

As with inscriptions in wood and bone, scholars are generally cautious about identifying the tool or tools used to carve runes into metal. "Sharp implements" are mentioned, and, a little more specifically, "metalworkers' tools", though that can cover a wide range of objects, from punches via hammer and chisel to gravers. The methods used will have varied according to the aims of the carver, the hardness of the metal and the situation. The inscription on the third-century Næsbjerg silver and bronze fibula (brooch) from western Jutland, for example, seems to have been part of the design, and was thus presumably made by a metalworker in a workshop. The runes are executed in so-called "tremolo" style, done with a sharp punch that is moved forward with a rocking or "trembling" action, producing a kind of zig-zag pattern. In many cases runic texts seem to have been added to a metal object long after its manufacture, as in the case of the Hunterston (Strathclyde, Scotland) and Penrith (Cumbria, England) silver brooches. The Hunterston brooch is dated stylistically to the late seventh or eighth century, whereas the runic inscription that now decorates part of its hoop, **malbriþaastilk:** 'Melbrigða owns ?', can hardly be older than the tenth. The Penrith brooch is dated to the late ninth or early tenth century and need not in theory be much older than the inscription – an almost complete sixteen-rune *fuþark* – but the runes show little sign of wear or abrasion and were thus probably carved when the brooch was no longer in everyday use. It is difficult to detect in either of these cases what kind of tool was used, but it is likely to have been whatever sharp implement was at hand – possibly some kind of knife. A Kufic coin from Hoen, Buskerud, Norway, one item in a large hoard of coins and jewellery discovered in the early nineteenth century, bears a brief runic inscription – **laku** '?long ago' – clearly cut with a knife. The coins in the hoard had been converted into jewellery, and some bear ornamental pattern graffiti – cut (almost certainly) with silver- or goldsmiths' engraving tools.

The Forsa iron door-ring (Hälsingland, Sweden) bears a long inscription that has been the subject of much discussion. It had been thought medieval, not least because of the supposed occurrence of the word *lærðir* 'learned' (normally applied to members of the clergy). More recently, however, it has been placed in the ninth century, greater emphasis being given to the consistent use of simpler variants of the younger-*fuþark* runes (pp. 61–3) and the occurrence of archaic linguistic forms. But key in the argument has been the reading of the word interpreted as *lærðiʀ*. Early runologists thought to see **lirþiʀ**, but a more recent study of the rune forms and the technique by which they were made concludes that **liuþiʀ** is the correct reading, giving the word *ljuðiʀ* 'men', and banishing all reference to the clergy and with it the medieval context. The study argues persuasively that the Forsa runes were cut with hammer and chisel, implements that in metal produce angular rather than rounded lines. In such circumstances the difference between ᚱ and ᚼ will reside chiefly in the direction(s) taken by the branch, in ᚱ right–left–right, as ᚴ, in ᚼ essentially right, as ᚾ. The rune concerned has been damaged by rust, but appears to have a branch coming off the right-hand side of the vertical about half way down. The branch descends in almost a straight line, with perhaps a slight kink lessening its rightward path. It is therefore likely to be ᚼ. This investigation indicates two important things: that hammer and chisel were sometimes used in the production of runic inscriptions in metal; that much can be revealed by close study of carving techniques.

Some metal inscriptions are made by rather different methods from the ones just outlined. 10.2 contained discussion of the Oslo church bell, whose runes were part of the mould from which the bell was cast (p. 104). Runic coins and bracteates were struck from dies. The dies were probably mostly made of metal (four bracteate dies have been found, all bronze), but it has been suggested that in a few instances wood and fired clay may have been used. The inscription formed part of the overall design and since most dies were intended for striking directly on to the surface (rather than right through the metal), the runes would have had to have been inscribed mirror-image into the die. Some unusual rune forms on bracteates may have arisen during this (presumably tricky) process. Not only coins and bracteates were stamped with runes. A third-century lance-head from Illerup, eastern Jutland, bears in relief the name **wagnijo** '?traveller', clearly struck with a die (the same name appears incised into two similar lance-heads, one from Illerup the other from Vimose, Fyn; cf. p. 29).

14.5 Inscriptions in other materials

Mention was made in chapter 10 of runic inscriptions in wax, plaster, brick, and leather (pp. 108–9, 117–18, 124–6). These belong first and foremost in the medieval period. Inscriptions in plaster and brick are quite common, in leather rare. No rune-inscribed lump of wax has been found, but the existence of hollowed-out pieces of wood or bone with runes in the recessed surface, suggests that wax writing tablets were used for runic as well as roman-alphabet messages. The procedure itself is well documented. A thin layer of liquid wax is poured into the shallow hollow and letters carved into the surface with the pointed end of a stylus. The blunt end can be used to smooth over the writing in preparation for the next message, or the wax can be melted and reused. The occasional occurrence of runes (or their remains) in the hollows of writing tablets indicates either that someone cut too hard and deep, or (as clearly the case with the Bergen tablet, pp. 108–9) that a message was deliberately incised into the hard surface and then hidden by a layer of wax.

Runic inscriptions in plaster and brick could be made while the material was still damp or after it had dried or been fired. It is not difficult to tell the difference. A finger or thin stick seem to have been the implements of choice for marking damp plaster or brick, and this tends to leave a tell-tale ridge on either side of the furrow. For cutting in dry plaster a knife was probably the handiest tool. Inscriptions in fired bricks seem chiefly to have been the work of stonemasons, and they doubtless used any suitable stone-cutting implement that was to hand.

One or two leather shoe uppers from medieval Bergen exhibit inscriptions lightly cut and then embroidered. Runic inscriptions in leather tend otherwise simply to be cut – a knife the most likely tool. The rarity of this material in the runic corpus may be due to the scarcity of leather objects on which there was any reason to write runes. But many such artefacts may of course have rotted away. Runic inscriptions could also be embroidered into textiles: there is one such example from Härjedalen, medieval Norway (now Sweden), which has a date range 900–1100.

14.6 Rune-carvers

As will be clear from the foregoing, rune-carvers were not a single category of people. Runes were used, frequently or infrequently, in a wide range of contexts and for diverse purposes, and those who used them will have varied correspondingly.

Relatively few inscriptions are preserved from the older-*fuþark* period. We have no idea how many might have been made (cf. p. 34), but the paucity of what survives is probably a reflection of the total number carved. Clearly, enough people must have written in runes between the second and eighth centuries AD for the skill to have been passed on from generation to generation. There has been much speculation about who these people were. Widespread literacy seems out of the question, so we have to think of the rune-carvers as a rather small and special group, some kind of elite perhaps. Those directly responsible for a good many of the older-*fuþark* inscriptions were clearly metal-workers of one kind or another, but some runologists have questioned how much they understood of what they inscribed or engraved. Not a few of the early runic inscriptions in metal appear to be bungled, and this has been ascribed to illiterate metal-workers, who had problems following the templates they were given. Many scholars do not accept this view, however, and consider metal-workers one of the main repositories of runic knowledge (though endowed with varying degrees of competence). If the average metal-worker did not know his runes, then who did? Who provided the templates? So far there is not enough evidence to answer this question, though clearly there were groups other than metal-workers capable on occasion of producing quite sophisticated inscriptions. The scattering of older-*fuþark* rune-stones suggests a rune-carving tradition – limited though it may have been – among certain stonemasons.

In the late Viking Age there were clearly professional rune-stone carvers (cf. 14.2). Where the demand for rune-stones was not great enough to sustain dedicated workshops, general stonemasons probably learnt the art and produced runic monuments as a sideline. The extent to which runes were used for other purposes in the Viking Age has been a matter of controversy. Quite a few inscriptions on loose objects are known, but it is unclear what kind of runic culture they represent. Some have extrapolated from the medieval situation and envisaged the widespread use of runes by merchants and other town-dwellers for everyday communication. The difficulty for those who espouse this view is the lack of positive evidence. It is argued, however, that wood would have been the primary material employed, and that the wood will have rotted away. Yet the absence of relevant finds is surprising if Viking-Age trading centres like Ribe in Jutland, Kaupang in Vestfold, Norway, and Birka in Uppland, Sweden, were once awash with runes in the way of medieval Bergen. Current understanding suggests a gradual increase in the use of runes as a means of everyday communication starting at the very end of the Viking Age. Such use seems to have been a feature of urban centres in particular, and was perhaps in part inspired by literacy in the roman alphabet – a literacy that began to develop in the eleventh century.

In the Middle Ages the ability to read and write runes becomes fairly general. Inscriptions are made by all kinds of people: the ruling elite, the clergy, churchgoers, fighting men, adventurers, travellers, merchants, stonemasons, metal-workers, comb-makers, moneyers, and yet others. Many of these appear to have been literate in both runic and roman script. In urban environments, in particular, runes seem to have become part of everyday life. Nevertheless, many must have remained illiterate or semi-literate. Some of the garbled medieval inscriptions (p. 112) can probably be ascribed to the latter group. As the Middle Ages progressed, a cultural shift took place: writing increasingly became the province of those trained in Latin and the roman alphabet. Runes declined in use until they became little more than an object of antiquarian interest and, for a few, a secret script (often no longer carved, but written with pen and ink).

Select reading list

Åhfeldt, Laila Kitzler 2002. *Work and Workshop: Laser Scanner Analysis of Viking Age Rune Stones* (Theses and Papers in Archaeology B:9). Stockholm: Archaeological Research Laboratory, Stockholm University.

Barnes, Michael P., and Page, R. I. 2005. 'The runic inscriptions of Scotland: preservation, documentation and interpretation'. In: (Sally M. Foster and Morag Cross, eds) *Able Minds and Practised Hands: Scotland's Early Medieval Sculpture in the 21st Century*. Edinburgh: Historic Scotland, 193–8. [Contains general observations on rune-carving in stone.]

Knirk, James E. 2003. 'The runes on a Kufic coin from Hoen in Buskerud, Norway'. In: (Wilhelm Heizmann and Astrid van Nahl, eds) *Runica – Germanica – Mediaevalia* (Ergänzungsbände zum Reallexikon der Germanischen Altertumskunde 37). Berlin/New York: de Gruyter, 348–55.

Meijer, Jan 1992. 'Planning in runic inscriptions'. In: (Lennart Elmevik and Lena Peterson, eds) *Blandade runstudier* 1 (Runrön 6). Uppsala: Institutionen för nordiska språk, Uppsala universitet, 37–66.

Moltke, Erik 1985. *Runes and their Origin: Denmark and Elsewhere*. Copenhagen: National Museum of Denmark, 391–7, 417–500. [These sections offer general observations on runic coins and their minting, and on inscriptions in plaster, brick, metal, and other materials.]

Parsons, David 1994. 'Anglo-Saxon runes in Continental manuscripts'. In: (Klaus Düwel, ed.) *Runische Schriftkultur in kontinental-skandinavischer und -angelsächsischer Wechselbeziehung* (Ergänzungsbände zum Reallexikon der Germanischen Altertumskunde 10). Berlin/New York: de Gruyter, 208–11. [On the Blythburgh, Suffolk, writing tablet.]

Spurkland, Terje 2005. *Norwegian Runes and Runic Inscriptions*. Woodbridge: Boydell Press, 47–51. [Asks who might have carved certain types of older-*fuþark* inscription, and suggests a few answers.]

Thompson, Claiborne W. 1975. *Studies in Upplandic Runography*. Austin/London: University of Texas Press, 69–75. [On the technical aspects of carving Viking-Age rune-stones.]

Wicker, Nancy L. 2006. 'Bracteate inscriptions through the looking glass: a microscopic view of manufacturing techniques'. In: (Marie Stoklund *et al.*, eds) *Runes and their Secrets: Studies in Runology*. Copenhagen: Museum Tusculanum Press, University of Copenhagen, 415–36.

15 The reading and interpretation of runic inscriptions

15.1 General considerations

Most inscriptions runologists deal with were found some time ago – many a very long time ago. Almost all of these will have received some kind of publication involving a reading and an attempt at interpretation. Much work in runology has been devoted to bettering the efforts of earlier scholars, in particular to providing new interpretations of difficult inscriptions. While we should not accept complacently the conclusions of our predecessors, we should be wary of constantly reinterpreting runic texts. There is little point in adding to an already existing stock a further interpretation of indemonstrable validity. The much-quoted "first law of runo-dynamics" states that "for every runic inscription there shall be as many interpretations as there are runologists studying it". There is unfortunately enough truth in this humorous observation to cause unease.

Serious runological endeavour concerns much more than interpretation. Scholarly documentation and publication of an inscription involves a series of questions and procedures whose aim is to throw as much light as possible on the runes and what they say. First to be considered are the find circumstances. Who discovered the object bearing the inscription, where and in what context? Was the inscription itself noticed at the same time? Elements of this information can be crucial in identifying the origin of object and/or inscription and tracing their history, in ascertaining the purpose of either or both, and determining whether the runes are from a genuine tradition or represent a more recent recreation of the script. Modern archaeological excavations will usually give rise to the most detailed and reliable reports. The approximate age of most of the Bergen wharf inscriptions, for example, has been determined by their position in the ground relative to a series of "fire layers" (p. 106), although the identification of the layers has been subject to reconsideration (as often with initial conclusions reached by archaeologists). At the other end of the scale we may learn nothing more of a runic artefact than that it was: "discovered in a field near X", "acquired by Y during a trip to Z", and so on. In such cases there is only the evidence of object and inscription themselves to go on. An example is the Hunterston brooch (Strathclyde, Scotland; cf. p. 172). All we know about its discovery is that it is said to have been found by two workmen in about 1830 on part of the Hunterston estate, West Kilbride parish. It was lying on the ground and covered by grass. No indication is given of how or why it came to be there.

Having ascertained as much as possible about the find circumstances, the runologist will go on to study object and inscription in detail. Important questions will be: What is the nature of the object? Does it have a purpose other than to bear the inscription? How far are object and inscription contemporary? In uncertain cases close scrutiny may offer clues about the relationship between the two. Height, width and depth of the object (as appropriate), length of the inscription and heights of individual runes will be measured, and object and inscription drawn and photographed. Runes, separators and other marks will be examined individually, under magnification where available and as necessary, and with raking light from different angles. From this emerges a *reading* – the writing the runologist thinks to see. The reading will comprise more than simply a presentation of the particular sequence of runes, separators, etc. encountered. The aim is to document the carving in its entirety. Any evidence that the runes were lightly scratched in before being carved, for example, must be recorded. The runologist will try to determine what kind or kinds of implement were used, and how that may have affected the finished product (dots, for instance, are more likely as separators in a text that is made with a punch). Sometimes it may be possible to decide whether the runes were carved top to base or base to top, or in both directions. The general appearance of the inscription will also be taken into account, whether it is formal or informal, carefully or carelessly made, and how far the layout as a whole, and/or particular rune or word forms, can be ascribed to the shape of the inscription-bearer, the space available on it, or difficulties the carver experienced with the material.

On the reading is based the *interpretation*. To interpret a runic inscription satisfactorily, the runologist needs of course to know the language in which it is written. S/he will also require knowledge *about* the language in order to recognise chronological and dialectal differences. Equally essential is familiarity with the development of runic writing. The runologist must know which runes are likely to occur at different periods and in different areas, and how they relate to the speech sounds and/or sound systems they were used to denote. Personal names are a recurring feature of runic inscriptions, so the would-be interpreter should have some acquaintance with name studies. Other fields that may be of importance include – archaeology apart – cultural, religious, legal, literary and art history, geology, mythology and cryptology. The runologist cannot be competent in all of these and must therefore seek help from experts in the relevant disciplines. Their help will often consist in the provision of bibliographical references. For runologists, as all academics, it is often more important to know where to find information than to have the information stored in one's brain.

An interpretation of a runic inscription will not only concern itself with what the inscription says, but with its age and wider context. On the basis of one or more of the following factors, a date may be assigned: find report (cf. above), archaeological context, historical context, rune forms, language forms, type of inscription, content of inscription, layout, style of ornamentation or art. In some cases the dating can be very narrow (e.g. the Vinje church inscription(s), pp. 118–19), in others (e.g. most of the rune-stones of the older-*fuþark* period; cf. p. 35 and 15.2) only the broadest estimate will be possible. The wider context of an inscription can include its genesis (who provided the text, who carved it, and in what circumstances); its provenance and how it came to be where it was found; its function (understanding what a sequence of runes says does not necessarily tell us why the runes were carved); its history (what happened to it after it was carved – whether it was in use for a long or a short time). The amount of contextual information that can be gathered will of course differ greatly from inscription to inscription.

Runologists vary in the ways they present their readings and interpretations. A fundamental rule is that the two should be separated as rigorously as possible. In reading we must strive for objectivity; in interpreting there is more scope, and sometimes necessity, for subjectivity. The reading must clearly come first, since it provides the basis for the interpretation. A practical way of presenting an inscription is as follows: (1) heading (including the name and/or number of the inscription, find spot, and current location); (2) find circumstances; (3) description of the object bearing the inscription, an account of where and how the runes are placed on it, and measurements of individual runes and the inscription as a whole; (4) reading, in the form of normalised runes and/or transliteration; (5) detailed discussion of the reading and how it was arrived at; (6) interpretation, including analysis of language, word forms, names, etc., and leading, where possible, to an edited text and translation into a modern language; (7) consideration of the age of the inscription.

Behind this innocuous list there lurk a good number of problems. For example, transliterations are not always wholly objective. Some editors, while basing their choice of roman-alphabet equivalent chiefly on distinctive runic shape, may occasionally use supposed sound value as an alternative: medieval ᛂ, for instance, is transliterated as both ø and ǫ in some works, the choice depending on the editor's understanding of the sound denoted. But that is to introduce an element of subjectivity into what should be an objective exercise – to indicate to the reader what the runologist has thought to see. It is also confusing, since with two different roman letters the reader may well assume two different runic characters are involved. Interpretations will to some extent be subjective, as already acknowledged. However, editors are seldom frank about, or possibly even aware of, the preconceptions they bring to their work. In Wolfgang Krause and Herbert Jankuhn's *Die Runeninschriften im älteren Futhark* (pp. 201, 216–17), for example, the background of cult and magic against which many of the inscriptions are seen appears as a fundamental premise (of unexplained origin) rather than a hypothesis to be demonstrated.

In the light of such hazards, it is desirable that runic corpus editions of the future – in addition to presenting individual inscriptions roughly as suggested above – fulfil certain general requirements. The first concerns explicitness. There should be an account of how the editor(s) moved from concept to end product, including discussion of: (1) the establishment of the corpus – what was admitted, what left out, and why; (2) the circumstances in which the editor(s) examined the inscriptions and how far these could have affected the reliability of their readings; (3) the way the inscriptions are presented and the reasoning that led to the particular choice of method; (4) the principles according to which runes are normalised and transliterations made; (5) the distinction between observation and interpretation, and how far it was possible to maintain it; (6) editorial preconceptions – do the editor or editors espouse a particular point of view that may affect their interpretations or are they agnostic? A second requirement is for caution. Authoritarian pronouncements about the meaning and age of inscriptions should be eschewed where no certainty exists. Editors will of course express their opinions, but it should be clear that that is what they are. The editor's chief task is to set out the data, allowing readers – as far as possible – to make their own judgements. Caution could usefully extend to consideration of how far the corpus reflects what was actually carved. If, as is clearly most often the case, the extant material represents a tiny fraction of the total number of inscriptions originally made, what conclusions about language, culture, technical competence, political and ethnic relationships, etc., can safely be drawn from it? A third requirement is for awareness of the pitfalls that confront the editor who dabbles in disciplines of which s/he has little experience. And as a corollary to this: circumspection in relying on assertions by scholars in fields the editor is not trained to assess. More than one runologist has depended on archaeological expertise to date an inscription, in blissful ignorance of the fact that the archaeological dating can ultimately be traced back to runological opinion.

To exemplify some of the points made above, three inscriptions are now presented and discussed. It should be stressed, however, that they are not necessarily treated in accordance with the guidelines just suggested. This is not a scholarly edition, and all three inscriptions have already been edited, two of them more than once. The aim here is to introduce a variety of runological problems and to illustrate different aspects of runological method.

15.2 Example 1: Kjølevik

The Kjølevik inscription came to light in 1882 on a farm in south-western Norway. It was observed on a granite slab in the ceiling of a cellar used for storing potatoes. People on the farm claimed the stone had once formed part of a small monument nearby, and that a second runic stone had stood not far away. No trace of this second object has been found. The extant stone is now in the possession of Kulturhistorisk museum ('The Museum of Cultural History'), University of Oslo, and is on display in the University of Oslo Library for Humanities and Social Sciences, Blindern, where it is likely to remain. The inscription is presented in chapter 4 (pp. 30–31) in the form of an illustration (Plate 2), transliteration, edited text and translation. The runes are of older-*fuþark* type, and are transliterated in accordance with the system set out in Fig. 1. The reading was established in the nineteenth century. There has been general agreement on it ever since, as also on the general outline of the interpretation, although there remain uncertainties about points of detail.

There are three lines of runes, and from the direction of the branches it is clear they run from right to left. In the uppermost line splintering at the edge of the stone has destroyed the tops of the characters, but more than enough survives for clear recognition. Rune 3 of the middle line is an Ⱨ with what appears to be an extraneous twig on the right descending to meet the vertical at about the height of the branch (which, unlike that of the **h** below, rises from right to left). The bottom line seems at first glance to begin with the sequence ⓘⓘⱨ – unexpected, because the same rune is rarely written twice in succession. However, there is a very short groove descending from the top of the second vertical of Ⱨ towards the first ⵌ, and it is surmised that this represents an attempt by the carver to correct a mistake he made: instead of placing the single branch of ⵌ on the character that follows Ⱨ, as he had intended, he confused it with the ⵌ that was to come next and carved two branches. To repair matters, he fashioned a bind-rune (p. 20) by placing the branch of ⵌ on the second vertical of Ⱨ. The only way of dealing with one of the surplus ⵌs, when he realised his mistake, would have been to obliterate it, but that would have caused a visible scar, so he left things as they were.

It is not immediately clear why the inscription is set out in three lines. The arrangement may have been dictated by the size, shape and quality of the face selected for carving. There is not a great deal of spare room, and the stone is rough in places. On the other hand, it is possible the carver wanted to separate elements of the text in order to give them prominence. The layout itself offers no obvious indication of the order in which the three lines should be read (runic inscriptions do not necessarily run from top to bottom; they may start at the bottom or even in a middle line). The sense of the text as it emerges shows fairly clearly that it begins at the top, but we need to acknowledge that in this respect our reading is based not on what we think to have seen, but on interpretation. An element of subjectivity has entered what should ideally be an objective exercise. The runic sequences that emerge are, in transliteration (repeated from p. 30):

> **hadulaikaz**
> **ekhagustadaz**
> **ĥlaaiwidomaguminino**

We now proceed to interpretation. The words are not divided from each other by separators, but there is a possibility the line breaks coincide with the ends and beginnings of words. The appearance of **z** at the end of lines one and two turns possibility into probability, /z/ being very common in word final position in the Scandinavian Germanic of the time. Runes 1–2 of line 2 give the sequence **ek**, which we can assume on the basis of its occurrence in several other older-*fuþark* inscriptions to represent the first person pronoun, nominative singular, 'I' (cf. Old Norse *ek*, German *ich*, Latin *ego*, etc.). What follows 'I' in these inscriptions is often a personal name. Since -**az** is a common nominative masculine singular ending, it is probable that **hagustadaz** and **ek** belong together syntactically: 'I **hagustadaz**' (the latter word a compound, conceivably a name, consisting of *haʒu* 'piece of land' and perhaps *staldaz* 'owner' 'administrator', with **l** omitted in error).

In the continuation we look for some statement about putative *Haʒustaldaz* (*haʒustaldaz*), which will almost certainly involve a verb. We know that in Germanic languages there are many verbs which form the past tense with [d], [ð] or [t], as English *liked*, *waited*, and we also know that in the Germanic current in Scandinavia before the seventh century the past of most such verbs had a suffix consisting of vowel + ð + the appropriate personal ending (1st, 2nd or 3rd, sg. or pl.). In accordance with this, the sequence **ido** in the Kjølevik inscription seems to mark out **ĥlaaiwido** as a 1st sg. past tense verb form, of which **ekhagustadaz** would be the subject. The root of **ĥlaaiwido** is a problem, for there is nothing in later Scandinavian suggestive of such a verb, but Gothic, an East Germanic language (p. 218), has the noun *hlaiw* 'grave', presumably cognate with the **hlaiwa** on the Bø stone (p. 30). That makes it plausible **ĥlaaiwido** means 'entombed' 'buried'. Further possible evidence for the existence of a verb with root *hlaiw-* in older-*fuþark* times comes from the apparent past participle **haiwidaz** on the Amla stone (p. 30), interpreted *hlaiwiðaz* (with **l** omitted in error), and taken to mean '[is] buried'.

We would expect the remainder of the third line to explain who or what ?Haʒustaldaz buried. The sequence **maguminino** looks as though it might contain some form of the first person possessive adjective 'my' (cf. ON *minn*, English *mine*), which would mean that **magu** was likely to be a noun with which **minino** agreed. Old Norse has *mǫgr*, a poetic word for 'son'. In the accusative (object) form this is *mǫg*, and its vowel *ǫ* (/ɔ/) is the product of so-called *u*-mutation, which involves the influence of an unstressed /u/ on a preceding /a/ (p. 219). In other words, if we were to reconstruct the earlier form of *mǫg* on the basis of our understanding of North Germanic language history, we would arrive at exactly the **magu** we find on the Kjølevik stone. From this we deduce that **minino**, if it is indeed a form of the possessive adjective, must be accusative masculine singular, although the ON acc. m. sg. *minn* cannot be derived directly from it.

There remains **hadulaikaz**. Form and context (a compound word in the nom. m. sg. standing on its own) indicate a personal name. That assumption is strengthened by the occurrence of the name *Heaðolac* in Old English, which would seem to be cognate (both have been taken to consist of the element 'battle', **hadu**-/*Heaðo*-, followed by 'play', -**laikaz**/-*lac*). Because the expected form of 'battle' in early Scandinavian is **haþu** rather than **hadu**, alternative interpretations have been suggested, most notably Handulaikaz (with **d** for /nd/, cf. p. 25, giving a name consisting of the elements 'hand' and 'play'), but many nevertheless still prefer to see here a word with a Germanic cognate rather than one that is otherwise unknown. Haðulaikaz/Handulaikaz is presumably to be identified as the buried son. The bare name is perhaps to be taken elliptically: 'Haðulaikaz/Handulaikaz [lies here]', or some such.

Apart from **hadulaikaz** and **hagustadaz**, both of which have been the subject of debate, the sense of the inscription thus seems clear enough: 'Haðulaikaz/Handulaikaz [lies here]. I ?Haʒustaldaz buried my son'. The interpretation has been pieced together from various sources, but principally from knowledge of: (1) the older *fuþark*; (2) the speech sounds denoted by this rune-row; (3) early forms of Germanic language more generally; (4) other runic inscriptions of similar age.

For all that, there is much in the wider context of the Kjølevik stone that is unclear. Because of the occurrence of *hlaiwiðo*, which we take to mean 'buried', and because we believe many, perhaps most, of the older-*fuþark* stones are of commemorative type (p. 30), we interpret its words as a memorial. Tradition on the farm where the stone was discovered suggests it was set up as part of a monument, perhaps over or near a burial chamber, and that there was a second runic stone close by, possibly also part of the monument. This leads us to consider whether it was a relatively common practice in the older-*fuþark* period to raise one or more commemorative stones over, or in connection with, a burial. There are a few inscriptions from this time that mention burials and graves (p. 30), and some that were found in connection with burials, but there is a striking difference in number between these and the commemorative stones of the late Viking Age (chapter 8) – which seem in any case to have functioned not so much as epitaphs, rather as public notices set up in places where they would be seen by as many people as possible. Nor can we know how much store to set by what people on Kjølevik farm related about the earlier history of the stone. It appears to have formed part of the cellar ceiling for some time before its runes were noticed, and there is no report of a monument or burial chamber having been found in the vicinity. The raising of two runic stones at the same site would be unusual, to say the least. No pairs of commemorative stones are otherwise known from the older-*fuþark* period, though they do occur in the Viking Age. Reasons can vary from ostentation to lack of space: for some the motivating factor was clearly that a single stone would not accommodate all the commissioners wanted to say. Kjølevik could of course have been one of a pair, but there is nothing to suggest its text is incomplete, and one wonders what the other stone might have said.

To sum up: the Kjølevik inscription offers no serious problems of reading and – the probable name **hagustadaz** apart – gives good linguistic sense (unlike many inscriptions in the older *fuþark*). Its primary purpose seems to be commemorative. It may have marked a burial site, but there is no direct evidence for this, and we do not know enough about the customs of the time to judge whether it is likely. Indeed, we have little idea what motivated people in this early period to raise rune-stones, or what they might have thought appropriate to record on them, beyond what the inscriptions themselves tell us. To put a date on "this early period" is difficult. The older *fuþark* appears to have remained in use in Scandinavia until about AD 700, but from around 600, or perhaps a little earlier, it began to undergo changes. There are no signs of these changes in the Kjølevik inscription, so on runological grounds we would assign it to a time before 550. The type of language employed supports that assumption. How much older than 550 the inscription could be is difficult to determine. It has been widely assumed that the oldest rune-stones are from around AD 400 (the previous century according to some), but the reasoning is often vague and generally unpersuasive. Recent work on the typology of rune forms (pp. 19–20) suggests a date range 160–560/70 for the oldest rune-stones as a group and 375/400–520/30 for Kjølevik in particular, but even this roughly 150-year slot is probably too precise.

15.3 Example 2: St Albans 2

The St Albans 2 inscription occurs on a fragment of bone, perhaps from a young sheep or roe deer. The fragment was discovered during excavations at St Albans Abbey in 1984. It comes from the occupational debris of a late tenth-century structure, which was demolished at the rebuilding of the abbey in the period 1077–88. The layer from which it was recovered was sealed by 1088. The bone is unlikely to derive from occupation of the site prior to the erection of the late tenth-century structure, so on these archaeological grounds its date range may be deduced as between *c.* 970 and 1088. The piece is currently in private hands.

The inscription consists of six runes in all (Fig. 30), almost certainly cut with a knife. The base of rune 4, the lower part of rune 5 and the lower half or perhaps two-thirds of rune 6 have been lost through breakage. Identification of runes 2–4 is straightforward. We have ⁿᴾR **ufr**. Rune 1 is a clear ᚹ, i.e. **w**. Rune 5 consists of a vertical and nothing more; enough of the lower part of this character is missing for there to be residual doubt about its identification as | **i**. Rune 6 appears to be a younger-*fuþark* ᚴ **k**, although so much of the character is lost that it might be identified as Anglo-Saxon ᚾ **n** with an unusually long branch, or a skewed Anglo-Saxon ᚷ **g**, or just possibly a fairly rare Anglo-Saxon **s**-form. We are faced here with problems of identification. The occurrence of ᚹ suggests an inscription in English runes, since ᚹ **w** was dropped from the Scandinavian *fuþark* by the early eighth century at the latest (pp. 56–9). Yet rune 6, from what remains of it, looks more like a Scandinavian ᚴ **k** than ᚾ or ᚷ, though the possibility of Anglo-Saxon ᚴ **s** must be kept open. Such uncertainty makes transliteration difficult: the roman equivalents chosen are not immutable, but vary, dependent on which runic system is being transliterated (pp. 3–4, 42–3, 52). In this particular case there is no problem with the first four runes ᚹⁿᴾR, which are to be transliterated **wufr** whatever the system. | too always has the same roman equivalent, so rune 5 can be rendered **i**, but with an indication that the reading is uncertain. Rune 6, as has been shown, is the real crux. If read as a damaged ᚴ, it is **s** in the Anglo-Saxon system, **k** in the Scandinavian. The editor can of course decide that ᚴ is more likely to be a Scandinavian **k** than the rare Anglo-Saxon **s**, or conversely, that since we already have **w**, the inscription should be deemed Anglo-Saxon and ᚴ taken as **s**, but these are matters of interpretation, not observation, and that should be made quite clear.

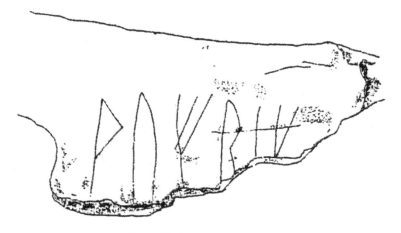

Fig. 30 The St Albans 2 inscription

An English rune in a Scandinavian text is unexpected and appears otherwise unexampled. The closest parallel is to be found in the twelfth-century Bridekirk font inscription from Cumbria, which mixes English bookhand characters with Scandinavian runes and is written in Middle English. It is nevertheless possible to envisage the sort of mixed cultural group that might have used runes from different traditions existing in late tenth- or eleventh-century St Albans (a town close to the border with the "Danelaw", the Scandinavian-administered area of England).

With such uncertainty about what has been read, interpretation can only be a matter of setting out the possibilities and weighing up their plausibility. None of the sequences **wufrin**, **wufrig**, **wufris** is easily interpretable as a Scandinavian or Anglo-Saxon word. Apart from anything else, initial [wu] does not occur in Viking-Age Scandinavian, /w/ having been lost in this position before rounded vowels (cf. OE *wulf*, ON *ulfr* 'wolf', OE *word*, ON *orð* 'word', etc.). If we take rune 6 as **k**, we might have an acceptable spelling of the common English personal name *Wulfric*, albeit written with the help of a Scandinavian runic character. The lack of /l/ is noteworthy, but *Wuf-* for *Wulf-* is documented in late Old English sources. Possible, but less likely, interpretations of the second element of the name are *-rinc* or *-ring*, when it is recalled that in the younger *fuþark* **k** can stand for /nk/ and /ng/ as well as /k/ and /g/ (p. 60). No *Wulfrinc* or *Wulfring* seems to be recorded, except possibly in place-names, but **-rink** occurs as the second element of what appears to be an English name, **iatrink** (?Eadrinc), inscribed on a medieval bone comb from Lund, Skåne, Denmark. Whatever putative **-rik** might represent in the St Albans 2 inscription, the first element is most plausibly taken as a way of writing *Wu(l)f-*. If done by a Scandinavian, we might surmise that he borrowed ᚹ from the Anglo-Saxon *fuþorc* in order to represent a specifically English name form. In Denmark, English moneyers with names ending in *-wini* tend to spell this **-uini** in runes, **u** being the usual way of writing [w] in the younger *fuþark*. Sometimes, however, the **u** is dotted, seemingly to mark it out as the semi-vowel [w]. Furthermore, the Lund moneyer Wulfgeat, when employing roman letters, can give the first element of his name as PVLF-, with roman 'P' to be interpreted as a romanised *wynn*, the Anglo-Saxon bookhand character developed from ᚹ (p. 153). It is perhaps conceivable that the ᚹ in St Albans 2 was a runic rendering of bookhand *wynn* rather than a direct borrowing from the English *fuþorc*, but it looks very convincing as a rune, in contrast to the bookhand P of the Bridekirk font.

A completely different interpretation of St Albans 2 is that it represents the garbled beginning of a *fuþark* inscription, with rune 1 as ᚦ with a much higher bow than usual and rune 5 as perhaps an incomplete ᚴ or ᛆ (cf. the damage described above). The bow of **þ** can vary considerably in height and length in the younger *fuþark*, since there is no danger of the character's being confused with **w**. Even so, **þ** rarely takes the form found in St Albans 2. Nor is there any sign of a branch in rune 5, which one might have expected if this had been some form of **ã/o**, given the positions of the other runes. The "incomplete *fuþark*" interpretation must thus be regarded as rather a long shot.

Finally to be considered is the wider context of the inscription. Who might have carved it and why? It is unclear whether the six characters we have are all that was written. Judging by the spacing it is perhaps unlikely any rune came after the present final character, but there could have been a gap or separation point that was followed by an additional word or more. If on the other hand the six runes give a personal name, there is no reason why it should not stand alone. Another bone inscription recovered from the same site in St Albans (St Albans 1) may hold a clue. This records what seems to be a name followed by the common phrase *risti runaʀ* 'carved runes'. On that analogy St Albans 2 may represent a bit of runic doodling. People might have been filling an idle hour carving their names, adding, as the mood took them or space allowed, an otiose statement about the activity in which they were engaged. Whether these people are to be thought of as Scandinavians, Englishmen or part of a mixed community, is hard to say. St Albans 1 is wholly Scandinavian, and its runes and language look to be of East Scandinavian type (which in the historical context suggests Danish involvement or inspiration). Thus St Albans 2 might have been carved by someone with an East Scandinavian cultural background, who, for whatever reason, bore an English name. But the carver could also have been an Englishman who had adopted Scandinavian culture to the extent of using Scandinavian rune forms. If the inscription was originally longer, there is of course less reason to suppose **wufrik** and the carver identical. Another individual may have been writing about **wufrik**.

15.4 Example 3: Birsay 1

Birsay 1 consists of a sequence or sequences of runes and rune-like characters (some of the latter possibly damaged runes) running along the narrow edge of an oblong block of sandstone (Fig. 31). The carvings were discovered in 1921 by Hugh Marwick, an Orcadian scholar, while making his first visit to the Brough of Birsay, a tidal island some 250 metres off the north-west corner of the Orkney Mainland. He noticed the stone lying horizontally in the outer face of the north chancel wall of the ruined church on the Brough, about 30 cm above the ground. On peeping in at the upper surface, mostly hidden by the stones built on top of it, Marwick thought he saw traces of letters. He managed to remove the stone from the wall without much difficulty, and was surprised to find that it bore Scandinavian runes. The tide was coming in and he and his six-year old son, whom he had taken with him, had little time left to return to the Mainland. Nothing if not determined, Marwick made his way back across

Fig. 31 The Birsay 1 inscription(s)

the slippery causeway, boy under one arm and stone (some 84 × 8 × 16 cm) under the other. Birsay 1 is now in the keeping of the Museum of Scotland.

The broad face of the stone adjacent to the tops of the runes is cut away round its edge to a width of anything from 1.5 to 2.6 cm and a depth of about 1 cm. This gives the face the appearance of having a central relief panel. In its present state the inscribed part of the runic edge contains three clearly defined sections. First there are some shallow runes or rune-like symbols; thereafter comes a section comprising a series of faint lines that have something of the appearance of runes, but few of their distinctive features; finally there is a sequence of bolder characters that seem indubitably runic. Preceding the inscription or inscriptions is a space of just over 32 cm in which hardly anything can now be seen but which might once have held some kind of writing. Among the vertical and diagonal lines that make up the first inscribed section certain runic shapes of Scandinavian type can be discerned. Other lines cannot easily be resolved into runes. What we have here is possibly an incompetent attempt to execute a runic carving; or wear and tear, including perhaps the reuse of the stone as building material, may have removed a number of distinctive features from the carving. Alternatively, we may be dealing with random shapes that by chance have come to look like characters of the *fuþark*. None of the "runes" that can be conjured up with the eye of faith suggests a Scandinavian word or words, but there are many indubitably runic inscriptions from Scandinavia of which the same is true. These slender indications make it well nigh impossible to decide whether to classify the relevant carving as runic or rune-like. The second section of Birsay 1 consists of sundry vertical and diagonal lines, but only in one or two places do they approximate to runes. The third section runs: **filibusrañru.** Judging by the relatively even line made by the tops of these characters compared with the more ragged line at their bases, the direction of carving was downward. The implement used in all three sections seems to have been a thick-bladed knife (one and the same or more than one).

Only for section three can an interpretation be offered. All who have studied Birsay 1 seem to agree that **filibus** gives the Latinised name *Filippus* 'Philip', first recorded in Norway in the early twelfth century and in Iceland in the early thirteenth. As Marwick points out, we should not be surprised at finding an apostolic name at an early church site. The final four runes are trickier. With so little to go on they have been taken as drastic abbreviation: either **ræru** for *ræist rúnar* 'carved runes'; or **rañru** for *ræist enn rúnar* 'carved runes in addition', where the first **r** stands for *ræist*, **añ** for [æn:], the assumed pronunciation of *enn*, and **ru** for *rúnar*. The former of these interpretations is impossible: ⴕ, the character read above as a bind of **a** and **n**, cannot, whatever else, be **æ**, which has the form ⴕ. The latter interpretation lacks specification of what it was Filippus carved runes in addition to: possibly the other carvings on the stone, but it is odd to have this only vaguely implied. More likely, should **rañru** really stand for *ræist enn rúnar*, *enn* means 'yet again', suggesting perhaps that Filippus was a dedicated graffito-merchant responsible for several boasting stones saying 'Filippus carved runes' or something similar. Rune-carvers do occasionally abbreviate, although it is usually clear when this has happened, as for example with the **ætþffssantætþffssant** in Gol stave-church (pp. 146–7), which gives the first letters of the Old Norwegian names of the numerals 1–20. Many explanations involving abbreviation, however, are far-fetched and appear to be based on little other than the desire to give meaning to apparently meaningless sequences of runes.

An alternative explanation of Birsay 1's **ra͡nru** is that it represents an unintentional anagram of **runar** 'runes', and that **a͡n** is a botched attempt to carve **a** and **n** rather than a deliberate bind-rune. Conceivably Filippus was a novice in the art of rune-writing, who had learnt to inscribe his name and little else. The idea perhaps gains in plausibility if it is assumed that several hands were responsible for the carvings on the stone. It could have been a surface on which several people tried their hand at writing inconsequential messages in runes. 'NN carved runes' is probably the most common of such messages.

Just as difficult as the interpretation of **ra͡nru** is the understanding of the wider context of Birsay 1. When were the various symbols inscribed on the stone, for what purpose, and what damage, if any, did they suffer over the years? There is no reason to doubt Marwick's account of how he made the find (though few of us have had our investigations rewarded quite so speedily and dramatically). He was a serious and reputable scholar. However, the fact that he managed to remove the stone from the wall without difficulty does mean that others in modern times could have been there before him and done the same. Such people would have had an opportunity to try their hand at carving – in emulation of one or more already existing inscriptions, or from scratch. Yet it is hard to see why anyone in the recent past should have adorned a stone with poorly executed runes, and/or rune-like characters and/or an abbreviated or garbled runic inscription, and then replaced it in the wall in such a position that whatever had been written was concealed from public view. Modern runic carvings tend to show greater competence than this, and are often imitations of well-known inscriptions or types of inscription. To that extent it seems likely the Birsay 1 carvings have a medieval origin, and, as suggested above, represent an attempt or attempts at runic writing by a novice or novices.

There are few indications of when in the Middle Ages the stone might have been inscribed. The latest date for the surviving but ruinous church building seems to be twelfth-century, though parts of the structure could be up to a century older. If the carvings post-date the building of the church, they are thus unlikely to have been made much before the twelfth century, though they could be from a considerably later period. They may, however, already have been on the stone at the time it was used as building material. The name *Filippus* points to a Christian milieu, as does the church in which the stone was found, making the reintroduction of Christianity into pagan Norse Orkney in perhaps the late tenth or early eleventh century the earliest likely date for the **filibusra͡nru** section, but there is no reason to think any of the writing on the stone as old as that.

The Birsay 1 carvings are instructive. They move uncertainly from the "rune-like" to the runic and force us to consider the distinction and what it implies. The stone and its inscriptions also raise questions of authenticity. While it is perhaps likely that the inscribing took place in the Middle Ages, there is too little evidence either from the inscriptions themselves, the find circumstances, or the wider context for us to be entirely sure.

15.5 Conclusion

These three case studies serve to illustrate how runologists approach – or should approach – the task of reading and interpreting runic inscriptions. The three have been chosen to exemplify different methodological problems that can arise in the course of their work. As the discussion in 15.1 makes clear, however, runological endeavour covers a far wider spectrum of questions than it has been possible to deal with here.

16 Runes and the imagination: literature and politics

16.1 Literature

In the M. R. James tale of the supernatural 'Casting the runes', we are introduced to a sinister gentleman by the name of Karswell. He has learnt how to direct runes against people, "for the purpose of gaining their affection or of getting them out of the way – perhaps more especially the latter", as the brother of one of his victims reports. The runes intended to bring about a person's death are marked on a strip of paper, in red and black, and the recipient, once he has taken the paper, is destined to die within a specified period. Based on the James story, the 1950s film *Night of the Demon* gives added emphasis to the runic menace. It opens with an image of a grey Stonehenge, through which the wind whistles eerily while a sinister voice intones: "It has been written since the beginning of time, even on to these ancient stones, that evil, supernatural creatures exist in a world of darkness. And it is also said, man using the magic power of the ancient runic symbols can call forth these powers of darkness: the demons of hell." With anachronistic implications, one of the stones sports a sequence of characters not unlike Anglo-Saxon runes.

J. R. R. Tolkien's celebrated works of fantasy present "runes" of various kinds. In *The Hobbit* mention is made of a runic script called *Dwarvish*, but the author goes on to reassure readers that *Dwarvish* characters are to be represented by their "English" counterparts. Such runes as are employed in the book do indeed differ only marginally in form and usage from those of the Anglo-Saxon *fuþorc*. In *The Lord of the Rings* the "runes" of a system called *Cirth* are set out. *Cirth* consists of actual runes and rune-like symbols, to which largely invented sound values have been assigned.

In 'Casting the runes' the primary function of the script is to work black magic; it is unclear whether it is also a writing system in the ordinary sense. Tolkien's "runes" are certainly characters for writing language, but they exist in a mythological world inspired by ancient lore. Both the James short story and Tolkien's more substantial works spring from the imagination of modern men steeped in old texts. No sensible person would view the "runes" they conjure up as anything other than motifs in pieces of fiction. Where runes appear in medieval stories, there has been greater willingness to believe some truth may lie behind whatever is told of them.

Medieval Icelandic literature, both prose and verse, has quite a lot to say on the subject. The Saga of Egill Skallagrímsson (*Egils saga skallagrímssonar*, set in the tenth century but composed in the thirteenth) recounts how its hero Egill, served with poisoned drink, carved runes on the horn containing the liquid and smeared them with his own blood, whereupon the horn shattered and the drink spilt on the ground. On a later occasion we find him carving a runic curse on a mocking pole he has raised as an insult to King Eiríkr Bloodaxe and his wife Queen Gunnhildr. Then he cures a sick woman of her illness by scraping ten cryptic runes off a whalebone concealed in her bed, burning both runes and bone, and placing other runes under her pillow. Finally, Egill's daughter urges him to compose a poem about the death of his son, the text of which she intends to carve on a stick (presumably in runes since the roman alphabet would hardly have been known in Iceland in the 900s). In the Saga of Grettir Ásmundarson (*Grettis saga Ásmundarsonar*, set in the early eleventh century but composed in the early fourteenth), we are introduced to an old woman skilled in witchcraft. In one scene, walking by the sea-shore, she comes upon a tree-stump. She has people prepare a small flat surface on the wood, into which she carves runes with a knife, rubbing her blood into them, and uttering a spell while walking withershins round the stump. She then has the stump pushed into the sea and directs it to float to an island off the coast where Grettir is holding out against his enemies. It is taken for firewood by one of Grettir's men, and while chopping it up Grettir cuts his leg, the wound ultimately leading to his death.

Norse heroic and mythological poetry contains a variety of references to runes, their origin, and uses. This poetry was preserved in Iceland, most of it in a single, late thirteenth-century manuscript, but some of the lays have been thought to go back to at least the early Viking Age. According to a couple of fairly murky verses in the didactic compilation *Hávamál* 'The Words of the High One [Óðinn]' (containing material of diverse origin and age), the runes and related knowledge were obtained through self-sacrifice by the god Óðinn. Certain of the verses that follow carry the implication that runes belong among the gods, the elves and the dwarfs, and a connection is made between the writing and reading of runes and worship of the heathen gods. In another section of *Hávamál* we find the phrase *rúnum ... inum reginkunnum* 'the runes stemming from the gods'. *Sigrdrífumál* 'The Lay of Sigrdrífa' (seemingly comprising material of different ages) contains some fourteen verses dealing with runes (all probably quite late). They describe (in the words of Sigrdrífa) many different kinds of runes and their purposes, but bear little obvious relation to the rest of the poem. We learn, for example, of *sigrúnar* 'victory runes', which those who would be victorious must know, of *bjargrúnar* 'helping runes', useful when assisting at childbirth, of *málrúnar* 'speech runes', handy in legal disputes, and of *ǫlrúnar* 'ale runes' a defence against trickery and deceit. To improve the chances of victory Týr (rune 12's designation) should be named twice; and to increase the protection against trickery *nauð* (rune 8's designation) should be marked on one's nail. In *Skírnismál* 'The Lay of Skírnir' (of uncertain age), Skírnir threatens to carve *þurs* 'giant' (rune 3's designation) and three 'staves': 'lust', 'passion' and '?unbearable pain', which, it is clear from the context, will cause harm to the giantess Gerðr against whom they are to be directed. *Atlamál* 'The Lay of Atli' (probably twelfth-century) tells of a warning message carved with runes; the characters are "distorted" by a hostile hand, but a woman skilled in runes manages to read and understand the message nevertheless.

This material, both prose and verse, has been taken with varying degrees of seriousness. There are probably few today who would claim that the events portrayed actually took place, or that the words attributed to supernatural beings, heroes, or others were in fact uttered. What some scholars assert is that the rune-lore these sources record is culturally true. By that they mean (a) it was believed runes were divinely inspired and could be used to affect the course of events, and (b) there were people who used runes in the ways described. This offers scope for much confusion. It would lead too far in the present context to try to unravel the many tangled strands, but a few thoughts will not be out of place.

Both sagas and verse may well preserve traditional lore about runes (as opposed to material invented on the spot by compilers or authors). What we do not know is how far either literary source reflects any kind of reality at any particular period. Ancient tales can contain elements of truth, but they are subject to constant change and embellishment as they are retold. Though the Icelandic family sagas doubtless preserve facts about tenth- and eleventh-century Iceland, the consensus seems to be that they present an imagined past, rather in the way the western film offers a romantic view of the old West. Some of the verse may go back three, four or five centuries beyond the time it was written down, but it is difficult to say precisely which parts of it existed in this early period, and in what form. Certainly a good deal of the verse material as we have it has been reworked and edited. Perhaps what sagas and verse tell us of runes reflects what twelfth-, thirteenth- and fourteenth-century Icelanders believed. That is not implausible, given the apparent distance of Iceland from the everyday runic usage of mainland Scandinavia. It is stretching credulity to think that those who employed runes to identify their property, keep a check on payments, write letters, record crude jokes, etc. can have thought of the characters they used as divinely inspired and endowed with magic powers. But the Icelanders might (or might at least have been disposed to exploit such notions as literary motifs).

As always, a clear distinction needs to be maintained between runes as magic symbols *per se* and their use in writing spells (cf. p. 8). Like all writing systems, the runic could be and was employed to set down magic formulas and sundry types of hocus pocus. Unfortunately the Icelandic sources often fail to make clear in what the supernatural resides. That runes were transmitted to mankind by Óðinn perhaps speaks for the potency of the symbols themselves, although belief in the divine origin of scripts is common to many cultures. Further evidence that the runes were credited with special powers might lie in the phrase *rúnum ... inum reginkunnum* 'the runes stemming from the gods' – although it is unclear exactly what this implies: is it saying that runes in general stem from the gods, or just a particular example, set or type? An almost identical form of words occurs on the supposedly early ninth-century Sparlösa stone from Västergötland, Sweden, and a related one on the perhaps sixth-century Noleby stone, also from Västergötland. The latter runs: **runofahiraginakudo** 'I ?paint/?make ?a rune/?a runic inscription/?runes stemming from the gods'. As the attempted translation indicates, it is uncertain whether **runo** is singular or plural, and what, if it is singular, the word means. If the sense could be substantiated as 'runic inscription' (which it cannot), the divine origin would most naturally apply to the text rather than the runes used to carve it. All we can safely say is that *Hávamál's rúnum ... inum reginkunnum* has epigraphic parallels, and to that extent probably reflects an ancient formulation.

The *sigrúnar, bjargrúnar, málrúnar, ǫlrúnar*, etc. of *Sigrdrífumál* hardly imply the existence of special types of runes – certainly there is no medieval evidence for such varieties. It is more likely the terms refer to runic texts formulated to achieve the particular aim the carver had in view. *Sigrdrífumál* offers helpful hints about where the different "runes" it identifies are to be placed. *Sigrúnar*, for example, should be carved on specific parts of a sword. This intelligence has led some people to wonder whether runic inscriptions on weapons in general might not be interpreted as 'victory runes'. But is it the mere carving of *runes* that aids victory, or the text – or a combination of both? Extant runic inscriptions on weapons do not help greatly. There is little in what they record suggestive of victory formulas. But equally, there do not appear to be many random assortments of runes, which is what one might expect if it was believed the mere presence of the characters on a weapon was enough to promote victory. The Illerup/Vimose lance-heads, with their identical text, offer a fairly typical example of a weapon inscription (p. 29). The text looks meaningful enough, but its purpose rather prosaic: to inform customers which workshop the lances came from. *Ǫlrúnar*, according to *Sigrdrífumál*, are to be carved on a horn (presumably a drinking horn) and on the back of one's hand. Possibly, as some have argued, we are dealing here with a medieval misinterpretation. 'Ale runes', according to them, are not a type of rune but a garbled reference to **alu**, a word of common occurrence (but uncertain import) in older-*fuþark* inscriptions (pp. 30, 32). If that is so, the significance of *ǫlrúnar* lies not in the runes themselves but in a particular type of runic text featuring **alu** (and perhaps in later times its reflex *ǫl*). That *ǫlrúnar* should be carved on a horn may be part of the misinterpretation, but why they should also be cut into the back of one's hand is unclear. The older-*fuþark* **alu** inscriptions are found on loose objects, mostly bracteates, and in one case on a stone.

The two saga texts in which runes play a part (cf. above) do not seem to portray the symbols themselves as bearers of supernatural power. In the Saga of Egill Skallagrímsson, Egill uses runes to carve magic formulas – at least that is a plausible interpretation of his dealings with the script as relayed by the author. The same is true of the Saga of Grettir Ásmundarson. What the old woman does is to carve a spell; whether the use of runes enhances its potency is unspecified. Some of the runic texts introduced in medieval Icelandic literature seem devoid of magical connotations of any kind. The written version of Egill's poem his daughter proposes is one such, the warning message in *Atlamál* another.

In the view of one runologist, the epigraphic and literary sources tell more or less the same story about the uses to which runes were put and the types of material into which they were carved. That is not entirely obvious, however. Runic inscriptions are rarely found on drinking horns, and no runes are known in which traces of blood survive. Of course blood is likely to disappear over time, as are human nails, human skin and the other perishable materials into which Icelandic sources suggest (or imply) runes should be carved. But that runes were actually used in the ways described must remain doubtful.

Cutting them into the back of one's hand, as recommended for 'ale runes' in *Sigrdrífumál*, for example, seems likely to have been an uncomfortable process.

There is certainly evidence that runes and magic were connected in the popular mind, not least in Iceland. The problem is to understand the nature of the connection in any particular case: from what cultural context does it spring – how far does it reflect actual practices, how far is it a product of the imagination? Above all, what general conclusions, if any, can be drawn from sources of widely varying date, type and trustworthiness? The answers people give to these questions will depend very much on their mental make-up. At one end of the spectrum are those eager to seize on every hint of sorcery as evidence of an intimate connection between runes and magic; at the other are the sceptics, who see runes as a writing system, no more no less. Whatever the starting-point, we should examine the evidence carefully and dispassionately, ever striving for precision and clarity.

Unfortunately that is not the manner in which scholars always proceed. *Runes, Magic and Religion* (cited at the end of chapter 12), for example, claims that stanza 6 of *Sigrdrífumál* "advocates inscribing the rune ↑ ... twice on one's sword as an invocation of Týr for victory" (p. 33). As noted above, what *Sigrdrífumál* actually says is that those who wish for victory should carve 'victory runes' on their sword and name Týr twice. Precisely what this involves is a matter of interpretation. In the same account, the threat in *Skírnismál* to carve *þurs* 'giant' and three 'staves': 'lust', 'passion' and '?unbearable pain', becomes "the threat to carve a triple ▶", prompting the conclusion: "the intensifying effect of repeating the runes was clearly still well understood" (p. 33). The conclusion is unwarranted because the text as it stands contains no threat to carve a triple ▶. The silent transformation of supposition into fact does little to advance understanding.

16.2 Politics

Surprising as it may seem, politics have at times intruded on runic research – or runes played a minor part in politics. National pride – rather than careful consideration of the evidence – is chiefly what motivated the seventeenth-century polemic between Danish and Swedish scholars over which of the two peoples had created the script (p. 204). The nineteenth century saw a vigorous debate about the type of Germanic language to be found in a (probably) fifth-century inscription on a gold horn. The horn was discovered in Gallehus, southern Jutland, in 1734, and in the context of the Schleswig-Holstein wars concerning the sovereignty and national affiliation of the two Duchies its text was declared German by German scholars and Scandinavian by Scandinavians. In this case too, patriotic zeal – the urge to document the Jutlandic ancestry of the one or the other group of people – seems to have taken precedence over dispassionate consideration of the evidence. The inscription, which runs **ekhlewagastiz:holtijaz:horna:tawido:** 'I Hlewaʒastiz [a man's name consisting of the elements 'protection' – or perhaps 'fame' – and 'guest'], ?son of/?related to Holta [or someone an element of whose name was Holta] made the horn' does not in fact exhibit conclusively West Germanic or Scandinavian features.

The most dramatic example of the entanglement of runes and politics comes from Nazi Germany. The emphasis in that society on "the Aryan" and "the Germanic" inspired some writers to portray runes as the original alphabetic writing system – the progenitor of Mediterranean alphabets such as the roman and greek. The use of runes as signs and emblems also found favour among elements of the National Socialist hierarchy. Great age could be ascribed to the runes by arguing (or asserting) that they were derived from symbols found in ancient rock carvings. It was not solely idle dreamers and zealous Nazis who championed this point of view. Influenced at least in part by the climate of the times, a number of serious scholars joined in. The more sober of the fraternity acknowledged that the runes as we have them are primarily characters of a writing system, but tended to argue that they had gradually been transformed from conceptual into alphabetic symbols, and that something of their original sense lingered on. On the wilder fringes, people with little or no understanding of runology treated runes as though they stood for concepts first and foremost, downgrading or ignoring their role as representations of speech sounds. ᛋ, for example, was widely employed as a 'victory' symbol – in defiance or ignorance of the fact that the name of this rune as far back as we can follow it is 'sun'. 'Victory'-ᛋ appeared on the uniforms of the SS and other organisations, on standards and banners, and on badges for sale to the general public. Another rune widely adopted as a symbol was ᛟ. Here only a gentle tweaking of the sense of the name (as understood by runologists) was necessary. With the designation 'inherited possession', ᛟ could be made to signify Aryan and Germanic heritage, power and life. In its new guise it was used as an emblem by among others members of the *Rasse- und Siedlungshauptamt* ('Race and Settlement Office') of the SS. It too appeared on badges for sale to all and sundry, its symbolic value explained as *Blut-Boden* 'blood-soil'. Further runes brought to prominence by the "Germanicisation" of society in the Nazi era included ᛏ, used by the SA and given the symbolic value 'struggle', ᛄ, borne on their uniform by adjutants in the Hitler Youth, and ᛉ signifying 'life'. Atop this heady mix stood the swastika, an ancient symbol appropriated by the Nazis. The fact that a good many people came to regard the swastika itself as a rune is an indication of the intellectual confusion that reigned.

The symbolic values attributed to certain runes by adherents of National Socialist ideology are the products of fantasy. Because of their associations these imaginings have taken on a sinister quality, but in essence they do not differ from many of the delusions about runes in circulation today. The titles of a selection of books making unjustified claims about runes are given on pp. 142–3. Anyone who taps "rune" or "runes" into an Internet search engine will need some foreknowledge and a good deal of patience to sort out the sense from the nonsense. In the latter category, a sample taken at random from a single page included: "Runes, Alphabet of Mystery", "FREE Rune Readings", "The Runic Journey", "Runes of Magic". On another page an entry with the innocuous title "Runes" began: "The origins of the Runes lays [*sic*] buried in distant [*sic*] past, predating the oldest religions. During that time those who practice [*sic*] this ancient system of magic...". The odd grammar, phraseology and spelling indicate that the writer is less than fastidious about presentation, and that is often a guide to the quality of the content, which in this instance is woeful. Apart from anything else, we have no way of knowing how old the oldest religions are. The writer goes on to bemoan the perverted use of runic symbolism under the Nazis, (wrongly) attributing to Adolf Hitler personally "a corrupted form of Runic occultism". S/he does not seem to realise that his/her words display exactly the same lack of intellectual rigour as that which allowed the Nazi fantasies to thrive. Indeed, the writer is at one with Nazi ideology in claiming an extraordinary age for the runes.

It may be argued that unwarranted beliefs in the nature and age of runic characters do no harm in themselves. Yet the flight from reason that is a prerequisite for holding such beliefs makes people vulnerable to persuasion of many different kinds. It is enough here to consider the more recent fate of ᛟ. The rune has been resuscitated as a symbol of white and/or Germanic supremacy, first through association with Óðinn and "the Vikings", and second by giving it the symbolic value "our inheritance" "our land" (which, interpreted, means "foreigners, keep out!"). Evidence-based understanding of runes and runic writing provides no warrant for any of this. The association of ᛟ with Óðinn and the new symbolic value attributed to it spring entirely from the imagination. The sources show ᛟ to be a rune of the older *fuþark* and the Anglo-Frisian *fuþorc*, denoting /o(:)/ and /ø(:)/ respectively – no more, no less.

16.3 Conclusion

This brief examination of the use of runes in literature and politics demonstrates how crucial it is not to accept what one is told without evidence. It also underlines the importance of clear thinking and unambiguous terminology. Runology is of course different from the natural sciences: we cannot do an experiment, repeat it, and arrive at the same result time and time again. In the study of runes and runic writing we are for the most part dealing not with certainty, but plausibility and probability. However, that should not be seen as an invitation to abandon intellectual rigour. Runologists have to abide by the same academic standards as students of any other subject. Their procedures must be clear and transparent, their approach impartial and questioning, and their conclusions based on careful consideration of whatever facts are available. Where there is too little evidence to allow conclusions safely to be drawn, this should be acknowledged. Nothing of intellectual value is gained by filling the vacuum of ignorance with products of the imagination.

17 A brief history of runology

17.1 Introduction

As was shown in chapter 11, serious study of runic writing began while runes continued in use in one or two outlying corners of the Scandinavian-speaking world – and while they were still known to a good few people in Scandinavian society in general. No question of decipherment thus arose, as it did in the case of many other early writing systems. The older *fuþark* had fallen into oblivion, but full understanding of it was regained during the nineteenth century with the help of the Vadstena bracteate *fuþark* (p. 17), early *runica manuscripta* (cf. pp. 154–5, 205), and the Anglo-Saxon *fuþorc*. Knowledge of the last persisted in one form or another over the years. In seventeenth-century England there were certainly people able to read Anglo-Saxon runes and transliterate them fairly accurately into roman letters.

Runic research takes many forms. An elementary division can be made into (1) the treatment of individual inscriptions (documentation, editing and publication), and (2) the study of broader runological questions (such as the origin of the runes or the relationship of different rune-rows to one another), but there can be a considerable degree of overlap between the two. Activities that do not fit easily into either category include the compiling of reference works and the dissemination of news about matters runic (including the presentation of new finds). In addition, there have of course been a multitude of smaller studies on all kinds of rune-related topics, but here we follow the main lines of development.

17.2 The documentation, editing and publication of inscriptions

The study of runes and runic inscriptions is generally taken to have begun at the end of the sixteenth century (concerning the publication of runic alphabets and rune-rows in the 1500s and 1600s, see 11.3). In Sweden the scholar Johan Bure (or Johannes Bureus in Latinised form) travelled widely in search of rune-stones. He worked from the 1590s until the middle of the following century, examining inscriptions and making drawings of them. On the basis of his field-work he compiled a number of manuscripts and copperplate engravings. Very little of this material was ever published, but most of it has survived into modern times. Part of what Bureus left to posterity can be seen as an embryonic corpus edition of the Swedish rune-stones. As well as providing illustrations of individual inscriptions, he wrote out their runes, rendered them into roman script (in the form of Old Swedish texts rather than transliterations), and gave Latin translations. For his time Bureus was a remarkably accurate recorder and capable interpreter of rune-stone inscriptions, although there were of course things he misunderstood. It is not for nothing he has been called the father of runology (see further 17.3).

Bureus had a rival in Denmark in the person of Ole Worm (Latinised as Olaus Wormius), doctor of medicine and antiquarian. In 1643 Worm published *Danicorum Monumentorum Libri Sex* 'Six Volumes of the Danish Monuments', primarily an edition of all the then known Danish, Norwegian and Gotlandic runic inscriptions (Norway and Gotland being at that time part of the Danish kingdom). The work includes drawings of the individual inscriptions, a rendering of the runes into roman (not a transliteration in the modern sense since there is considerable editorial intervention), a translation into Latin, and commentary. Worm gets reasonably close to the sense of most of the runic monuments he treats, but as one might expect there are misreadings and misinterpretations. In the case of the fourth- or fifth-century older-*fuþark* Tune stone (Østfold, Norway) he is all at sea. The inscription is barely recognisable in the schematic drawings he prints, and he despairs, he says, of being able to offer an interpretation. It must be remembered, though, that Worm was working almost 200 years before the first serious attempts to get to grips with the older *fuþark* (see 17.1 above)

Two of Bureus's successors in Sweden were Olaus Verelius, who published a *Manuductio* 'Handbook' of runes and runic writing, exemplified by various Swedish rune-stone inscriptions (1675), and Johan Göransson, whose work *Bautil* 'Memorial Stone' (1750) presents a large number of Swedish rune-stones – in the form of woodcuts (of varying reliability depending in part on who made the original drawing), printed runic texts (with stylised rune forms), and Swedish translations. Verelius's work is largely discursive, though he offers independent readings and interpretations of several inscriptions. In the face of the unknown, Verelius, like Worm, admits defeat. He reproduces Bureus's careful drawings of the staveless Malsta and Hälsingtuna inscriptions (Hälsingland, Sweden, probably eleventh century; see 7.6), but declares that such *Willoruner* 'cryptic runes' are not meant to be understood and that effort spent on trying to decipher them has little point (cf. p. 205). In *Bautil* it is the illustrations that assume particular importance since some of the inscriptions portrayed have since disappeared or been damaged in one way or other. This is not a feature peculiar to *Bautil*: a good number of printed works, manuscripts and drawings preserve runic inscriptions, and the odd *runicum manuscriptum* (chapter 13), that would otherwise have been lost. One important example is the text on the gold horn from Gallehus (pp. 194–5). The object itself was stolen in 1802 and melted down, but fortunately three independent drawings were made shortly after the horn was discovered in 1734. The Anglo-Saxon *Rune Poem*, preserved only in a printed book of 1705 after the destruction of the manuscript source in 1731 (p. 159), is another case.

The nineteenth century saw an increase in the number of works devoted to the publication of runic inscriptions. In most cases there was also an increase in quality. The Swedish antiquarian Johan Liljegren's *Run-urkunder* 'Runic records' (1833) makes reference to 3,000 inscriptions, Swedish and other, some 2,000 of which are transliterated into the roman alphabet. Although Liljegren's transliterations are not as precise as modern scholarship demands, there is nothing in them of the confusion with edited text and interpretation we find earlier. Liljegren, in fact, offers no interpretations at all, nor does he include drawings.

Svenska run-urkunder 'Swedish runic records' (1855–7) and *Sverikes run-urkunder* 'The runic records of Sweden' (1860–76) were the work of the Swedish historian and archaeologist Richard Dybeck. They present a selection of Swedish rune-stone inscriptions in the form of drawing, normalised runes, and transliteration, but offer little in the way of interpretation. The drawings and readings are reasonably accurate; the transliterations are slightly less precise than those of Liljegren in that Dybeck inserts spaces between words in place of the separators of the inscriptions.

The Danish historian P. G. Thorsen's *De danske Runemindesmærker* 'The Runic Monuments of Denmark' (1864–80) provides a fairly comprehensive account of the Danish rune-stones known at the time the work was published. It also deals with other types of runic writing found in Denmark and discusses general questions arising from some of the inscriptions. There are illustrations (drawings and lithographs), transliterations or 'readings', and interpretations, some detailed, some more summary. The illustrations are by and large reliable; the renderings of the inscriptions into roman less so, often coming closer to an edited text than a transliteration; the interpretations are sometimes fanciful, but mostly sober and well considered.

Unlike Liljegren, Dybeck and Thorsen, the Norwegian historian P. A. Munch did not compile a runic corpus edition. He did, though, contribute to a publication on the Orkney Maeshowe inscriptions (pp. 119–20), offering readings and interpretations of virtually the whole corpus (cf. James Farrer, *Notice of Runic Inscriptions Discovered during Recent Excavations in the Orkneys*, 1862). Munch's approach is critical and cautious, and it is clear he understood better than the other contributors to the volume (and anyone else at the time) what the inscriptions say. As a transliterator Munch is less convincing. His readings, like those of so many of his contemporaries, combine the reproduction of the runes in roman with editorial features such as word spacing, punctuation and capitalisation, and he is not averse to taking other liberties, such as rendering one and the same rune with different roman letters, or, conversely, giving different runes the same roman equivalent.

A runic corpus edition on a grand scale is the Copenhagen professor George Stephens's four-volume *The Old-Northern Runic Monuments of Scandinavia and England* (1866–1901). This takes in inscriptions in the older and younger *fuþark*s and also the Anglo-Saxon *fuþorc* (indeed, it is the nearest thing we have to an edition of the Anglo-Saxon inscriptions). Many readers will see it as an advantage that the work is written in English. For all that, it cannot be recommended. While the illustrations are generally reliable, and on occasion show inscriptions or features no longer extant, the readings and interpretations are idiosyncratic, often wildly so. Serious runologists today regard Stephens's edition as little more than a curiosity.

With the Danish comparative philologist and runic scholar Ludvig Wimmer's *De danske runemindesmærker* 'The Runic Monuments of Denmark' (1895–1908), we enter the era of the modern runic corpus edition. The work concentrates on commemorative rune-stones to the exclusion of much else, but one of its merits is that each of the inscriptions included is treated according to a set format, closely adhered to. The inscription is described, and the size, shapes and peculiarities of individual runes commented on as appropriate. There follows a transliteration into lower-case, wide-spaced roman, with separators shown. Rounded brackets indicate uncertain readings, square brackets editorial expansions or readings taken from earlier accounts (the functional distinction between the two types of bracket is not in fact absolute). Next comes discussion of the reading, leading to an edited text in Old Danish followed by a translation into modern Danish placed within double inverted commas. Thereafter the wider context of the inscription is considered. Each runic object is illustrated by a drawing. Treatment of the individual inscriptions is preceded by a lengthy introduction in which the Danish commemorative rune-stones are discussed as a group. Themes here include: the purpose of the stones; their general appearance; the age, geographical spread, names and current locations of the inscriptions; rune-carvers; the art of the rune-stones; stones with rune-like symbols; Danish runic monuments abroad (i.e. monuments outside Denmark for which Danes can be considered responsible). Although Wimmer's edition lacks discussion of the principles on which it was based, and an account of how it was compiled, in most respects it marks a giant leap forward compared with what went before.

Runic research has of course moved on in the more than 100 years that have elapsed since *De danske runemindesmærker* was completed, and the work has been superseded by newer editions, but many of the differences between these and Wimmer's concern details rather than fundamentals: the corpus has been expanded with numerous new finds; more secure datings have (in some cases) been achieved; there is fuller understanding of the contexts in which many inscriptions were made; greater stress is placed on coverage of the whole corpus (and not merely commemorative rune-stones); modern photography has considerably improved the quality of illustrations.

Contemporary with Wimmer's edition and similar to it in methodology is *Norges Indskrifter med de ældre Runer* 'The Inscriptions of Norway with the Older Runes [i.e. in the older *fuþark*]' (1891–1924). This extensive work was begun by the Norwegian philologist, Sophus Bugge, and completed by his pupil, Magnus Olsen. The presentation of the individual inscriptions differs slightly from Wimmer's. First comes detailed discussion of the reading (as required). There follows a reproduction of the runes in normalised form and a precise transliteration into bold lower-case roman (although uncertainty of reading is not normally indicated). Out of the ensuing discussion, which takes in runography, language, meaning and context, emerges what might be termed a modified transliteration incorporating word separation, which is then translated into Dano-Norwegian (the Danish-based written language used in Norway at the time). Illustration is by photograph as well as drawing. As *De danske runemindesmærker* in Denmark, *Norges Indskrifter med de ældre Runer* marked the beginning in Norway of the modern runic corpus edition.

From these two seminal works we move to the editions that are still by and large used today (listed at the end of chapter 18) – notwithstanding some of the volumes go back seventy years or more and are sorely in need of updating.

One thing the "modern" editions have in common is that they aim (by and large) for comprehensive coverage of the corpus. In structure and approach they can differ considerably. *Sveriges runinskrifter* 'The Runic Inscriptions of Sweden' and *Norges innskrifter med de yngre runer* 'The Inscriptions of Norway with the Younger Runes' concentrate on the individual inscriptions, consigning the broader aspects of their material to introductory remarks, final reflections, indices or asides. *Sveriges runinskrifter*, not least because of the size of the corpus, has a range of compilers. Perhaps because of that, it is less subject to editorial whim than *Norges innskrifter med de yngre runer*, which up to and including vol. 5 was virtually the private province of Magnus Olsen (cf. above). Certain of the editorial procedures in *Sveriges runinskrifter* can be traced back to the editions of Liljegren and Dybeck, and some of those in *Norges innskrifter med de yngre runer* to the earlier *Norges Indskrifter med de ældre Runer*.

Danmarks runeindskrifter 'The Runic Inscriptions of Denmark', compiled by the Danish runologists Lis Jacobsen and Erik Moltke, is organised very differently from its Swedish and Norwegian counterparts. More like an encyclopaedia, it is much easier to use for those seeking specific details. The disadvantage is that the story of an individual inscription may have to be teased out of different parts of the work. Nevertheless, *Danmarks runeindskrifter* contains a much wider spectrum of information than *Sveriges runinskrifter* and *Norges innskrifter med de yngre runer*, and this information is presented in more systematised and accessible form. Moltke's *Runes and their Origin: Denmark and Elsewhere* provides a supplement to *Danmarks runeindskrifter*, and for English-language readers a useful alternative, though it is far from being a corpus edition.

Wolfgang Krause and Herbert Jankuhn's *Die Runeninschriften im älteren Futhark* 'The Runic Inscriptions in the Older *Fuþark*', like *Sveriges runinskrifter* and *Norges innskrifter med de yngre runer*, is structured round the individual inscription. The work does, however, begin with a general introduction, and there are short preambles to each of the ten categories into which the inscriptions are divided. Because so much of the older-*fuþark* material is hard to understand (cf. chapter 4), the temptation to offer speculative interpretations is always present, and it is a temptation the compilers of *Die Runeninschriften im älteren Futhark* are not always able to resist (cf. 15.1). To a limited extent this edition overlaps with an earlier one, *Die einheimischen Runendenkmäler des Fastlandes* 'The Runic Monuments belonging to the Mainland of Europe' (1939). However, as the title suggests, the authors of this work, the historical linguist, Helmut Arntz, and the prehistorian Hans Zeiss, concentrate exclusively on the Continental material (in which the Frisian is included).

Anders Bæksted's *Islands runeindskrifter* 'The Runic Inscriptions of Iceland' is in some respects the most advanced of all the early and mid-twentieth century runic corpus editions. It is more explicit about procedure and in general more rigorous and consistent in its treatment of the material. Unusually, the compiler explains the principle underlying his transliteration practice. The Icelanders, he maintains, used runes as roman-alphabet equivalents, 'as simple replacements for the corresponding latin letter'. His system of transliteration thus takes the roman letters as its starting point rather than the runes – a reversal of the normal procedure. While clear and explicit enough, such an approach raises problems. It is hardly self-evident, for example, that ᛁ and ᚼ should both be transliterated **o**, but that is how they are treated in *Islands runeindskrifter* because the compiler considers 'o' to be the letter an Icelander writing in the roman alphabet would have used in the relevant contexts.

All of these twentieth-century editions are copiously illustrated, though the quality of the photographs and drawings, in particular in vol. 1 of *Norges innskrifter med de yngre runer* and the early volumes of *Sveriges runinskrifter*, may leave something to be desired. In comparison with the earlier editions they mark a clear improvement, not least because the compilers were able to build upon the work (and learn from the mistakes) of their predecessors. Most of the volumes, however, are far from fulfilling the ideals set out in the penultimate paragraph of 15.1. It was with those ideals firmly in mind that the compilers of recent editions of the Scandinavian runic inscriptions of the British Isles proceeded (*The Runic Inscriptions of Maeshowe, Orkney*; *The Runic Inscriptions of Viking Age Dublin*; *The Scandinavian Runic Inscriptions of Britain*; listed at the end of chapter 18). But it is of course for others to decide how far these authors achieved their aims.

There currently exist no corpus editions of the Anglo-Saxon, Frisian, Greenlandic or Manx runic inscriptions. For the Anglo-Saxon corpus, R. I. Page's *An Introduction to English Runes* offers a wide range of valuable insights; for the Frisian, Tineke Looijenga's article 'Checklist Frisian runic inscriptions' sets out the basics (both cited at the end of chapter 18, and in other reading lists). A rudimentary introduction to the inscriptions on the Manx crosses will be found in Page's article 'The Manx rune-stones' (reference at the end of chapter 8), and a guide to important parts of the Greenlandic corpus in Marie Stoklund's paper 'Greenland runes: isolation or cultural contact?' (listed at the end of chapter 10). Þorgunnur Snædal's article 'Rúnaristur á Íslandi' (cited at the end of chapter 18) provides an up-to-date list of the Icelandic runic inscriptions with transliterations and brief notes, and Marie Stoklund's paper 'Faroese runic inscriptions' (reference at the end of chapter 10) performs a similar service for the small Faroese corpus.

The editing of runic inscriptions continues. Further volumes of *Sveriges runinskrifter* and *Norges innskrifter med de yngre runer* are planned, as are new editions of the Danish and Icelandic corpora and the inscriptions in the older *fuþark*. One reason new editions are needed is the large number of finds that have accrued since the existing works saw the light of day. It is unclear how many of the projected volumes will appear in book form. Internet publishing is significantly cheaper and allows regular updates. Important on-line runic data-bases already exist (for which references are provided at the end of this chapter).

17.3 Broader runological research

The study of runes and runic inscriptions can include an array of topics. The following brief survey will concentrate on the way scholars have approached what may be considered the core questions of runology: the origin and age of the runes, the development of the different rune-rows and their relationship to one another; the purposes and uses of runes; runes and language; the dating of inscriptions; the recording of runes in manuscripts. The survey will only be mildly topic-based, however. In order to give the reader an idea of how runological studies evolved and progressed, it will proceed more or less chronologically in the manner of 17.2.

Antiquarian interest in runes seems to go back as far as the Middle Ages, but it is in the early post-Reformation period this develops into a learned interest (11.3, 17.2). In the sixteenth and seventeenth centuries, scholars begin to write and publish on runes. They speculate about the origin and uses of the script, consider how runic writing relates to speech, and record and interpret individual runic inscriptions. It is important to remember that this was a discipline in its infancy. Very little was known or understood, which made possible all kinds of assumptions and claims that to us seem totally misguided. Early runic research must also be viewed in the context of Sweden's "age of greatness" – and its rivalry with Denmark, which had been the principal Scandinavian power in the Middle Ages.

Writing in the 1550s, the brothers Johannes and Olaus Magnus ascribe great antiquity to runic script – or at least to the "Alphabetum gothicum" they present (11.3). According to Johannes it arose shortly before or after the Flood. Olaus considers it was in use in 'a primeval age, when there were giants in the northern lands'. Their accounts, together with those of various seventeenth- and eighteenth-century Swedish scholars, suggest a two-fold origin for the runes: ancient hebrew script and native invention. "Native" in this context encompassed the Goths as well as the Swedes, as the title the Magnus brothers bestowed on their runic alphabet shows. Scholarly thinking at the time made a connection between the East Germanic Goths and the part of southern Sweden called Götaland. The Goths were supposed to have had their origin in this region, and the later inhabitants were deemed a remnant of the same people. For many the distinction between "Swede" and "Goth" became totally blurred, a state of mind which made it possible to confer great antiquity on the Swedish nation and language and to claim all the deeds of the Goths as a Swedish inheritance. It is in this spirit Johannes Magnus's 1554 work is entitled *De omnibus Gothorum Sveonumque regibus etc.* 'Concerning all the Kings of the Goths and the Swedes etc.'. It should be stressed, however, that the runes to which such a long and venerable descent was attributed were, naturally enough, those with which Swedish scholars of the sixteenth to eighteenth centuries were familiar: the younger *fuþark*, with or without the expansions and changes it underwent during the Middle Ages. There is no sign here of the older *fuþark* or its Anglo-Saxon offshoot.

Early research on runes and runic writing encompassed much besides speculation about the origin and age of the script. The work of recording and editing inscriptions is described in 17.2. In addition to his work as a recorder, the Swedish pioneer, Johannes Bureus, furnished a detailed account of the sound or sounds each rune could stand for (though based more on the Swedish spoken in his day than the language of the late Viking Age or Middle Ages, of which he would have known little). Bureus also attempted to reintroduce runic script as an alternative to roman, in furtherance of which he in 1611 published *Rvna ABC boken* 'The Runic ABC Book'. This contains a brief introduction showing how the runes correspond to roman letters, followed by a number of short religious texts such as the Lord's Prayer and the Creed, most of them set out in runes and roman.

In Denmark Ole Worm wrote and published extensively on runes and runic writing. His most significant general work is ᚱᚢᚾᚼᛆ *seu danica literatura antiqvissima* 'Runes, or the most ancient Danish alphabet' (1636). Here he goes into a wide range of topics, including the origin of the runes, the nature of the characters, their purpose and use, the materials into which they were carved, their names, and the *fuþark* order in which they appear. Although patriotic zeal is less in evidence here than in the Swedish research, Worm is in no doubt that runic writing originated among the Danes. Like his Swedish counterparts, he traces the runes back to hebrew script, but he considers hebrew writing to have split into several branches. One branch spread north from the Mediterranean, picking up various features on the way, and ultimately reached Denmark. Out of this the Danes fashioned the runes. Similarities between particular runes and characters of other writing systems are explained by the long journey from hebrew to runic script. Worm's views led to acrimonious debate with Bureus. And other Swedish scholars continued the polemic, not least Bureus's immediate successor, Verelius, who had much to say in his *Manuductio* 'Handbook' (p. 198). Taken as a whole, Worm's runic scholarship is an eclectic mix, combining shrewd observation and sound reasoning with fanciful speculation. He is not above contradicting himself, and this can lead to lack of clarity as can the generally unsystematic presentation of such a wide range of ideas and material. Regarding the type of runes the Danes invented, however, Worm is totally clear: it is the younger *fuþark* that represents the oldest form of runic writing.

Worm's publications stimulated an interest in runes as far a-field as Britain, though not in a productive way. Many British writers began to associate "runes" and "runic" with Scandinavia in general, and extended the terms to language and literature, which did little to aid understanding. There were nevertheless people in seventeenth- and eighteenth-century Britain who recognised runes as a writing system pure and simple, and also realised they were not an exclusively Scandinavian phenomenon. In the early 1600s the Anglo-Saxon runes on the (now) lost head of the Bewcastle cross (Cumbria) were copied and transliterated reasonably accurately into roman letters, and in 1705 the Anglo-Saxon *Rune Poem* and much other runic material were given tolerably careful publication in George Hickes's encyclopaedic *Thesaurus* (p. 159). It would, however, take a long time before runic studies in Britain moved forward from these modest beginnings.

In his 1675 'Handbook' (cf. above), Verelius had declared the staveless runes to be *Willoruner* 'cryptic runes', not intended to be understood and therefore not worth bothering with. By an unfortunate coincidence 1675 was the very year the Swedish mathematician Magnus Celsius delivered his oration 'De runis helsingicis' 'Concerning the Hälsingland runes', given on the occasion of his retirement from the vice-chancellorship of the University of Uppsala. In this lecture (published in 1707 by his son, Olof Celsius) he unlocked the secret of the staveless runes, showing them to be what we recognise them as today: a version of the younger *fuþark* from which most of the verticals have been removed.

The eighteenth century saw little progress in runic research. In 1821, however, the German philologist Wilhelm Grimm published *Ueber deutsche Runen* 'Concerning German Runes', in which he argued on the basis of early *runica manuscripta* that the Germans had possessed a rune-row different from both the Scandinavian (younger) *fuþark* and the Anglo-Saxon *fuþorc*, and that these manuscript runes must reflect a German epigraphic tradition (no German inscriptions were known at the time). Grimm concluded that the younger-*fuþark* runes were the oldest type (brought from Central Asia and related to the greek alphabet) because they exhibited the simplest system and bore the original names (the latter a wholly incorrect assumption). He thought it likely the German runes developed in northern *Germania*, close to Scandinavian culture, from where they spread northwards, southwards, and westwards, reaching England with the Saxon invaders. Grimm's "German" runes are in fact those of the older *fuþark*. Notwithstanding this misapprehension, and the primacy he gives to the younger *fuþark*, his study is often said to mark the beginning of "scientific" runic research. Gone is the wild speculation of earlier times, to be replaced by careful and critical analysis of the evidence. That Grimm nevertheless reached a false conclusion could be due to the power of habitual thinking. So entrenched was the idea that the sixteen runes of the younger *fuþark* represented the original state, that he may have looked for confirmation of this view rather than reasons to challenge it.

Yet Grimm did have a contemporary who was prepared to think along more radical lines. In two studies (1822 and 1839) the Danish natural historian and philologist Jakob Bredsdorff argued persuasively that the runes we know as the older *fuþark* represented the earliest form of runic writing. He was also able to offer an interpretation of the fourth- or fifth-century Gallehus gold horn inscription (pp. 194–5) not far removed from the one accepted today – at all events a drastic improvement on previous attempts. In one important respect Bredsdorff and several of his contemporaries were still on the wrong track. They assumed older-*fuþark* Y to stand for /m/ (its value in the younger *fuþark*), notwithstanding the presence of ᛗ **m** in the older rune-row. Around the middle of the nineteenth century this misconception was put right by the Norwegian historian P. A. Munch and the Danish antiquarian C. C. Rafn. To begin with Munch had taken Y as **m**, just as his fellow scholars. The linguistic forms that emerged from this identification had led him to the conclusion that the language of the older-*fuþark* inscriptions was Gothic, and that the younger *fuþark* represented a rival runic writing system introduced

by Scandinavian invaders. Subsequent detailed consideration of several older-
fuþark inscriptions persuaded him that Ⴤ must in fact stand for some kind
of [z]- or "rs"-sound, although he still maintained the language they were
written in was Gothic. For Rafn, the existence of older-*fuþark* ᛗ **m** meant
Ⴤ was unlikely to stand for [m]. Looking at the occurrence of Ⴤ in various
inscriptions in the older runes he concluded it must represent [r] (in spite of
the existence of ᚱ **r**). These ideas were taken up by the Norwegian philologist
Sophus Bugge, who ultimately opted to transliterate Ⴤ **R**, although, following
Munch, he conceded it might stand for some kind of [z].

The scholar who is credited with establishing once and for all the
relationship of the different rune-rows to each other is the Danish
comparative philologist and runologist, Ludvig Wimmer. In his seminal work
'Runeskriftens Oprindelse og Udvikling i Norden' 'The origin and development
of runic writing in Scandinavia' (1874), expanded and translated into German
as *Die Runenschrift* 'The Runic Script' (1887), Wimmer showed conclusively
that the twenty-four character *fuþark* was the oldest rune-row, from which
the sixteen-character Scandinavian row derived. He placed the origin of the
script at around AD 200, and argued that the runes were based on latin capitals
(neither of which positions is far removed from common opinion today –
cf. pp. 4–6, 14 – though his dating of the oldest preserved inscriptions to the
fourth century is far too late). He also sought to explain the development
that led from the older to the younger *fuþark*. He saw it as a gradual process:
ᛁ, ᚴ, ◇ were eliminated early through lack of use; later ᚷ, ᛗ, ᛉ, ᛜ were dropped,
ᚷ, ᛗ, ᛜ following changes to the initial sound of their names, ᛉ in part at
least because of the common change /o/ > /u/ in word endings; finally, around
800, ᛈ was replaced by ᚾ. It is instructive to compare Wimmer's account
with the discussion on pp. 56–9. Many would agree that he showed foresight
in ascribing the loss of certain runes to changes in the form of their names,
though they would add ᛈ to that group, perhaps also ᛁ, ◇, ᛉ, while excluding
ᚷ and ᛜ. Much of what Wimmer has to say here is still worthy of consideration,
not least given the lack of consensus that continues to exist about the causes
or the process of the change that led from the older to the younger *fuþark*.
Few, though, would now put the emergence of the new rune-row as late
as *c.* 800.

In the course of the twentieth century runic research became more diverse.
One of the topics most widely debated was the origin and age of the runes (see
chapter 2 for presentation and discussion of the principal hypotheses). The
debate had – and still has – many participants. Here only a few of them can be
mentioned. The belief that runes were derived from the classical greek alphabet
is chiefly associated with the Swedish language historian and runologist Otto
von Friesen, who published articles on the subject in 1904 ('Om runskriftens
härkomst' 'Concerning the origin of runic script') and 1913 ('Runskriftens
härkomst' 'The origin of runic script'). His view became very influential for
a time not least through his encyclopaedia articles on runes. The realisation
that some runic inscriptions were older than the date at which greek writing
could have inspired the creation of the script in von Friesen's scenario, spelt
the end of this line of thinking. The north etruscan derivation was proposed

by the Norwegian Celtic scholar Carl Marstrander in a 1928 article ('Om runene og runenavnenes oprindelse' 'Concerning the origin of the runes and the rune names'). It drew support from the Finnish philologist Magnus Hammarström in a paper published the following year ('Om runskriftens härkomst' 'Concerning the origin of runic script'), and remained influential until long after the Second World War (an attempt has of late been made to revive it; cf. the reference to Mees at the end of chapter 2). In recent years many scholars have returned to Wimmer's view that the runes are (in the main, at least) derived from latin capitals. Proponents of this idea include the Danish runologist Erik Moltke and the Swedish language historian and runologist Henrik Williams (references at the end of chapter 2). A hypothesis that the runes go back to an archaic form of the greek alphabet in use *c.* 400–300 BC was launched by two American historical linguists, Elmer Antonsen and Richard Morris (see, e.g., Morris's book *Runic and Mediterranean Epigraphy*, cited at the end of chapter 2). This idea relies not only on similarities of form between archaic greek characters and runes and between the archaic greek and early runic writing systems, but on the belief that the older *fuþark* reflects the phonology of Germanic as it was some centuries before the Christian era. The absence of runic inscriptions that can be dated earlier than AD *c.* 160 has led most runologists to reject the proposal.

The purposes for which runes were invented and the uses to which they were originally put are briefly considered in chapter 2. The ideas put forward there are however by no means the only ones. In the first half of the twentieth century many scholars associated runes with cult and magic. So convinced were they these were the contexts in which runes were used that they hardly bothered to argue the case. Much was thereby left unclear. Were runes adopted for magic purposes or were they invented with such purposes in mind? Were they used for profane purposes as well? A couple of quotations will give the flavour of the "argument". In his 1912 article 'En indskrift med ældre runer fra Huglen i Søndhordland' 'An inscription with older runes from Huglen [Nordhuglo] in Sunnhordland' the Norwegian runologist Magnus Olsen wrote of 'the distinctly magical character of runic writing', and in a contribution to a 1930 paper felt able to affirm: 'priest and rune magician are united in one and the same person' (author's translations). In the same year his fellow-countryman Carl Marstrander made a series of assertions of similar type in the article 'Tunestenen' 'The Tune stone'. He claims, *inter alia*: '*There* [in southern Europe] the inscriptions belong to mankind, *here* they are all part of the world of the gods, they are *ragina-kundoʀ* [pp. 191–3], born of divine powers'; 'Among the Germanic peoples the runes have always evoked particular religious and mythical associations; they were sacred symbols rather than letters' (author's translations). As late as 1966 the German runologist Wolfgang Krause was promoting similar ideas (pp. 179, 201). These scholars allowed their conviction to form the starting point of the debate, and pressed anything and everything into service in support of that conviction, leaving little or no room for counter-argument. Fortunately this was provided by the Danish runologist Anders Bæksted in his 1952 book *Målruner og troldruner* 'Language runes and magic runes'. Bæksted conducted a forensic examination of the whole gamut of rune magic, and found arguments in its favour wanting. Although aspects of the book were criticised by some, it became much more difficult after its appearance to make unsupported assertions about the magical or divine nature of runes. Scholars today, by and large, tread more carefully (cf. the work by Flowers, cited at the end of this chapter).

The Danish runologist Erik Moltke argued widely that trade was the key to understanding the genesis of the runes. He saw them as a neutral means of communication, invented by Germanic speakers who recognised how useful a writing system could be in keeping track of clients, stock, payments, etc. He was convinced that even in their infancy runes had been employed much as they came to be in medieval Bergen (pp. 106–15). Against this it has been pointed out that few, if any, of the earliest inscriptions are reminiscent of those found in Bergen or comparable Scandinavian towns. One or two are suggestive of the world of trade, but as a whole the extant corpus offers little evidence to help us understand why runes were invented. Their original purpose, most would probably agree, remains elusive (see pp. 11–12, 14).

An important question for modern runic research has been how to date individual inscriptions. Scholars of the sixteenth, seventeenth and eighteenth centuries tended not to trouble themselves greatly about chronology or the absolute or relative age of runic artefacts. Many of them were happy in the belief that things runic must of necessity be ancient. Some eighteenth-century voices were raised against this unreflecting approach. It was pointed out, for example, that the Viking-Age inscriptions appeared for the most part to spring from a Christian environment, and could not therefore be anything like as old as had often been supposed. Serious attempts to date individual inscriptions began with the corpus editions of the nineteenth century. A variety of criteria were used – runological, linguistic, archaeological, historical, and genealogical for the most part. As knowledge of runic writing increased, it could be shown that certain rune forms belonged to particular periods, and a rough chronology established. Understanding of linguistic history grew too, making it possible to assign approximate dates to many inscriptions on the basis of their language forms. Some runic artefacts came from reasonably well-documented archaeological contexts, and could be dated on that basis. A few inscriptions mentioned historical characters or events (or what were taken to be such), which placed them within fairly narrowly defined periods. The close absolute dating of certain inscriptions allowed the relative dating of many of the rest (the presence or absence of particular features meant they could be categorised as contemporary with, earlier, or later than such inscriptions as had been fixed in time). Alternatively, inscriptions that mentioned different generations of the same family could be used to document relative age within a small group of texts. However carefully argued, these early attempts at dating were often ad hoc and unsystematic. Criteria relevant to particular inscriptions were seized upon as and where they could be found, but there was little attempt to establish a general framework within which one dating could be judged against another.

The compilers of the mid-twentieth century corpus edition, *Danmarks runeindskrifter* 'The Runic Inscriptions of Denmark' (p. 201), attempted to remedy this position. Taking as the starting point inscriptions to which they felt an absolute date could be assigned, they sorted the Danish corpus into four different periods. Period 1 encompassed inscriptions written in runes of the older *fuþark* and exhibiting a pre-Old Norse type of language. Period 2 covered the Viking Age (*c.* 750/800–1050), period 4 the Middle Ages (beginning early in the twelfth century), with period 3 representing the transition between 2 and 4. Period 2 was subdivided into 2a (*c.* 750/800–900), 2b (*c.* 900–1000), 2c (*c.* 1000–1050), and 3 into 3a (*c.* 1050–1100) and 3b (*c.* 1100–1150; 3b thus overlapped with 4). The methodology (described briefly in 8.2) distinguishes carefully between absolute and relative dating, but the temptation to conflate the two has often proved too strong. Thus many a scholar noting the period to which a particular inscription is assigned in *Danmarks runeindskrifter* has happily given the inscription the date range allotted to that period (or an even narrower one). That an inscription is assigned to a particular period, however, does not necessarily imply it was made within the relevant date range, rather that it has features in common with one or more other inscriptions which have been dated absolutely within the range. And there can of course be other than chronological reasons for the occurrence of shared features. New finds, altered datings, and reinterpretations, coupled with concern about the way in which *Danmarks runeindskrifter*s periodisation was being misunderstood and/or misused, have led to attempts to provide a revised chronology for the Danish inscriptions. While progress has undoubtedly been made, there is still much that remains uncertain.

In Sweden, the main effort has gone into trying to establish a rough chronology of the Viking-Age rune-stones, though nothing like the Danish periodisation has been suggested. To begin with, a crude distinction was made between the bulk of the inscriptions, dated somewhen in the eleventh century, and a small group dated in the ninth or tenth, with the oldest placed on rather uncertain grounds around 800. Many fell back upon this basic distinction when late twentieth-century studies exposed flaws in various runological and linguistic criteria used to support more precise datings. Recently attempts have been made to establish a chronology of the "eleventh-century" inscriptions using variation in ornamental style as a guide. Six stylistic types have been identified. Together with a group of unornamented stones, this gives seven periods of about thirty years each extending, with some degree of overlap, from about 980 to 1130. As with the Danish periodisation, the proposed chronology is relative, but with such comparatively narrow date ranges the urge to place particular inscriptions firmly within one of the roughly thirty-year spans has proved powerful. The stylistic method of classification has elicited some criticism. Attention has been drawn in particular to conflicts between the "stylistic age" of certain rune-stones and the approximate date that might reasonably be assigned to them on other grounds.

Norwegian runologists continue to date inscriptions by a variety of criteria. Although no general framework has so far been proposed, the large number of finds made since the middle of the twentieth century in controlled archaeological excavations (cf. p. 106) has provided a solid basis for the dating of much of the medieval runic material.

Among the most difficult runic inscriptions to date are some in the older *fuþark*. This is partly because they are so far removed from us in time and often difficult to understand, partly because there are relatively few of them, offering little basis for comparison. Wolfgang Krause in his edition *Die Runeninschriften im älteren Futhark* (p. 201) used runic form as one of the principal dating criteria. He thought he could identify a chronological development in the shapes of several runes, and felt able to assign absolute, if approximate, dates to a number of forms. New finds, often archaeologically dated, together with various reappraisals of the chronology of the older-*fuþark* inscriptions, have largely discredited Krause's system, though recent work suggests that some rune forms may offer limited guidance to age.

One or two individual efforts apart, Anglo-Saxon runic studies remained moribund until the twentieth century (on the work of George Stephens, see p. 199). During that century important work was done on a number of individual inscriptions or groups of inscriptions, a system of transliteration for Anglo-Saxon runes was elaborated (in which each rune is given a lower-case roman equivalent set between single inverted commas), and a thorough survey of English runic coins published. The name most associated with Anglo-Saxon runic scholarship in the second half of the twentieth century is R. I. Page. He published widely on many aspects of the subject, and his *Introduction to English Runes* (1st ed. 1973, 2nd ed. 1999; p. 53) can be seen as a preliminary to the corpus edition he had been preparing for a number of years but which he never completed. A significant contribution to the understanding of how the Anglo-Saxon runes developed is David Parsons's *Recasting the Runes* (1999). The author argues cogently that the Anglo-Saxon *fuþorc* was reformed in the late seventh century, and contrasts developments in England with those in Scandinavia (cf. pp. 39–41, 58–9). He also offers a detailed reappraisal of the relationship of the earliest Anglo-Saxon runes to those found on the Continent.

1954 saw the production of a rather different kind of work dealing with Anglo-Saxon runes – René Derolez's *Runica Manuscripta: The English Tradition*. As indicated by the title, the book deals almost entirely with runes in manuscripts. Its significance lies in the wealth of material it placed before the runological community, and the prominence it gave to what up to the time it appeared had been a rather neglected subject. Although subtitled *The English Tradition*, the work does have something to say about "Norse runic cryptography". Scandinavian epigraphic and manuscript evidence is compared with the English cryptographic tradition as it emerges from the *runica manuscripta*. The Scandinavian manuscript material consists of an extract from the eighteenth-century Icelander Jón Ólafsson's treatise *Runologia*. Like many of the English *runica manuscripta*, post-Reformation Icelandic writing on runes, their forms and uses, was little known at the time Derolez published his book. In recent years considerable interest has developed in this late Icelandic tradition, but it is as yet unclear what connection it has to earlier runic writing and rune-lore.

With the rise of linguistic science in the twentieth century some runologists began to study rune-rows more systematically, and to analyse the way particular sets of runes were deployed to denote particular sound systems. Questions were asked that had been little considered earlier. What constitutes a rune – how does one tell the difference between two variants of the same rune and two different runes? What status do the dotted runes have – are they independent characters or variants of other runes? How do runes denote the speech sounds of medieval Scandinavian as compared with the letters of the roman alphabet? Like much else in runology, these and related questions have yet to find a definitive answer.

17.4 Reference works

Runological reference works have been few and far between. A series planned and published in Göttingen, Germany, *Bibliographie der Runeninschriften nach Fundorten* 'Bibliography of Runic Inscriptions by Find-Place' has not gone beyond two volumes, one covering the British Isles (plus a supplement on the 'alleged runic inscriptions from North America', 1961) and one the Continent (1973). For Swedish inscriptions there is Jan Owe's *Svensk runbibliografi 1880–1993* 'Swedish Runic Bibliography 1880–1993' (1995). The runic newsletter *Nytt om runer* 'News about Runes', published by the Oslo Runic Archive since 1986, contains a bibliography of runic studies, continually updated (its chief function otherwise is to serve as a vehicle for the reporting and discussion of new finds; from issue no. 20 it has become an on-line publication only). Other useful reference works are the Swedish runologist Lena Peterson's *Svenskt runordsregister* 'Word Index to the Swedish Runic Inscriptions' (1st ed. 1989, 2nd ed. 1994; 3rd ed. on-line, see the reading list below) and *Nordiskt runnamnslexikon* 'Dictionary of Proper Names in Scandinavian Runic Inscriptions' (2007). Both these works, in spite of their titles, are limited to words from Viking-Age inscriptions. Peterson has, however, published an on-line dictionary of pre-Viking Age personal names, *Lexikon över urnordiska personnamn* (2004). A number of runic databases have been compiled in recent years, of which the most comprehensive and useful so far is *Samnordisk runtextdatabas* 'Pan-Scandinavian Runic Text Database', included in the on-line resource list below.

Select reading list

Flowers, Stephen E. 1986. *Runes and Magic: Magical Formulaic Elements in the Older Runic Tradition* (American University Studies, Series 1: Germanic Languages and Literature, vol. 53). New York: Lang. [A modern attempt to clarify the relationship between runic writing and magic.]

Gräslund, Anne-Sofie 2006. 'Dating the Swedish Viking-Age rune stones on stylistic grounds'. In: (Marie Stoklund *et al.*, eds) *Runes and their Secrets: Studies in Runology*. Copenhagen: Museum Tusculanum Press, 117–39.

Jacobsen, Lis, and Moltke, Erik 1947. *The Runic Inscriptions of Denmark: Summary*. Copenhagen: Munksgaard. [Explains the background to the corpus edition *Danmarks runeindskrifter*, and gives a detailed account of the periodisation of Danish runic inscriptions followed in that edition.]

Moltke, Erik 1985. *Runes and their Origin: Denmark and Elsewhere*. Copenhagen: The National Museum of Denmark, 504–9. [Offers a brief history of runic studies in Denmark.]

Page, R. I. 1999. *An Introduction to English Runes* (2nd ed.). Woodbridge: Boydell Press, 1–10. [Offers a brief history of runic studies in England.]

Stoklund, Marie 2006. 'Chronology and typology of the Danish runic inscriptions'. In: (Marie Stoklund *et al.*, eds) *Runes and their Secrets: Studies in Runology*. Copenhagen: Museum Tusculanum Press, 355–83. [Proposes a revision of the chronology and typology of the Danish runic inscriptions.]

On-line resources

Database of older-*fuþark* inscriptions:
http://www.runenprojekt.uni-kiel.de

Nytt om runer 'News about Runes':
http://www.khm.uio.no/forskning/publikasjoner/runenews

Peterson, Lena. *Lexikon över urnordiska personnamn*:
http://www.sofi.se/images/NA/pdf/urnord.pdf

Peterson, Lena. *Svenskt runordsregister* (3rd ed.):
http://uu.diva-portal.org/smash/record.jsf?pid=diva2:437203

Samnordisk runtextdatabas 'Pan-Scandinavian Runic Text Database':
http://www.nordiska.uu.se/forskn/samnord.htm

18 Where to find runic inscriptions

The majority of runic inscriptions are to be found in Denmark, Norway and Sweden. There are also a fair number preserved in Iceland, Germany, and different parts of the British Isles. Holland has a few, and there is a handful in the Faroe Islands, France and Russia. Bosnia, Hungary, Romania and Switzerland hold one or more examples. Most of the Greenlandic inscriptions are currently kept in Nationalmuseet ('The National Museum of Denmark'), Copenhagen, though some forty are held by Grønlands Nationalmuseum og Arkiv ('Greenland's National Museum and Archives') in Nuuk, Greenland. This distribution means that those interested in seeing a large number and a wide variety of runic inscriptions should visit Denmark, Norway or Sweden, ideally all three. Most Anglo-Saxon examples, unsurprisingly, are to be found in England; for first-hand study of the Anglo-Frisian tradition a trip to Holland is also essential.

Commonly, runic inscriptions are housed in museums. A great many, however, are located in churches. In Scandinavia the sheer number of sizeable stone monuments has made it impractical to move everything indoors, and many rune-stones (in Sweden the majority) stand out in the open. Some, situated in parks or churchyards, or by the roadside, are readily accessible; others are located in remote fields or hidden away in forests. In Sweden it is the custom to paint the carvings on rune-stones (usually in red), making such monuments relatively easy to spot among the myriad of stones littering the landscape. Detailed maps will often mark the location of ancient monuments (though not of rune-stones in particular). Some areas of Sweden and Denmark are richer in rune-stones than others. In Sweden the interested layman would do well to focus on the provinces of Uppland, Södermanland, Östergötland, Västergötland and Skåne, and the island of Gotland. In Denmark, northern, especially north-eastern, Jutland and the island of Bornholm have the biggest concentrations of rune-stones still standing outdoors. Most of Norway's relatively few runic stone monuments are now kept in museums. In the British Isles a small number of such inscriptions still stand in the open, but the majority are indoors. Some rune-stones, or fragments thereof, have been incorporated into church buildings (either for pious reasons or because they offered suitable material) and now form part of the structure. In Sweden, with its abundance of commemorative stone inscriptions, this is a particularly common phenomenon.

Some museums house large collections of runic material, others no more than a few objects, many just a single runic artefact. Mention will be made here chiefly of museums that hold a sizeable number of inscriptions. A slightly higher level of detail will be offered in the case of the British Isles, since English, Irish and Scottish museums are likely to lie within easier reach of most readers than those in other countries. A comprehensive list of Continental museums holding runic artefacts is provided in Klaus Düwel's *Runenkunde*, cited at the end of this chapter. Although the book is in German, those without knowledge of the language should experience no difficulty in using the list, which includes the names of the principal inscriptions held by each institution. Few of the Continental museums have substantial collections.

While certain museums display a good selection of their runic inscriptions in public galleries, this is by no means the rule. Often much is kept in store. What is on public view may vary from time to time. Not infrequently, objects are loaned to exhibitions and may be on their travels for several months. It is as well to make enquiry about availability before setting out. Preliminary contact should always be made with the relevant museum by anyone keen to examine specific inscriptions.

In Denmark, two museums in particular house a significant collection of runic objects: Nationalmuseet ('The National Museum of Denmark'), Copenhagen, and Moesgård Museum, outside Århus, Jutland. Both of these contain, *inter alia*, Viking-Age rune-stones and loose objects with older-*fuþark* inscriptions. Norway boasts at least five museums with important accumulations of runic material: Kulturhistorisk museum ('The Museum of Cultural History'), University of Oslo; Bergen museum; Bryggens museum ('The Wharf's Museum'), Bergen; Vitenskapsmuseet ('The Museum of Science and the Humanities'), Trondheim; Arkeologisk museum ('The Archaeological Museum'), University of Stavanger. Kulturhistorisk museum, Oslo, has only a small number of inscriptions on display relative to its total holdings. Currently most of the rune-stones owned by the Museum (which includes a number in the older *fuþark*) are in store awaiting a suitable venue where more of them can be exhibited. Bergen museum, likewise, keeps most of its rune-stones in store. Bryggens museum houses (on behalf of Bergen museum) the loose objects found during excavations at the medieval wharf site following the fire of 1955 (p. 106): a fair number are on display at any given time, but the majority are in store. A variety of runic inscriptions are held by Statens historiska museum ('The National Historical Museum'), Stockholm, and of these a reasonable selection is usually on display. That is also true of "Kulturen" – Lunds universitets historiska museum ('Lund University's Historical Museum'), Lund, Skåne, Sweden. Gotlands museum ('The Gotland Museum'), Visby, contains some important inscriptions, but the bulk of the Gotlandic runic material will be found distributed across the island's many churches (and identified by the name of the relevant church). The majority of the Icelandic runic artefacts are kept in Þjóðminjasafn Íslands ('The National Museum of Iceland'). Føroya fornminnissavn ('The Historical Museum of the Faroe Islands') is now home to most of the few extant Faroese inscriptions, and they are generally on display.

The runic inscriptions of Ireland come chiefly from the Dublin excavations of the 1970s and 80s, and these are held (mostly in store) by the National Museum of Ireland, Dublin. The British Museum, London, has a number of – mainly Anglo-Saxon – runic artefacts, some of which are customarily on display. North of the border, The Museum of Scotland, Edinburgh, holds a small collection of Scandinavian inscriptions, most of which are usually on show to the public. Smaller still are the collections in the Orkney Museum, Kirkwall, and the Shetland Museum, Lerwick, but for those interested in the runic heritage of the Northern Isles these are both valuable resources. The Manx Museum, Douglas, Isle of Man, holds a few runic inscriptions (mainly fragments), but the Manx material is mainly to be found in church contexts (see below).

Churches preserve a great many runic inscriptions. They may be found on gravestones, on church furnishings, carved into the walls, or on runic commemorative stones incorporated into the buildings. In some cases standing runic stones have been moved into churches for safe-keeping. Notable collections of inscriptions are found in Borgund stave-church, Sogn og Fjordane, Norway (carved into the wooden walls), and in Lye church, Gotland (cut into the plaster). Gol stave-church, now in the Norwegian Folk Museum, Bygdøy, Oslo, has a smaller number of inscriptions than Borgund, but is for most people an easier place to get to. Many of the runic carvings in stave-churches are hard to spot, and it is therefore wise to try to identify the approximate location of inscriptions before making a visit. Essential equipment is a good torch – raking light can bring out incisions scarcely visible to the naked eye. This applies not merely in the stave-church context but to faint runic carvings in general (indeed, good, variable lighting can give prominence to features even in boldly cut, well-preserved inscriptions). The Isle of Man commemorative stone crosses are almost all located in, or immediately outside, parish churches in the northern half of the island. The whereabouts of most can (as in Gotland) be ascertained from the name by which they are commonly known (Andreas 1–4, for example, will be found in Andreas parish church, those named Michael in Kirk Michael parish church, and so on).

There are one or two places in addition to churches and museums that boast collections of runic inscriptions. These are sites where people congregated, rested or sheltered, and found time to carve messages. A striking example from the British Isles is Maeshowe, the famous prehistoric chambered cairn on the Mainland of Orkney, whose walls carry over thirty inscriptions (pp. 119–20). Access to Maeshowe is limited, so there is little opportunity for detailed examination of the runes except by special arrangement with Historic Scotland, who manage the site. At least eight runic inscriptions are carved into a rock overhang on Holy Island, off the east coast of Arran, but this is quite a remote spot and can be difficult to get to or from in adverse weather conditions. In Norway there are several collections of runic inscriptions out in the open (see, e.g., p. 119), but none of them is easily accessible.

The principal runic corpus editions will almost always indicate where the inscriptions they include are to be found (see the annotated list below). However, it is well to be aware that runic inscriptions are not necessarily static – not even the larger stone monuments. They may be moved for a variety of reasons: for better protection or conservation, because of redevelopment (of institutions or land), because a local community demands the return of an artefact spirited off to a major museum at an earlier period, and so on. This means the more recent a corpus edition, the more accurate its information on the whereabouts of particular inscriptions is likely to be. The following list comprises editions and other works that will help readers in their searches (several, though, are in languages other than English). It should be noted that the location of inscriptions is not always given prominently at the outset of an account (as in Barnes and Page 2006, for example). It may sometimes be tucked away in the body of the text.

Useful works for ascertaining the location of runic inscriptions

Bæksted, Anders 1942. *Islands runeindskrifter* ['The Runic Inscriptions of Iceland'] (Bibliotheca Arnamagnæana 2). Copenhagen: Munksgaard. [This edition of the Icelandic runic inscriptions is in Danish. The beginning of the individual treatment of each inscription gives its early 1940s location.]

Barnes, Michael P. 1994. *The Runic Inscriptions of Maeshowe, Orkney* (Runrön 8). Uppsala: Institutionen för nordiska språk, Uppsala universitet. [Indicates the precise location in the cairn of each of the Maeshowe inscriptions.]

Barnes, Michael P., Hagland, Jan Ragnar, and Page, R. I. 1997. *The Runic Inscriptions of Viking Age Dublin*. Dublin: Royal Irish Academy. [The 1996 locations of Irish inscriptions other than those held by the National Museum of Ireland are noted at the beginning of the individual treatment of the relevant item.]

Barnes, Michael P., and Page, R. I. 2006. *The Scandinavian Runic Inscriptions of Britain* (Runrön 19). Uppsala: Institutionen för nordiska språk, Uppsala universitet. [The heading preceding the individual treatment of each inscription gives its 2005 location.]

Düwel, Klaus 2008. *Runenkunde* ['The Study of Runes'] (Sammlung Metzler 72, 4th ed.). Stuttgart/Weimar: Metzler. [This wide-ranging introduction to runic studies is in German. On pp. 226–9 it lists the Continental museums in which runic inscriptions are kept, together with the names of the most important runic artefacts held by each institution. The list goes on (pp. 229–30) to include the location of some important British and Scandinavian inscriptions, but there is a bias towards those in the older *fuþark* and the Anglo-Saxon *fuþorc*.]

Jacobsen, Lis, and Moltke, Erik 1941–2. *Danmarks runeindskrifter* ['The Runic Inscriptions of Denmark'] (2 vols + index). Copenhagen: Munksgaard. [This is the principal edition of the Danish inscriptions and is in Danish. The brief individual treatment of each inscription gives its location in the early 1940s.]

Jansson, Sven B. F. 1987. *Runes in Sweden*. Stockholm: Gidlunds. [Gives the approximate location of the inscriptions discussed – mainly a selection of rune-stones. A handy guide for those who do not have access to *Sveriges runinskrifter* (see below), or who have difficulty negotiating a work in Swedish.]

Krause, Wolfgang, and Jankuhn, Herbert 1966. *Die Runeninschriften im älteren Futhark* ['The Runic Inscriptions in the Older *Fuþark*'] (2 vols). Göttingen: Vandenhoeck & Ruprecht. [This is the standard edition of inscriptions in the older *fuþark*, although a good number have been discovered since it was published. It is in German. The beginning of the individual treatment of each inscription gives its 1960s location.]

Looijenga, Tineke 1994. 'Checklist Frisian runic inscriptions'. In: (Tineke Looijenga and Arend Quak, eds) *Frisian Runes and Neighbouring Traditions* (Amsterdamer Beiträge zur älteren Germanistik 45). Amsterdam/Atlanta: Rodopi, 91–108. [Offers a brief account of the Frisian inscriptions and notes the early 1990s location of each item.]

Moltke, Erik 1985. *Runes and their Origin: Denmark and Elsewhere.* Copenhagen: The National Museum of Denmark. [More up-to-date than Jacobsen and Moltke's 1941–2 edition, and in English, this book has a "Table of Inscriptions" (pp. 516–52), which gives the location of all the Danish examples mentioned. The table includes almost all new finds made between the compiling of *Danmarks runeindskrifter* and 1984.]

Olsen, Magnus *et al.* 1941 (in progress). *Norges innskrifter med de yngre runer* ['The Inscriptions of Norway with the Younger Runes'] (6 vols). Oslo: Kjeldeskriftfondet. [This is the principal edition of the Norwegian inscriptions – excepting those in the older *fuþark* – and is in Norwegian. The individual treatment of most inscriptions gives their location at the time the relevant volume was published. The information is usually appended to the history of the artefact concerned.]

Page, R. I. 1999. *An Introduction to English Runes* (2nd ed.). Woodbridge: Boydell Press. [References to the whereabouts of runic artefacts are scattered throughout the book. The location of most Anglo-Saxon inscriptions and Scandinavian inscriptions from England can be found by following up the page references under "Index of Inscriptions", pp. 241–3.]

Spurkland, Terje 2005. *Norwegian Runes and Runic Inscriptions.* Woodbridge: Boydell Press. [Gives the approximate location of many of the inscriptions discussed – chiefly the rune-stones and those carved into buildings. A handy guide for people who do not have access to *Die Runeninschriften im älteren Futhark* or *Norges innskrifter med de yngre runer* (see above), or who have difficulty negotiating works in German or Norwegian.]

Þorgunnur Snædal 2003. 'Rúnaristur á Íslandi', *Árbók hins íslenzka fornleifafélags* 2000–2001, 5–68. [An up-to-date list of the Icelandic inscriptions, written in Icelandic. The rudimentary account of each inscription includes an indication of its location at the beginning of the twenty-first century.]

[Various editors] 1900 (in progress). Sveriges runinskrifter ['The Runic Inscriptions of Sweden'] (14 vols). Stockholm: Kungl. Vitterhets Historie och Antikvitets Akademien. [This is the principal edition of the Swedish inscriptions and is in Swedish. Information about the location of inscriptions is much as in *Norges innskrifter med de yngre runer*.]

Glossary

Bracteate: an archaeological term for a one-sided medallion.

Cursive: a continuous form of writing, done without raising the pen between each letter.

Epenthetic vowel: a linguistic term referring to a new vowel that arises between two consonants. One such can be heard in the common Irish pronunciation of *film*, which could be rendered /filem/ in **phonemic notation**.

Etruscan: a non-Indo-European language spoken in north-central Italy. With the rise of the Roman Empire, the Etruscans became Roman citizens and began to speak Latin, and their own language died out. The Etruscans developed an alphabet based on the greek, and from this were derived the north etruscan and other north italic alphabets, used to write a variety of languages.

Etymon: an earlier language form from which one or more later forms are directly derived; Old English *cyning*, for example, is the etymon of modern English *king* (cf. **reflex**).

Fibula: an archaeological term used to refer to various types of brooch.

Gemination: the repeating (doubling) of written characters, as 'nn' in English *funny*, 'tt' in Old Norse *þetta* 'this [nom/acc. n.]'.

Germania: a name applied to the area of the Continent of Europe occupied by **Germanic**-speaking peoples at the time of the Roman Empire. The area concerned corresponded very roughly with modern Germany and Austria. However, there were no fixed borders at this period; tribes were often on the move and centres of power shifted. The southernmost part of *Germania* gradually came under Roman occupation, the larger, northern, part, known as *Germania libera* 'free *Germania*', remained independent of the Romans.

Germanic: a branch of the **Indo-European** language family, comprising an eastern, northern and western variety. East Germanic is known chiefly from fourth-century Gothic, preserved in manuscripts of the sixth and seventh centuries, but subsequently unrecorded and now extinct. North Germanic is the ancestor of the modern Scandinavian languages: Danish, Faroese, Icelandic, Norwegian and Swedish. West Germanic gave rise to Dutch, English, Frisian and High and Low German (the modern form of the latter often known as *Plattdeutsch*).

Grammatical terminology: used as sparingly as possible in this book, but sometimes unavoidable. Readers unsure of the meaning of basic terms such as "noun", "pronoun", "verb", "subject", "object", etc. should consult a grammar of English. "Grammatical case" in nouns, adjectives and pronouns refers to changes of form according to function. English distinguishes, for example, between *I* and *me*, *she* and *her*, as in *I like her and she likes me*, where *I* and *she* are the subject and *her* and *me* the object. All **Germanic** languages distinguished at one time between four "cases", nominative, accusative, genitive, dative, corresponding roughly to subject, object, possessive (as the *'s* in *John's car*), and indirect object (as *John* in *I gave John the book*, cf. the alternative phrasing: *I gave the book to John*). Person in verbs is a grammatical category that distinguishes speaker(s) – *I* or *we* – from addressee(s) – *you* (singular) or *you* (plural) – and both from other individuals or things – *he, she, it, they*. *I, we* is called 1st person, *you* 2nd person, and *he, she, it, they* 3rd person.

Ideograph: a character symbolising an idea or concept (e.g. + meaning 'plus'); in the runic context a character representing a complete word, usually the name of the rune concerned.

Indo-European: a family of languages spoken in an area stretching from Ireland in the west to northern India in the east. Most of the modern languages of Europe belong to the Indo-European family: notable exceptions are Finnish, Hungarian and Basque.

Middle Ages: refers in this book to the period roughly AD 1050–1525 – from the end of the **Viking Age** to the Reformation in Scandinavia.

Mutation: a sound change whereby the vowel of a stressed syllable adopts one or more of the features of the vowel or semi-vowel of the immediately following unstressed syllable. The Old Norse noun *saga* 'story' 'saga', for example, has the plural form *sǫgur*, in which the root vowel /a/ has been changed to a sound something like the vowel in English *hot* under the influence of the following /u/; one of the features of /u/ is lip-rounding, and that has been transferred to the original /a/. The unstressed vowel causing the mutation may disappear. Old Norse *fœtr* 'feet', plural of *fótr* 'foot', comes from an earlier **fōtiz*; the root vowel /o:/ (formed by raising the back of the tongue) has been changed to /ø:/ (formed by raising the front of the tongue), under the influence of /i/, a vowel in which the front of the tongue is raised to almost its maximum height. The same mutation has affected English, where the plural of *foot* is *feet*. (See further **phonetic** and **phonemic notation**, and p. 223.)

Phonemic notation: a means of rendering distinctive speech sounds in writing. A "distinctive speech sound" (often called a "phoneme") is the smallest segment of sound that can distinguish two words in a given language. The *l* in standard English *light* or *clear*, for example, has a different sound from the *l* in *cold* or *pile* (and different symbols may be used to denote them in a phonetic transcription). However, the contrast between the two can never be used to distinguish words in English because of their distribution: the type of *l* in *light* or *clear* occurs before vowels, the type in *cold* or *pile* before consonants or at the end of a word (the final vowel symbol in *pile* is of course silent). Phonemic notation is placed between forward slashes, e.g. /lait/, /pail/ for *light, pile*, where /l/ suffices for both varieties.

Phonetic notation: a means of rendering speech sounds in writing. Traditional spelling, especially English, is often a poor guide to pronunciation. The word *should*, for example, consists of three sounds: what is written 'sh' represents a single consonant, 'ou' stands for a single vowel, and *l* is "silent". Phonetic notation represents speech sounds on the principle that one symbol denotes one sound and one sound only. Thus *should* might be written [ʃud], square brackets being the usual way of marking a phonetic transcription. As can be seen, phonetic notation makes use of special characters in addition to those of the roman alphabet. In a "narrow" (more precise) transcription *should* would be rendered [ʃʊd] to mark the particular character of the *u*-sound. Roman letters may also have values other than those commonly associated with them in English orthography. The phonetic symbols used in this book are set out and their values given on pp. 221–2.

Phonetics: the study of the nature, production and perception of speech sounds. It employs **phonetic notation**.

Phonology: the study of the sound systems of individual languages. It employs **phonemic notation**.

Reflex: a later language form, derived directly from an earlier one; modern English *king*, for example, is the reflex of Old English *cyning* (cf. **etymon**).

Viking Age: refers in this book to the period roughly AD 700–1050. Other writers operate with different dates.

Phonetic and phonemic symbols

The following list shows the phonetic symbols used in this book, and offers an approximate guide to their pronunciation. Phonemes are contrastive units in the sound system of a given language (p. 219), and can thus encompass a range of speech sounds in the area of the phonetic equivalent. While [o], for example, denotes a particular vowel sound more or less precisely, /o/ stands for vowels close enough to [o] to contrast with other vowels. Phonemic notation (which makes use of the same symbols as its phonetic counterpart) is often preferable in discussions of languages no longer spoken since it is easier to gain a view of their sound systems than the precise shades of sound employed. Those with only a passing interest in the subject may simply regard phonemes as less precise equivalents of the relevant speech sounds.

1 Vowels

[a] As *a* in English *father*.

[e] As *é* in French *été* 'been' or *e* in German *lesen* '[to] read'.

[i] As *ea* in English *eat*.

[o] As *o* in German *los* 'loose'; similar to *oa* in Scottish pronunciation of *coat*.

[u] As *ou* in French *bouche* 'mouth' or German *u* in *suchen* '[to] seek'; similar to *oo* in English *cool*.

[æ] As English *a* in *hat*.

[ø] As French *eu* in *peuple* 'people' or German *ö* in *schön* 'beautiful'.

[y] As French *u* in *tu* 'you [sg.]' or German *ü* in *Bücher* 'books'.

[ɔ] As English *o* in *hot*.

[ə] As English *er* in *father*, or *o* in *police*.

2 Consonants

[b] As English *b* in *big*.

[c] As English *k* in *kit*.

[d] As English *d* in *dog*.

[f] As English *f* in *fun*.

[g] As English *g* in *gull*.

[h] As English *h* in *hot*.

[k] As English *c* in *cart*.

[l] As English *l* in *life*.

[m] As English *m* in *man*.

[n] As English *n* in *no*.

[p] As English *p* in *put*.

[r] Rolled, as the *r* in Scottish *run*.

[s] As English *s* in *sun*.

[t] As English *t* in *take*.

[v] As English *v* in *vote*.

[w] As English *w* in *wait*.

[z] As English *z* in *zip*.

[β] A continuous sound pronounced with both lips, as Spanish *b* or *v* in *hablar* '[to] speak', *vuelo* 'flight'.

[ç] As German *ch* in *ich* 'I'; roughly as English *h* in *huge*.

[tʃ] As English *ch* in *church*.

[ð] As English *th* in *the*.

[ɣ] As *ch* in Scots *loch*, but voiced (p. 223); as *g* in some pronunciations of German *sagen* '[to] say'.

[x] As *ch* in Scots *loch* or German *lachen* '[to] laugh'.

[j] As *y* in English *year*.

[ŋ] As *ng* in southern English *sing*.

[ʀ] Somewhere between [z] and standard English *r* as in *run*.

[θ] As English *th* in *thin*.

Where a colon immediately follows a phonetic or phonemic symbol, it indicates that the sound or phoneme concerned is long. The vowel in English *pit*, for example, is short relative to that in *peat*, and the two words might be contrasted [pit]/[pi:t] in broad (i.e. rough-and-ready) phonetic notation. English words do not normally contain long consonants, but they can occur in compounds, as in *penknife* [pen:aif], where the [n:] is much more prolonged than in *penny* [peni], *puny* [pju:ni].

The sign ˜ placed above a vowel denotes nasal articulation, as in French *danse* [dãs] 'dance'. (See further p. 223.)

Special characters other than phonetic symbols are occasionally used in this book. Their forms and values are as follows.

œ As French *eu* in *peuple* 'people' or German *ö* in *schön* 'beautiful' (= [ø]).

ǫ As English *o* in *hot* (= [ɔ]).

ƀ A continuous sound pronounced with both lips, as Spanish *b* or *v* in *hablar* '[to] speak', *vuelo* 'flight' (= [ß]).

ȝ As *ch* in Scots *loch*, but voiced (p. 223); as *g* in some pronunciations of German *sagen* '[to] say'(= [ɣ]).

þ As English *th* in *thin* (=[θ]).

Vowel length may be indicated in non-phonetic representation by placing a macron over the relevant symbol (e.g. *ī, ō*). An exception is made for Old West Norse (effectively Old Icelandic and Old Norwegian), where following well-established convention an acute accent is used instead (e.g. *í, ó*).

The articulation of speech sounds

Speech sounds are made through an interaction of the tongue with different parts of the mouth, or by the lips, as air is expelled from the lungs. Vowels are articulated without blockage of the flow of air; consonants are produced by blocking the flow of air partially or completely.

Differences of vowel sound depend primarily on three factors: (1) tongue height; (2) the part of the tongue raised or lowered; (3) the shape of the lips (rounded or spread). Vowels may therefore be described as high, mid-, or low; as front, central, or back; and as rounded or unrounded. Examples: [i] is a high, front, unrounded vowel, because the front of the tongue is raised about as high as it will go and the lips are spread; [u] is a high, back, rounded vowel – the back of the tongue is raised about as high as it will go and the lips are rounded; [ø] is a mid-, front, rounded vowel – the front of the tongue is raised to about mid-height and the lips are rounded; [a] is a low, back unrounded vowel – the back of the tongue is lowered about as far as it will go and the lips are relaxed.

Consonants are described in terms of their place and mode of articulation. Those made by the lips are called labial. Others are mainly produced by contact between the tongue and one or other part of the mouth: between tongue and teeth = dental; between tongue and hard palate = palatal; between tongue and soft palate or velum = velar. Consonants made by blocking the flow of air completely and then releasing it are called stops or plosives; those produced by constricting the passage of air are called continuants, and subdivided according to the manner of the constriction. Examples: [b] is a bilabial stop, because it is made by momentarily stopping the flow of air with both lips; [f] is a labio-dental continuant (fricative/spirant) – the sound is made by placing the top front teeth against the lower lip, thus constricting the flow of air and producing audible friction; [r] is a dental continuant (rolled or flapped) – the sound is made by placing the tip of the tongue against the ridge behind the top front teeth, and letting it flap backwards and forwards; [k] is a velar stop – the flow of air is momentarily stopped by placing the back of the tongue against the soft palate or velum ([k] may also denote the corresponding palatal stop where it is unnecessary to distinguish this from the velar variety, otherwise [c] is used for the latter).

The vocal cords may be used in the production of speech sounds, in which case the sound concerned is called voiced. If the vocal cords are not used the sound is called unvoiced. Vowels are mostly voiced. Consonants may be voiced or unvoiced: [b], [r], for example, are voiced, [f], [k], are unvoiced.

During the production of speech sounds, air may be expelled through the mouth or through mouth and nose together. Where air passes through the mouth alone, the designation oral is used; where it passes through mouth and nose, the sounds concerned are called nasal. [i], [u], [ø], [a] are oral vowels, and [b], [f], [r], [k] oral consonants. Nasal vowels are common in French, as [ã] in *danse* [dãs] 'dance', [õ] in *don* [dõn] 'gift'. Examples of nasal consonants are the voiced bilabial continuant [m] and the voiced dental continuant [n].

Transliteration conventions

(1) Transliterated runes and separation marks are given in **bold type**.

(2) Unless precise shape and number are important to the discussion, separation marks are reproduced as **:** regardless of how they appear in an inscription. That is also the convention where separation marks occur in a sequence of normalised runes.

(3) Line division may be reproduced exactly as in the original, or, where more convenient, signalled by **|**. In insignificant cases it may be left unmarked.

(4) A gap in an inscription is indicated by a gap in the transliteration.

(5) Uncertain runes or separation marks are placed in round brackets, e.g. (**m**).

(6) Unreadable but countable runes are given as mid-height asterisks (*).

(7) Unreadable and uncountable runes are marked ... That is also the convention where part of an inscription has been omitted.

(8) Runes conjectured, or supplied from earlier drawings and/or photographs, are placed in square brackets, e.g. **m[u]þu[r]**.

(9) A lacuna at the start of a line is signalled by], and at the end of a line by [.

(10) Bind-runes (p. 20) are indicated by placing a slur over the relevant letters, e.g. **h͡l**.

These are the conventions used in *Runes: A Handbook*. Some runologists will differ on points of detail. Uncertain runes, for example, are often indicated by placing a dot beneath the relevant characters, while unreadable but countable runes may be given as xxx, - - -, or something other. A very different system has commonly been used for transliterating English runes. Instead of bold type spaced roman is employed, placed within single inverted commas, thus 'p a d a' rather than **pada**. This system also differs from the one used here in several other respects. The merits of the different conventions and the desirability of a single, unified system are discussed in Claiborne W. Thompson, 'On transcribing runic inscriptions', *Michigan Germanic Studies* 7:1 (1981), 89–95.

The spelling of edited texts

At the times and places runic inscriptions were made there was no standardised spelling. In converting inscriptions into texts suitable for the non-specialist, the editor thus has some freedom of choice. The aim should be to give as accurate an indication as possible of the assumed pronunciation. For Old Icelandic and Old Norwegian texts there exist established systems of normalisation, based to a greater or lesser degree on modern Icelandic spelling. There is no generally accepted way of normalising other types of language found in runic inscriptions, primarily pre-Viking Age North or North-West Germanic (pp. 22–3), Old Danish, Old Swedish, Old English, and Old High German (the forerunner of modern German). In this book account has been taken of previous practice, but the author has not adhered to any particular conventions. The principal considerations governing choice of spelling have been explicitness and accessibility. The texts thus highlight notable linguistic features while otherwise retaining a form that will be familiar to those acquainted with earlier forms of Germanic.

Index of inscriptions

In this Index, inscriptions are identified in different ways. Those included in the Pan-Scandinavian Runic Text Database (*Samnordisk runtextdatabas*, p. 212) have a so-called "signature" (e.g. U 729, meaning an inscription from Uppland, Sweden, numbered 729 in the standard edition, *Upplands runinskrifter*), and where such a signature exists, it is quoted in the Index in virtually all cases. Inscriptions not in the database have been given other forms of reference. All references are explained in the Key that complements the Index. This should enable those keen to find out more about a particular inscription to locate suitable material (the database will provide detailed information in English and Swedish on all the inscriptions it contains). In the Select Reading Lists that accompany most chapters emphasis has been placed on works in English. In the Index and Key, on the other hand, the chief aims have been to identify the inscriptions mentioned in the book and to lead the reader to the standard editions or, in the absence of such, to other primary accounts. Reference is thus of necessity to works in a number of languages. Underscored page numbers indicate illustrations.

Key to references in the Index of inscriptions

In the Select Reading Lists, where reference is often made to works that have appeared recently, publisher as well as place of publication is given. Many of the books included in this Key are of some age, and since the name of the publisher is seldom of much help in locating such volumes, it is here omitted.

Åhlén 1986: Marit Åhlén, 'On the younger and the youngest runic inscriptions in Sweden', *Saga-Book* 22:1 (1986), 73–9. (Reference is to the article as a whole.)

Bågenholm 1999: Gösta Bågenholm, *Arkeologi och språk i norra Östersjöområdet* (Gotarc Series B. Arkeologiska skrifter no. 12). Göteborg (1999). (Reference is to the initial page number of the relevant section of the book.)

Bæksted 1939: Anders Bæksted, 'Vore yngste runeindskrifter', *Danske studier* 1939, 111–38. (Reference is to the article as a whole.)

Barnes and Page 2006: (details given in the list following chapter 18, under "Barnes, Michael P., and Page, R. I. 2006"). (Reference is to the relevant page numbers in the book.)

By Fv1970: An inscription from Byzantium published in the Swedish periodical *Fornvännen* 65 (1970). (Reference is to the initial page number of the relevant piece in the periodical.)

By NOR1999: An inscription from Byzantium published in the Norwegian runic newsletter *Nytt om runer* 14 (1999). (Reference is to the initial page number of the relevant piece in the newsletter.)

FR: An inscription from the Faroes published in: Marie Stoklund, 'Faroese runic inscriptions'; in: Andras Mortensen and Símun V. Arge (eds), *Viking and Norse in the North Atlantic: Select Papers from the Proceedings of the Fourteenth Viking Congress, Tórshavn, 19–30 July 2001.* Tórshavn (2005), 109–24. (Reference is to the number of the inscription in the article.)

G: An inscription from Gotland, Sweden, included in the standard edition *Gotlands runinskrifter* 1–3 (Sveriges runinskrifter 11–12, eds Sven B. F. Jansson *et al.*, 1962–78, vol. 3 not yet completed; further details given in the list following chapter 18, under "Sveriges runinskrifter"). (Reference is to the number of the inscription in the edition.)

GR: An inscription from Greenland. (Reference is to the number of the inscription as used in the Pan-Scandinavian Runic Text Database.)

Gustavson 2003: Helmer Gustavson, 'Runorna som officerens hemliga skrift och allmogens vardagsvara', *Gamla och nya runor: Artiklar 1982–2001.* Stockholm (2003), 113–21 (article originally published 1995). (Reference is to the article as a whole.)

Hagland 1989: Jan Ragnar Hagland, '"Dei yngste runene" i ein variant frå Karmsund'; in: Bjørn Eithun *et al.* (eds), *Festskrift til Finn Hødnebø 29. desember 1989.* Oslo (1989), 91–101. (Reference is to the article as a whole.)

Hagland 2006: Jan Ragnar Hagland, 'Runic writing and Latin literacy at the end of the Middle Ages: a case study'; in: Marie Stoklund *et al.* (eds), *Runes and their Secrets: Studies in Runology.* Copenhagen (2006), 141–57. (Reference is to the article as a whole.)

Haugen 1981: Einar Haugen, 'The youngest runes: from Oppdal to Waukegan', *Michigan Germanic Studies* 7:1 (1981), 148–75. (Reference is to the article as a whole.)

Hickes's *Thesaurus*: George Hickes, *Linguarum Vett. Septentrionalium Thesaurus ...* (2 vols). Oxford (1705).

HrPeterson2006: Lena Peterson, 'Runorna på Överhogdalsbonaden I a: En snärjig historia med ett förslag till tolkning'; in: Lena Peterson *et al.* (eds), *Namn och runor: Uppsalastudier i onomastik och runologi till Lennart Elmevik på 70-årsdagen 2 februari 2006.* Uppsala (2006), 147–62. (Reference is to the article as a whole.)

Hs: An inscription from Hälsingland, Sweden, to be included in a future volume of Sveriges runinskrifter (details given in the list following chapter 18). (Reference is to the number of the inscription as used by Runverket, the section of the Swedish National Heritage Board in charge of runic inscriptions.)

IM MM: An inscription from the Isle of Man (see the reference to Page 1983 in the Select Reading List following chapter 8.) (Reference is to the Manx Museum number applied to the artefact.)

N: An inscription from Norway included in the standard edition *Norges innskrifter med de yngre runer 1–6* (full details given in the list following chapter 18, under "Olsen, Magnus *et al.* 1941 (in progress)"). (Reference is to the number of the inscription in the edition.)

N A: An inscription from Norway with a pre-publication number for those found in places other than Bryggen, Bergen. (Reference is to the number of the inscription.)

N B: An inscription from Norway with a pre-publication number for those found at Bryggen, Bergen. (Reference is to the number of the inscription.)

Nielsen 1987: Karl Martin Nielsen, 'The numerals in the Kensington inscription'; in: *Runor och runinskrifter: Föredrag vid Riksantikvarieämbetets och Vitterhetsakademiens symposium 8–11 september 1985*. Stockholm (1987), 175–83. (Reference is to the article as a whole.)

N IK: A bracteate inscription from Norway included in: Karl Hauck *et al.*, *Die Goldbrakteaten der Völkerwanderungszeit: Ikonographischer Katalog* (3 vols + introduction, Münstersche Mittelalter-schriften 24.1.1–24.3.2). München 1985–9. (Reference is to the number of the bracteate in the catalogue.)

N KJ: An inscription from Norway included in the standard edition *Die Runeninschriften im älteren Futhark* (see KJ above). (Reference is to the number of the inscription in the edition.)

Nordby 2001: An inscription included in the University of Oslo (Germanistisk institutt) thesis: K. Jonas Nordby, *Etterreformatoriske runeinnskrifter i Norge: Opphav og tradisjon*. Oslo (2001). (Reference is to the number allotted to the inscription in the thesis, which is prefaced by "E".)

Ög: An inscription from Östergötland, Sweden, included in the standard edition *Östergötlands runinskrifter* (Sveriges runinskrifter 2, ed. Erik Brate, 1911–18; further details given in the list following chapter 18, under "Sveriges runinskrifter"). (Reference is to the number of the inscription in the edition.)

Ög N: An inscription from Östergötland, Sweden, included in: Arthur Nordén, *Östergötlands runinskrifter*, an unpublished supplement to the standard edition *Östergötlands runinskrifter* (see Ög above). (Reference is to the number of the inscription in the manuscript.)

Öl: An inscription from Öland, Sweden, included in the standard edition *Ölands runinskrifter* (Sveriges runinskrifter 1, eds Sven Söderberg and Erik Brate, 1900–06; further details given in the list following chapter 18, under "Sveriges runinskrifter"). (Reference is to the number of the inscription in the edition.)

Or: A Scandinavian inscription from Orkney published in the standard edition *The Scandinavian Runic Inscriptions of Britain* (Barnes and Page 2006, see above). (Reference is to the number of the inscription in the edition.)

Or Barnes: A Scandinavian inscription from Maeshowe, Orkney, published in the standard edition *The Runic Inscriptions of Maeshowe, Orkney* (details given in the list following chapter 18, under "Barnes, Michael P. 1994"). (Reference is to the number of the inscription in the edition.)

Or Barnes Farrer: A carving from Maeshowe, Orkney, published in the standard edition *The Runic Inscriptions of Maeshowe, Orkney* (see "Or Barnes" above), but not considered indubitably runic. (Reference is to the number of the carving as established by James Farrer in his 1862 edition of the Maeshowe inscriptions, *Notice of Runic Inscriptions Discovered during Recent Excavations in the Orkneys.*)

Page 1998/1999: R. I. Page, 'The Icelandic Rune-Poem', *Nottingham Medieval Studies* 42 (1998), 1–37 (also published separately as *The Icelandic Rune-Poem*. London, 1999). (Reference is to the article/monograph as a whole.)

Page 1999: *An Introduction to English Runes* (2nd ed.). Woodbridge (1999). (Reference is to the book as a whole; individual items can be located through the index.)

Page 2003: R. I. Page, 'On the Norwegian Rune-poem'; in: Wilhelm Heizmann and Astrid van Nahl (eds), *Runica – Germanica – Mediaevalia* (Ergänzungsbände zum Reallexikon der Germanischen Altertumskunde 37). Berlin/New York (2003), 553–66. (Reference is to the article as a whole.)

Page and Hagland 1998: R. I. Page and Jan Ragnar Hagland, 'Runica manuscripta and runic dating: the expansion of the younger fuþąrk'; in: Audun Dybdahl and Jan Ragnar Hagland (eds), *Innskrifter og datering/ Dating Inscriptions* (Senter for middelalderstudier, Skrifter nr. 8). Trondheim (1998), 55–71. (Reference is to the article as a whole.)

Quak 1987: Arend Quak, 'Zum altschwedischen Runengedicht', *Skandinavistik* 17 (1987), 81–92. (Reference is to the article as a whole.)

Raschellà 1993: Fabrizio D. Raschellà, 'Grammatical treatises'; in: Phillip Pulsiano and Kirsten Wolf (eds), *Medieval Scandinavia: An Encyclopedia*. New York/London (1993), 235–7. (Reference is to the article as a whole.)

RiD 1985: Helmer Gustavson and Sven-Göran Hallonquist, *Runor i Dalarna*. Stockholm (1985). (Reference is to the relevant page number in the publication.)

Sc: A Scandinavian inscription from Scotland published in the standard edition *The Scandinavian Runic Inscriptions of Britain* (Barnes and Page 2006, see above). (Reference is to the number of the inscription in the edition.)

Sköld 2003: Tryggve Sköld, 'Edward Larssons alfabet', 'Edward Larssons alfabet och Kensingtonstenens', *DAUM-Katta: Vinterblad från dialekt-, ortnamns- och folkminnesarkivet i Umeå, 2003*, 5–11. (Reference is to both articles in their entirety.)

Sm: An inscription from Småland, Sweden, included in the standard edition
Smålands runinskrifter (Sveriges runinskrifter 4, ed. Ragnar Kinander,
1935–61; further details given in the list following chapter 18, under
"Sveriges runinskrifter"). (Reference is to the number of the inscription in
the edition.)

Sö: An inscription from Södermanland, Sweden, included in the standard
edition *Södermanlands runinskrifter* (Sveriges runinskrifter 3, eds Erik
Brate and Elias Wessén, 1924–36; further details given in the list following
chapter 18, under "Sveriges runinskrifter"). (Reference is to the number of
the inscription in the edition.)

Thompson 1978: Claiborne W. Thompson, 'The runes in *Bósa saga ok
Herrauðs*', *Scandinavian Studies* 50 (1978), 50–56. (Reference is to the
article as a whole.)

U: An inscription from Uppland, Sweden, included in the standard edition
Upplands runinskrifter 1–4 (Sveriges runinskrifter 6–9, eds Elias Wessén
and Sven B. F. Jansson, 1940–58; further details given in the list following
chapter 18, under "Sveriges runinskrifter"). (Reference is to the number of
the inscription in the edition.)

U Fv: An inscription from Uppland, Sweden, published in the Swedish
periodical *Fornvännen*. (Reference is to the initial page number of the
relevant piece in the periodical.)

Vg: An inscription from Västergötland, Sweden, included in the standard
edition *Västergötlands runinskrifter* (Sveriges runinskrifter 5, eds Hugo
Jungner and Elisabeth Svärdström, 1940–70; further details given in the list
following chapter 18, under "Sveriges runinskrifter"). (Reference is to the
number of the inscription in the edition.)

Zimmerman 2008: Larry J. Zimmerman, 'Unusual or "extreme" beliefs about
the past, community identity, and dealing with the fringe'; in: Chip Colwell-
Chanthaphonh and T. J. Ferguson (eds), *Collaboration in Archaeological
Practice: Engaging Descendent Communities*. Lanham MD (2008), 55–86.